ROMANTICISM IN PERSPECTIVE:
TEXTS, CULTURES, HISTORIES

General Editors:
Marilyn Gaull, *Professor of English,*
Temple University/New York University
Stephen Prickett, *Regius Professor of English Language and Literature,*
University of Glasgow

This series aims to offer a fresh assessment of Romanticism by
looking at it from a wide variety of perspectives. Both
comparative and interdisciplinary, it will bring together cognate
themes from architecture, art history, landscape gardening,
linguistics, literature, philosophy, politics, science, social and
political history and theology to deal with original, contentious or
as yet unexplored aspects of Romanticism as a Europe-wide
phenomenon.

Titles include

Richard Cronin (*editor*)
1798: THE YEAR OF THE *LYRICAL BALLADS*

Péter Dávidházi
THE ROMANTIC CULT OF SHAKESPEARE: Literary
Reception in Anthropological Perspective

David Jasper
THE SACRED AND SECULAR CANON IN ROMANTICISM
Preserving the Sacred Truths

Malcolm Kelsall
JEFFERSON AND THE ICONOGRAPHY OF ROMANTICISM
Folk, Land, Culture and the Romantic Nation

Andrew McCann
CULTURAL POLITICS IN THE 1790s: Literature, Radicalism
and the Public Sphere

Ashton Nichols
THE REVOLUTIONARY 'I': Wordsworth and the Politics of
Self-Presentation

Jeffrey C. Robinson
RECEPTION AND POETICS IN KEATS: 'My Ended Poet'

Anya Taylor
BACCHUS IN ROMANTIC ENGLAND: Writers and Drink,
1780–1830

Michael Wiley
ROMANTIC GEOGRAPHY: Wordsworth and
Anglo-European Spaces

Eric Wilson
EMERSON'S SUBLIME SCIENCE

Romanticism in Perspective
Series Standing Order ISBN 0–333–71490–3
(*outside North America only*)

You can receive future titles in this series as they are published by placing a standing order. Please contact your bookseller or, in case of difficulty, write to us at the address below with your name and address, the title of the series and the ISBN quoted above.

Customer Services Department, Macmillan Distribution Ltd
Houndmills, Basingstoke, Hampshire RG21 6XS, England

Cultural Politics in the 1790s

Literature, Radicalism and the Public Sphere

Andrew McCann
Department of English
University of Queensland

First published in Great Britain 1999 by
MACMILLAN PRESS LTD
Houndmills, Basingstoke, Hampshire RG21 6XS and London
Companies and representatives throughout the world

A catalogue record for this book is available from the British Library.

ISBN 0–333–73498–X

First published in the United States of America 1999 by
ST. MARTIN'S PRESS, INC.,
Scholarly and Reference Division,
175 Fifth Avenue, New York, N.Y. 10010

ISBN 0–312–21645–9

Library of Congress Cataloging-in-Publication Data
McCann, Andrew.
Cultural politics in the 1790's : literature, radicalism, and the
public sphere / Andrew McCann.
p.   cm. — (Romanticism in perspective : texts, cultures,
histories)
Includes bibliographical references and index.
ISBN 0–312–21645–9
1. English literature—18th century—History and criticism.
2. Politics and literature—Great Britain—History—18th century.
3. Wollstonecraft, Mary, 1759–1797—Political and social views.
4. Edgeworth, Maria, 1767–1849—Political and social views.
5. Godwin, William, 1756–1836—Political and social views.
6. Thelwall, John, 1764–1834—Political and social views.   7. Great
Britain—Politics and government—18th century.   8. Authors,
English—18th century—Political activity.   9. Political fiction,
English—History and criticism.   10. Political poetry, English–
–History and criticism.   11. Romanticism—Great Britain–
–History—18th century.   I. Title.   II. Series.
PR448.P6M36   1998
820.9'358—DC21   98–22100
                                                              CIP

This book is printed on paper suitable for recycling and made from fully managed and
sustained forest sources.

10   9   8   7   6   5   4   3   2   1
08   07   06   05   04   03   02   01   00   99

Printed and bound in Great Britain by Antony Rowe Ltd.

for Rachel

Contents

List of Illustrations

Acknowledgements

Several of the chapters in this book have been published previously. Chapter 2 was originally published in both *Prose Studies* vol. 18, no. 3 (December 1995), pp. 199–222 and in *The Intersections of the Public and Private Spheres in Early Modern England*, eds Paula R. Backscheider and Timothy Dykstal (London: Frank Cass, 1996), pp. 199–222; Chapter 3 was originally published in *Romanticism*, vol. 3, no. 1 (Spring 1997), pp. 35–52; and Chapter 6 originally appeared in *Novel: A Forum on Fiction*, vol. 30, no. 1 (1996), pp. 55–77. I am grateful to Frank Cass and Company, Edinburgh University Press and NOVEL Corp. for permission to reprint this material. I am also grateful to the British Museum, which has allowed me to use the prints that appear in Chapter 4.

This book began its life as a doctoral dissertation at Cornell University. My most immediate debts are to teachers and friends there who read and commented on parts of it in those early stages, or whose energy and rigour provided an indispensable context for my thinking. I would like to thank Laura Brown, Reeve Parker, Satya Mohanty, Peter Hohendahl, Neil Saccamano, Claudia Johnson, Mary Jacobus, Anna Neill, Anne Mallory and Chris Nealon. I would also like to thank Nicholas Roe and Timothy Dykstal, who encountered chapters along the way, the students in my honours seminars at the University of Queensland, who have provided me with a regular audience and sounding board, and Julian Honer and Charmian Hearne at Macmillan. The completion of this project would not have been possible without the enthusiasm and support of Marilyn Gaull. I wish to thank her especially. The book is dedicated to my family and to Rachel Roze.

List of Abbreviations

Belinda   Maria Edgeworth, *Belinda* (1801; Oxford: Oxford University Press, 1994)

CW   William Godwin, *Caleb Williams* (1794; Harmondsworth: Penguin Books, 1988)

EPJ   William Godwin, *Enquiry Concerning Political Justice and its Influence on Modern Morals and Happiness* (1793; Harmondsworth: Penguin Books, 1985)

Monk   Matthew Lewis, *The Monk* (1796; New York: Grove Press, 1952)

PL   John Thelwall, *Political Lectures. No. 1. On the Moral Tendency of a System of Spies and Informers* (London, 1794)

Poems   John Thelwall, *Poems, Chiefly Written in Retirement* (London, 1801; republished in facsimile form, Oxford: Woodstock Books, 1989)

PP   John Thelwall, *The Peripatetic. Sketches of the Heart, of Nature and Society; in a Series of Politico-Sentimental Journals*, 3 vols. (London, 1793)

PSE   Oskar Negt and Alexander Kluge, *The Public Sphere and Experience: Toward an Analysis of the Bourgeois and Proletarian Public Sphere* trans. Peter Labanyi, Jamie Oswen Daniel and Assenka Oskiloff (Minneapolis: University of Minnesota Press, 1993)

RN   John Thelwall, *The Rights of Nature Against the Usurpation of Establishments* (1796) in *The Political Writings of John Thelwall*, ed. Gregory Claeys (University Park: Pennsylvania State University Press, 1995) pp. 390–500

RRF   Edmund Burke, *Reflections on the Revolution in France* (1790; Harmondsworth: Penguin Books, 1988)

RW   Mary Wollstonecraft, *A Vindication of the Rights of Woman* (1792; Harmondsworth: Penguin Books, 1992)

ST   Jürgen Habermas, *The Structural Transformation of the Public Sphere: an Inquiry into a Category of Bourgeois Society* trans. Thomas Burger (Cambridge, Mass.: MIT Press, 1991)

W&S   Edmund Burke, *The Writings and Speeches of Edmund Burke*, vols 2, 4–5, 8–9 (Oxford: Clarendon Press, 1981–91)

WW   Mary Wollstonecraft, *Mary* and *The Wrongs of Woman* (Oxford: Oxford University Press, 1980)

Introduction:
Literature and the Public
Sphere in the 1790s

In recent years the study of late eighteenth- and early nineteenth-century British literature has been invigorated by work on the public sphere which takes its cue principally from Jürgen Habermas's *The Structural Transformation of the Public Sphere*. As James Chandler reminds us, this orientation to notions of publicity is not new to British literary studies.[1] In the 1950s and 1960s Raymond Williams made the idea of the public central to such studies as *The Long Revolution* and *Culture and Society 1780–1950*. Nevertheless it has certainly taken the English translation of Habermas, and of his Marxist revisionists Oskar Negt and Alexander Kluge, before the category of the public could emerge as the basis of a historicism capable of competing with the rhetorical reading practices that have dominated the study of Romanticism, at least in the American academy.[2] Yet just as Habermasian notions of the public have gained currency in the study of Romanticism, so too have they been quickly called into question from a number of political and disciplinary perspectives. In fact scholars across a wide range of disciplines now agree that Habermas's formulation of the bourgeois public sphere is flawed in fundamental ways. Not only is it apparently insensitive to the ways in which hegemonic definitions of community excluded certain segments of the population, like women and workers, but, worse, it also establishes and validates particular norms for social and communicative interaction, which a priori disqualify what Oskar Negt and Alexander Kluge call counterpublic spheres capable of embodying the interests and experiences of these marginalized and oppressed groups.

In the 1790s, the period with which this book is concerned, these theoretical issues take on a very tangible form. The period not only saw, as Raymond Williams points out, an increasing number of writers and intellectuals concerned with the 'public' and its related term the 'market' as general and abstract entities,[3] it also saw the proliferation of dissident or radical public discourses with very specific forms of interaction and production involving, as Kevin Gilmartin writes, the extension of a network 'from vigorous print arguments about public opinion, into concrete assemblies of that opinion in meetings, debating societies, political clubs, petition campaigns, and organized boycotts'.[4] The communicative networks associated with late-eighteenth-century radicalism seem to explode the idea of a single, monolithic public. As Terry Eagleton writes:

> what is emerging in the England of the late-eighteenth and early-nineteenth centuries, in that whole epoch of intensive class struggle charted in E. P. Thompson's *The Making of the English Working Class*, is already nothing less than a 'counterpublic sphere'. In the Corresponding Societies, the radical press, Owenism, Cobbett's *Political Register* and Paine's *Rights of Man*, feminism and the dissenting churches, a whole oppositional network of journals, clubs, pamphlets, debates and institutions invades the dominant consensus, threatening to fragment it from within.[5]

Contemporary scholars working at the intersection of critical theory, history and literary studies, and largely inspired by E. P. Thompson's *The Making of the English Working Class*, have developed Eagleton's observation into detailed and tangible accounts of specific counterpublics.[6] Orrin Wang describes this as scholarship's 'romance' with the possibility of oppositional politics embodied in the idea of a counterpublic sphere or spheres.[7] The present study in some ways continues that romance. One of my aims is to examine the consolidation of what might be called a plebeian or proletarian public sphere in the 1790s and the very specific forms of cultural production, dissemination and reception that informed it. Yet for all our contemporary scepticism about the idea of a dominant, consensus oriented public sphere in the period, the 1790s was also the decade in which a climate of political unease and military conflict enabled orators like Edmund Burke and the slew of conservative pamphleteers who imitated his hyperbolic, Gothic-sentimental style, to address with confidence a national community steeled against the Jacobin menace. It was also the period in which the production of Gothic-sentimental literature reached its acme and in which, relatedly, private reading became a dominant mode of culture-consumption and one integral to the formation of bourgeois subjectivity. As Habermas argues the bourgeois public sphere was one composed of essentially private subjects increasingly integrated into the institutions of emergent capitalism (the family, private property and possessive individuality), and certainly forms of cultural production oriented to private consumption have a role to play in this story. If the period directs our attention towards radical counterpublics, it also demands a new investigation of exactly what a 'dominant' or 'hegemonic' public might look like – an investigation of exactly what economies of cultural production and reception could be justly called dominant in their resistance to the formation of radical counterpublics, and of how mass produced literary forms, like the Gothic novel, might have been implicated in them. Given, moreover, that the cultural revolution of late-eighteenth-century Britain was most emphatically, as Gary Kelly has argued, a middle class revolution directed against the vestiges of aristocratic and courtly culture, we also need to be careful about reading the institutions of bourgeois culture as politically regressive.[8] While bourgeois and plebeian or proletarian forms of public political activity were often distinct, involving structurally differentiated forms of discursive production and reception, they were just as often imbricated with each other or even, at moments, indistinguishable. At the end of the eighteenth century many members of an emergent middle class were as politically disempowered as the workers and it wasn't until the first reform bill of 1832 that something like bourgeois political enfranchisement became a reality. Given this situation it may be more accurate, and politically relevant, to supplement oppositions between 'dominant' and 'oppositional', 'bourgeois' and 'proletarian' publics, with the distinction between forms of cultural production that fostered engaged and progressive political activity, and those that impeded this. The difficulty of analysing the bourgeois public sphere in the 1790s is that it was quite clearly informed by both. In examining these issues we can read the ideological manifestation of the actual political struggles, in Britain and its colonies, that have made the 1790s such a complex and compelling decade for literary scholars and social historians alike: a decade which saw the emergence of both activist political and cultural practices (bourgeois, proletarian and feminist) in opposition to both the residual forms of courtly culture and the emergent forms of an increasingly homogenized culture industry. It is only by understanding the tensions between these, not by wishing them away, that our present romance with radical counterpublics retains its political relevancy.

The great usefulness of Habermas's study of the public sphere and the theoretical debates it has generated, is that they suggest a framework with which to discuss the different ways in which texts are implicated in the construction of community, imagined or otherwise. In this introduction I want to discuss this framework and its relevance to the literary and cultural material that I focus on in the following chapters. If we are to understand the materiality of discursive production and reception in the 1790s, the ways in which publics and counterpublics were imagined, represented and constructed in the period, it is imperative that we remember that the original utility of these terms in critical theory is that they let us specify the cultural dimension of the political struggles and antagonisms that inform the consolidation of capitalism in the early modern period.

LITERATURE, CULTURE-CONSUMPTION AND THE BOURGEOIS PUBLIC SPHERE

By the end of the eighteenth century the idea that culture – in the sense of art, music and literature – had a profoundly redemptive social function was a mainstay of Romantic aesthetic theory, in Britain and on the continent. For contemporary critical theorists Friedrich Schiller's *On the Aesthetic Education of Man* is the text that makes this claim in its most emphatic form. Schiller held that art's non-utilitarian character, its distance from power-relations and means–end rationality, made it the reserve of freedom and the medium through which to overcome the alienated nature of human potentialities in the attainment of a utopian wholeness. Writing in 1795, in the wake of the French Revolution and the subsequent Terror, Schiller saw the political sphere as one given over, alternately, to perverseness and brutality, and responded by developing Kant's work on the disinterestedness of the aesthetic faculty, ultimately proposing, as John Brenkman writes, 'to redirect the general process of human emancipation and self-realization into what he called aesthetic education'.[9] The development of Romantic thought in Britain, at least in its canonical Wordsworthian and Coleridgian forms, is informed by a similar move away from the political to the aesthetic as the basis of redemption and emancipation. Wordsworth claimed his 'spots of time' have a 'renovating virtue' that is sharply juxtaposed with the realm of necessity, 'trivial occupations' and 'ordinary intercourse'; Coleridge's notion of the imagination, in both the *Biographia Literaria* and in early poems like 'Dejection: an

Ode', tends towards a realm of idealism that links the human imagination to a universal and transcendental force beyond the reach of the 'loveless ever anxious crowd'.[10] Both demarcate the space of the aesthetic as one removed from the banal necessities of everyday life or the more destructive realm of public politics. As it was for Schiller this move seems to have been one urged by the climate of violence in France, which signalled an end to the emancipatory promise of the French Revolution. *The Prelude*, for example, recounts very specifically Wordsworth's disillusionment with revolutionary politics and Godwinian philosophy as crucial moments in his development as a poet.[11] One of the striking things about these moments in high Romanticism is that the public value of a cultural form like poetry is premised on a rejection of public political life, conceptualized in a very abstract and impressionistic way to include city life, market economics, popular politics and popular entertainment, and a corresponding orientation to private feeling, virtue, sensibility and pleasure. The aesthetic, in this very specific sense, develops, in part at least, as a valorization of the private and a move away from a certain conception of the public. A generation later Keatsian images of reading and writing poetry as distinctly pastoral practices present this dynamic in its most objectified form.

Of course this notion of art as inherently redemptive was not unique to high Romanticism. In sentimental literature we find a more intuitive formulation of the same idea. Here escapist pleasure seems to go hand in hand with a moral dimension similar to the one that informs the thinking of Wordsworth and Coleridge. In her 1790 novel *Julia*, for example, Helen Maria Williams writes that 'the most precious property of poetry is, that of leading the mind from gloomy mists of care, or the black clouds of misfortune, which sometimes gather round the path of life, to scenes bright with sunshine, and blooming with beauty'.[12] A subsequent 'Address to Poetry' rehearses the standard oppositions in which poetry, defined against selfish and anti-social passions, has a deeply renovating effect that extends universally to embrace non-European societies:

> Ye southern isles, emerg'd so late
> Where the pacific billow rolls,
> Witness, tho' rude your simple state,
> How heav'n-taught verse can melt your souls:
> Say, when you hear the wand'ring bard,
> How thrill'd ye listen to his lay,

> By what kind arts ye court his stay,
> All savage life affords, his sure reward.[13]

In this passage the transcendental nature of poetry, its disinterested distance from avarice and its simple orientation to beauty, also mediates a certain myth of community. The receptiveness of Europeans and Pacific islanders to poetry is a sure index of the humanity they hold in common. In Williams's enlightened universalism we can begin to see some of the contradictory claims being made for poetry and the aesthetic faculty: on the one hand it is a private retreat, on the other hand, it is a guarantee of a commonality that promises some kind of cosmopolitan bond that overcomes cultural specificity – a utopian community of man very similar to the one that informs Wordsworth's views on sympathy in the 1802 'Preface' to *Lyrical Ballads*.

> In spite of difference of soil and climate, of language and manners, of laws and customs, in spite of things silently gone out of mind and things violently destroyed, the Poet binds together by passion and knowledge the vast empire of human society, as it is spread over the whole earth, and over all time.[14]

Herbert Marcuse's seminal essay 'The Affirmative Character of Culture' has pointed out the ideological dimension of culture in its Schillerian sense. Marcuse argues that the assumption of culture's disinterested autonomy from other aspects of social life was becoming increasingly dominant by the end of the eighteenth century, and that culture's function in society is subsequently linked to the assumption of this autonomy. Art and literature seem to negate social relations based on exchange-value in bourgeois society and seem to offer a retreat into a realm of universal freedom and beauty. Yet one accesses this world only on the condition that one withdraw, momentarily, from actual, material social relations, such that in this withdrawal the status quo remains undisturbed. Affirmative culture's 'decisive characteristic is the assertion of a universally obligatory, eternally better and more valuable world that must be unconditionally affirmed: a world essentially different from the factual world of the daily struggle for existence, yet realizable by every individual "from within," without any transformation of the state of fact'.[15] Through acts of private culture-consumption one can experience the ideals of bourgeois society, ideals that are essentially

unrealizable in a society given over to market forces and exploitation. Culture, by this reckoning, is affirmative in two senses: it
affirms values that cannot be articulated in social life more generally, and it affirms the prevailing mode of production by bracketing
these ideals within the space of culture.

> Only in art has bourgeois society tolerated its own ideals and
> taken them seriously as a general demand. What counts as
> utopia, phantasy, and rebellion in the world of fact is allowed in
> art. There affirmative culture has displayed the forgotten truths
> over which 'realism' triumphs in daily life.[16]

Marcuse's essay directs us towards a consideration of the materiality of reading and the ways in which it normalizes the association
between pleasure, freedom and privacy removed from the realm of
necessity.[17] Yet as I suggested in the above discussion of Helen
Maria Williams's 'Address to Poetry', this stress on privacy is also
implicated in the consolidation of a certain kind of imagined community based around a very abstract humanism, yet nevertheless
experienced in a very tangible way. Habermas's *Structural
Transformation*, in which reading plays a crucial role, enables us to
develop Marcuse's account of affirmative culture and to suggest the
ways in which it was important in the realization of this form of
communality.

Habermas begins his study by recounting the transition from
what he calls the publicity of representation to the rational public of
the bourgeoisie, which he locates in the eighteenth century and in
Britain particularly. In this account the publicity of representation
involves the visible, ritualized presentation of feudal or monarchic
authority as nothing more than a physical presence linked to the
concrete existence of the lord. This authority was staged and
embodied in the personal attributes of the lord – insignias, dress,
deportment, rhetoric, etc. – and hence had no particular location
reserved for its display. It was perhaps most evident at court and in
public occasions and ceremonies, but was also disseminated
throughout society as a 'knightly code of conduct' that was
'common as a norm to all nobles' (*ST*, p. 8). With the erosion of
feudal structures and the rise of centralized state authority, this
form of representation became limited to the space of the court, an
enclave in the midst of a new form of publicness developing simultaneously with the constitution of individuals as the bearers of

private economic interests. The private space of economic activity had to take on a public dimension because 'the economic activity that had become private had to be oriented toward a commodity market that had expanded under public direction and supervision; the economic conditions under which this activity now took place lay outside the confines of the single household' (*ST*, p. 19). Radical responses to the French Revolution and, relatedly, to the monarchy preceding it, retell the history of civil society precisely in these terms, as a move away from the performative, aural displays of courtly chivalry to more rational and democratic forms of political authority. Mary Wollstonecraft's *An Historical and Moral View of the Origin and Progress of the French Revolution*, with its detailed accounts of the 'quixoticism' of courtly life, the moral perversions of official chivalry and especially of the pageantry produced at court by Marie Antoinette, is exemplary in this respect. Domestic and Gothic-sentimental novels of the late-eighteenth century, such as Burney's *Eveline*, Williams's *Julia* or Radcliffe's *A Sicilian Romance*, also stigmatize these codes of chivalry and public display, producing an opposition between public, aristocratic performances of power, beauty and authority, the moral enervation they produce, and the authentic intercourses of domestic life. Such texts essentially recast radical histories of civil society as accounts of the development of enlightened domesticity and testify to a literary culture intent on imagining more rational forms of social interaction beyond the realm of courtly representation.

According to Habermas, such literary fictions played an important role in the consolidation of the public sphere, validating the norms of privacy, domesticity and conjugality that together formed the bedrock of bourgeois subjectivity. Economic interests developing in an increasingly free market outside of residual client-based relations compelled private individuals to collectively assert themselves against state authority, in order to secure their own economic autonomy and freedom, and to debate 'the general rules governing relations in a basically privatized but publicly relevant sphere of commodity exchange and social labour' (*ST*, p. 27). These economic shifts encouraged the growth of public institutions like clubs and associations which developed as a way of perpetuating and safeguarding these economic interests. 'Club', John Brewer notes, suggested in the eighteenth century 'clubbing together', in the sense of pooling financial resources, and indeed part of the function of coffee-shop clubs, Masonic lodges and subscription societies was as a means of economic mobilization, fund-raising for collective invest-ments, and mutual protection in the midst of conditions that were as economically promising as they were threatening.[18] What distin-guishes the public in Habermas's account is its use of reason (*öffentliches Räsonnement*) as its guiding principle. It is this that seems to allow him to claim a normative dimension for the bourgeois public – a dimension subsequently lost as the public sphere disinte-grates into the modern culture industry.

The conditions for rational public interaction developed first, Habermas claims, in what he calls the literary public sphere, or the public sphere in the realm of letters, which functioned partly as an ideological mode of validation through which the emerging bour-geois identity, that defined and was defined through the public sphere, could imagine itself in universal terms. It constituted the public sphere of private individuals as an ideologically legitimated interest because it managed to conceal the economic and social specificity that enabled one to construct oneself as a private econ-omic interest engaged in a world of commodity exchange in the first place. In the literary public sphere, which in the eighteenth century was supposedly built-up around coffee-houses, debating societies, and the circulation of news and culture-commodities (journals like the *Spectator* and the *Tatler*), reason implied a free and economically unmediated discussion of those aesthetic and philosophical issues that affected the private individual not as the bearer of an economic interest, but as a human being. In this respect the structure of the public sphere assumed a universality not attenuated by class. In that membership appeared linked to the deployment of cultural capital only – to the ability to purchase textual commodities, read them and discuss them in public – it 'established the public as in principle inclusive': 'The issues discussed became "general" not merely in their significance, but also in their accessibility: everyone had to be able to participate' (*ST*, p. 37). Needless to say the literary public sphere's own self-image effaced the extent to which the deployment of cultural capital was itself linked to one's ability to participate in the market of commodity exchange. Thus 'the masses were not only largely illiterate but also so pauperized that they could not even pay for literature. They did not have at their dis-posal the buying power needed for even the most modest participa-tion in the market of cultural goods' (*ST*, p. 38). More substantive research suggests that the political public sphere and the literary public sphere were actually simultaneous. Brewer, for example, argues that the growing number of early-eighteenth-century news and periodical commodities also attempted to offer codes of conduct, linked to a notion of civility that legitimized the emerging public of bourgeois economic agents, and to reconcile the otherwise egocentric and thus incompatible interests of individuals through notions of propriety and morality. The newspaper, he writes, 'served not only as a business seismograph, informing merchants, middlemen and traders of tremors that could lead to a financial earthquake, but also taught precisely those virtues and values that were necessary for survival in an economically expansive though debt-ridden society.'[19] These values linked individual economic freedom to civic responsibility based on acknowledging the rights, as property owners, of one's peers. The institutions of the public sphere – the press and associational organizations – thus managed to meld the realization of specific economic interests with a new kind of freedom: freedom from state intervention and from aristo-cratic client-relations, the freedom to associate outside of and in spite of these, and the freedom to realize one's own interests and economic aspirations in an open market.

The ideological normalization of this public, via its experience of itself as universal in ways that denied its specificity and exclusive-ness, was secured also through the construction of domestic space, in the sense of the intimate space of family and hearth. The private household was the space in which the subjectivity that the literary public sphere discussed and reproduced textually was formed. The autonomy of the private economic agent found its moral and psy-chological correlative in the fictional autonomy of the individuals who came together freely to form the family unit. The family seemed to be established 'voluntarily and by free individuals and to be maintained without coercion; it seemed to rest on the lasting community of love on the part of the two spouses; it seemed to permit the non-instrumental development of all faculties that mark the cultivated personality' (*ST*, p. 46–7). The male family head thus returned to the hearth not as patriarch nor as an economic agent, but as a human being characterized by the uncoerced rationality and affection that he shared in common with other family members. Accordingly, this myth of the bourgeois family also managed to efface both the conditions that secured the legal author-ity of the male family head, and the residual economic relations in which marriage was seen as a contractual exchange of property, women, status and social legitimation. A novel like Richardson's

Pamela, for example, works out the space of domesticity as antithetical to class division and instrumental relations, and as premised on a moral community built on the common humanity of husband and wife. Pamela and Mr. B. transcend their social and economic specificity to form a family.[20] Moreover the novel itself, in its circulation as a culture-commodity, defined the realm of human subjectivity it represented as a sociological fact in the form of an empathetic bourgeois readership. With the popularity of similarly affective works towards the end of the century, such as Gothic-sentimental novels, and Romantic prose like Goethe's *The Sorrows of Young Werther*, 'relations between author, work, and public changed. They became intimate mutual relationships between privatized individuals who were psychologically interested in what was "human," in self-knowledge, and in empathy' (*ST*, p. 50). In the eighteenth century the connection between empathy and sociability was a constant focus of aesthetic theory and political philosophy. Sympathy, or the cult of sensibility, implying a kind of visceral response to external stimuli that indexed the moral resources of the respondent, suggested, in Hume's *A Treatise of Human Nature* for example, the 'intercourse of sentiments' which 'in society and conversation, makes us form some general and inalterable standard by which we may approve and disapprove of characters and manners'.[21] The sympathy generated in the literary public sphere, in other words, could be grasped as the basis of normative sociability – of humanity, morality, civic harmony, all that binds monadic interests together into a community. In this respect we can see how the apparently 'disinterested' realm of the aesthetic – as formulated by Schiller – worked in tandem with the development of class interests and the class-based distribution of cultural capital and literacy, forming, as Habermas writes, the *'fictitious identity of the two roles assumed by the privatized individuals who came together to form a public: the role of property owners and the role of human beings pure and simple'* (*ST*, p. 56). Habermas's conceptualization of the printed text as primarily a commodity foregrounds the slippage between reading and economic exchange as activities that both imply property ownership, together forming a structure in which class identity was constituted partly through the production and consumption of texts.

The crucial point we need to grasp here, one that Habermas's account actually elides to some extent, is that privacy, private reading, and private culture-consumption become the mediums of a public now understood as an imagined community of private individuals.[22] Jon Klancher makes this very point when, discussing James Anderson's journal the Edinburgh *Bee*, he argues that the journal became a 'portable coffeehouse' offering a simulated public to private readers: 'This "society of the text" brings into the after-hours realm of familial privacy the wider discourse of the public sphere.'[23] By the end of the eighteenth century, in other words, public space was no longer essential to a public sphere that had become 'an image to be consumed' rather than a place to frequent. Klancher quotes Anderson to this effect:

> A man, after the fatigues of the day are over, may thus sit down in his elbow chair, and together with his wife and family, be introduced, as it were, into a spacious coffee house, which is frequented by men of all nations, who meet together for their mutual entertainment and improvement.[24]

In this process the institutions of emerging capitalism – the nuclear family, private property and possessive individualism – were normalized and universalized as essentially 'human'. The monadic subjectivity of the bourgeois citizen was rehearsed in the act of reading and the myths of privacy, autonomous and disinterested, it fostered. This is why Max Horkheimer can describe the family as the reserve of utopian impulses, as cultivating 'the dream of a better condition for mankind' despite its otherwise obvious relations to power.[25] In the family man can be imagined as some kind of ideal communal creature. If, as Pheng Cheah writes, Kantian notions of enlightened publicity imply a 'sense of progressive time ... reaching through the future into the timeless ideal of social stability', then, ironically, the family and its attendant myth of disinterested privacy, so closely bound up with the development of aesthetic sensibility, provide the enlightenment's most tangible version of how this stability beyond history was imagined.[26] The public, in other words, can become a stable and harmonizing collective precisely because it only exists as a series of private individuals or family units imagining community through private consumption and, periodically, in public entertainments like the theatre. The bourgeois public sphere, by this reckoning, was as reliant on private imaginings or simulations of the 'humanity' supposed to be explored in actual interactive space, as it was on forms of public discussion and organization. As we will see, actual public spaces devoted to political debate and education became the focus of official paranoia and invigilation in the 1790s. These tangible forms of public activity, indicative of a radical political culture encompassing, sometimes uneasily, bourgeois and proletarian interests, might be thought of as oppositional in their resistance both to the exclusive ambit of parliamentary politics in the late-eighteenth century, and to the orientation of bourgeois life to private culture-consumption.

BOURGEOIS PUBLICITY BEYOND SENTIMENTAL HUMANISM

Habermas's discussion of the public sphere gives us a somewhat prudish account of the cultural forms mediating the consolidation of private, monadic subjects in the period. In *The Structural Transformation* Richardson and Goethe emerge as the two exemplary models of affective cultural production, sentiment and feeling. Needless to say the more general frame Habermas establishes, in which the bourgeois public sphere is subsequently degraded by the invasiveness of the culture industry, necessitates the exclusion of more obviously mass cultural forms – like the Gothic novel for instance – from the scope of bourgeois publicity in the eighteenth century, in order to preserve it as the lost horizon of normative-utopian potential in which the idealism of Romantic and neo-Platonic thought is still hopefully posited. It is for this reason, of course, that the literary becomes central to the public sphere's normative dimension, despite Habermas's stress on public reason as the essence of bourgeois humanism's idealism. In the late-eighteenth century, however, culture-consumption was more diverse than this account allows for. In the following chapters I will argue that forms of discourse and entertainment, that at a glance seem a world away from the idealism of Schiller's *Kultur*, or Wordsworth's 'spots of time', also consolidated the monadic subject, allowing us to argue, against Habermas's account of the public as a *Verfallsgeschichte* (a history of decline), that an emerging culture industry, realized in mass cultural forms that were prurient and voyeuristic, had a significant role to play in the construction and dissemination of bourgeois humanist ideals.

Edmund Burke's speech at the impeachment of Warren Hastings, and his subsequent attacks on the French Revolution, both in and out of parliament, provide a good example of what I mean here. Burke's career at the end of the 1780s and through the early 1790s until his death in 1797 has been seen as indicative of the ways in which political discourse – parliamentary and pertaining to the security and management of the state – was Gothicized and sentimentalized, that is infused with a kind of performativity and literariness that effectively made the disinterested realm of the aesthetic the medium of national and colonial policy. Burke, Claudia Johnson writes, in drawing on sentimentalized images of suffering females, incited pathos as a 'momentous national duty', and in so doing attempted to consolidate a form of community, or at least communal outrage, around images of threatened privacy. Johnson rightly points out that Burke's speeches and writings evoke public consciousness as an effect of aesthetic strategies that moulded emotional responses in a way conducive to the maintenance of civic order:

> For Burke, the continuance of civil order resulted not from our conviction of the rational or metaphysical rightness of certain moral obligations and arrangements, but rather from our attachment to customary practices, practices which are unconflictually sustained because we feel emotions of veneration, awe, desire, solicitude, gratitude, loyalty, endearment towards them and towards the persons who represent them.[27]

But the way in which this happened was not just a matter of one's veneration of Marie Antoinette and the ideal she represented for Burke. In the following chapter I'll argue that Burke's speech at the impeachment of Warren Hasting in 1788 deployed images of female suffering in ways that also appealed to the prurient and voyeuristic pleasure of the public. In so doing it consolidated an imagined community by implicitly appealing to a sense of collective guilt closely linked to the lurid pleasures of contemplating scenes of extreme sadistic violence. The speech and the kind of communal identity it consolidated exemplify Slavoj Žižek's idea that what binds a community together most emphatically is the 'solidarity-in-guilt induced by participation in common transgression'.[28] By this reckoning the intrinsic humanity suggested by sympathy and sensibility is confirmed as a response to the guilt one feels at having derived some sort of pleasure from the spectacle of another's suffering. Burke's speech ends up being much closer to sensationalized, exploitative forms of mass culture than to the idealism of aesthetic education, yet the forms of subjectivity and communal identity fostered by each were ultimately, I'll argue, very similar. By emphasizing this similarity we are also revealing what Habermas's account of the public sphere represses – namely that the normative-utopian realm of bourgeois subjectivity was already thoroughly implicated in and mediated through what critical theorists would today call the culture industry.

Late-eighteenth-century Gothic novels provide perhaps the best example of this complicity between bourgeois privacy and the culture industry. In *Madness and Civilization* Michel Foucault provides a compelling account of how the Gothic aesthetic developed alongside forms of discipline and social control that he identifies as typical of the enlightenment. Foucault argues that the enlightenment, the age of reason, involves the development of a disciplinary infrastructure oriented to the confinement of a complex of social and moral disorders that are simply defined as reason's negation – unreason. What counted as unreason here, what was confinable, was defined through a web of moral imperatives linked to processes of economic rationalization, the related formalization of law and the dream of synchronicity between these and human will itself. Accordingly individuals or groups that counted as symptomatic of a rejection of this synchronicity (the idle, the unproductive, and the transient as well as the insane) found themselves bound to reason's reintegrative infrastructure, bound 'to the rules of morality and their monotonous nights' – stasis, disciplinary fixity, morally redemptive labour.[29] It is not difficult to see how reason and unreason are categories that function in the normalization of a certain set of social and economic relations broadly synonymous with the instrumentalized relations that inform emerging capitalism. The experience of unreason, Foucault argues, is defined largely through this process of normalization, which manifests itself in policing practices oriented to the incarceration and containment of unreason. It is the material forms of these policing practices – from actual modes of incarceration, to textual forms of representation – which become reworked into literature as the imaginative rehearsal of a space antithetical to reason's hegemony. If reason is the principle that characterizes productive integration into society as an organic whole and galvanizes the illusory collective will of the public sphere, then unreason designates a space at once 'outside' of reason's redemptively integrative structures, but also a space defined as such by the disciplinary practices that mediate public or civic awareness. The imagery and iconography of unreason can thus become the locus of a dissidence that attempts to realize the excess occluded by reason. Unreason itself is recuperated in a different discursive space – a space equivalent to what Marcuse calls affirmative culture – as a symbolic or spectacular negation of alienating structures. Max Byrd, discussing the role of places of confinement in eighteenth-century fiction, arrives at a similar conclusion: 'Within the confines of a sometimes dogmatic eighteenth-century humanism, in other words, runs a countercurrent of literary energy, straining against precisely what we sometimes strain against in writing.'[30] In the 1790s this dynamic is perhaps most evident in the prophetic poetry of William Blake, in which political and erotic liberation are associated with sometimes dangerous forms of violence or unreason. Orc's political and sexual energy in 'America' and Oothoon's defence of free love in 'Visions of the Daughters of Albion' both oppose the tyranny of law and reason, which is embodied in the figure of Urizen, and indeed the broader scope of Blake's worldview implies the complicity between colonial exploitation, capitalism and a law-bound society.[31]

Foucault's discussion of the emergence of literature at the end of the eighteenth century forces us to expand our definition of affirmative culture and our ideas about how it functions. *Madness and Civilization* suggests that something like affirmative textual production, by the end of the eighteenth century, became a discursive practice marked by the grotesque, the sadistic, the sublime and the transgressive, as well as by sentimental humanism. If the castle of confinement, as the material form of unreason's containment, became a site of disease, insanity and criminality in the paranoid imagination of the emerging nation-state,

> These same dangers, at the same time, fascinated men's imaginations and their desires. Morality dreams of exorcising them, but there is something in man which makes him dream of experiencing them, or at least of approaching them and releasing their hallucinations. The horror that now surrounded the fortress of confinement also exercised an irresistible attraction. Such nights were peopled with inaccessible pleasures; such corrupt and ravaged faces became masks of voluptuousness; against these dark landscapes appeared forms – pains and delights – which echoed Hieronymous Bosch and his delirious gardens.[32]

The public production of unreason as the antithesis of society can thus also be read as the preservation of the possibility of transgression once this production has been recuperated from policing and judicial practices in the form of literature. Late-eighteenth-century Gothic literature clearly utilizes the iconography of unreason as its content – 'the Fortress, the Cell, the Cellar, the Convent, the inaccessible Island which thus form, as it were, the natural habitat of unreason'.[33] Sade is of course the strong articulation of this. However, Foucault wants to claim more than merely the return of unreason as literature. He is suggesting that literature itself as a discursive formation comes into existence with these textual forms, with the Gothic or Sadean moment. While language becomes increasingly 'traversed' with knowledge in, say, the human sciences, it also reconstitutes itself as the negation of this process. At the end of the eighteenth and the beginning of the nineteenth century,

> literature becomes progressively more differentiated from the discourse of ideas, and encloses itself within a radical intransitivity; it becomes detached from the values which were able to keep it in general circulation during the classical age (taste, pleasure, naturalness, truth), and creates within its own space everything that will ensure a ludic denial of them (the scandalous, the ugly, the impossible).[34]

It is in his 1963 essay 'Language to Infinity' that Foucault gives his most systematic account of this argument. In its attempt to create a sensuous-material experience utilizing the related aesthetics of sadism and the sublime, Gothic literature is bound into the contradictions of its own linguistic constitution. It must, on the one hand, deny its own textuality in order to allow the reader access to unmediated sensation, and, on the other, deploy its textuality as the mode in which sensation is possible. As Simon During writes, 'In trying to disengage themselves from the linguistic, using and evoking terror calmly, these works which attempt to exceed language, to pass themselves off as sensations, become all the more linguistic.'[35] For Foucault the works of Sade and 'the tales of terror' are composed of

> languages which are constantly drawn out of themselves by the overwhelming, the unspeakable, by thrills, stupefaction, ecstasy, dumbness, pure violence, wordless gestures, and which are calculated with the greatest economy and precision to produce effects (so that they make themselves as transparent as possible at this

limit of language toward which they hurry, erasing themselves in their writing of the exclusive sovereignty of that which they wish to say and which lies outside of words) – these languages very strangely represent themselves in a slow, meticulous, and infinitely extendible ceremony.[36]

Literature then, in the very specific sense that Foucault discusses it, has a dual relationship to functionalized discursive practices. Firstly, it recuperates a vision of transgression from practices that are un-ambiguously prescriptive or authoritarian, and, secondly, it presents this vision in a sensationalized medium that reinscribes its material-ity (textuality) at the very moment that it promises an unmediated experience of terror. To the extent that it offers the reader a kind of escape into sensationalism, it too can be understood as performing an affirmative function. The negation of the instrumentalizing structures of emerging capitalism is enacted in a spectacle of vio-lence that itself presupposes the economy of commodification, cir-culation and private consumption in which textual objects mediate the stabilization of society. The very forms of culture-consumption that seem to transgress Habermas's reason-bound public in fact re-inforce it by consolidating notions of privacy, private pleasure and private consumption as redemptive and ultimately therapeutic. As is the case in Marcuse's theory of affirmative culture, pleasure, re-gardless of whether it is refined or populist, is a matter for private subjects, and it is this privacy that was becoming increasingly imbri-cated with culture-consumption in the eighteenth century.

Habermas's account of the bourgeois public sphere and the role of culture in it is one that I think remains crucial to our understand-ing of the late-eighteenth century. Yet it only does so if we are able to expand this model to suggest the ways in which more diverse forms of textual and discursive production functioned in the consol-idation of bourgeois privacy and how these potentially undermine or disorganize the public culture of political activism that emerged during the 1790s. By looking at the Gothic aesthetic – with its explicit debts to sometimes extreme images of transgression – we are also forced to consider the ways in which culture-consumption could embody a symbolic refusal of societal norms and, precisely in this refusal, stabilize those norms just as emphatically as those forms of culture that appear more explicitly committed to the maintenance of civic order. A text like Matthew Lewis's *The Monk*, I'll argue, functioned in this way – that is as part of a discursive formation that defined transgression and private reading as virtually synonymous.

TOWARDS A PROLETARIAN PUBLIC SPHERE

By Habermas's own admission the bourgeois public sphere was exclusionary. To participate in the public's fictitious equation of *bourgeois* and *homme* one needed a certain level of cultural literacy and, relatedly, a certain degree of financial security. While the public could, in theory, include everyone, its reality marginalized lower class men and, one would expect, all but an elite of extremely privileged women. In the 1790s radical writers repeatedly pointed out that official definitions of the 'public' excluded the vast majority of Britons. When Burke calculated the British public, which he defined as members of the population with the leisure to engage in rational discussion, at four hundred thousand, the radical orator John Thelwall responded by claiming that Burke had condemned nine-tenths of the population to political annihilation: 'This the British public! – and what are all the rest? Political non-entities! – a dash of the pen has blotted them out of the book of life' (*RN*, p. 397). But recent criticism of the model goes significantly further than just corroborating the bourgeois public's exclusionary nature. Habermas is, after all, very clear about the dialectical nature of his model and his most lucidly argued sections turn on an analysis of the relationship between the idea of the public (its normative-utopian moment) and its practice (its ideological moment). What characterizes a good deal of the revisionist work on Habermas, especially that written from a Marxist perspective, is a profound ambivalence about whether or not integration into a dominant public is desirable and, beyond this, whether it is sufficient to offer multiple or counterhegemonic public spheres, oriented to engagement with the political and social institutions of the dominant public sphere, as a viable way of conducting oppositional politics.[37] The problem is this: if the imagined community of the bourgeois public sphere is the medium in which bourgeois class hegemony is secured and normalized, it is also characterized by fundamental mystifications at the level of social and economic relations. The worker, for example, can only be integrated into the public to the extent to which he becomes a privatized property owner, which means the reification of his or her own body in the form of wage-labour. In this way the naturalization of the bourgeois monad can compel the assimilation of other groups into a form of sociability that clearly alienates them from their own class interests, which reside in a transformation of the structures of ownership, rather than mere assimilation into them. By conceptualizing political opposition as an interrogation of the boundaries of the public sphere, is one merely reproducing reified, oppressive and alienating structures as the basis of reformist politics? As we will see this question goes to the heart of radical politics in the 1790s, in which we can read proto-socialist elements formulating a critique of property relations that threatened to go beyond demands for an extended franchise and parliamentary reform.

Oskar Negt and Alexander Kluge's 1972 *The Public Sphere and Experience: Towards an Analysis of the Bourgeois and Proletarian Public Sphere* perhaps goes furthest in examining these problems at a theoretical level. The two long chapters that commence their book read like a critique of Habermas that proceeds by reproducing, expanding and developing upon the dialectical frame that Habermas's first four chapters established, but in a manner that clearly rejects Habermas's faith in the normative dimension of bourgeois publicity and his attempts to reconcile this with Marxist politics. Negt and Kluge depart from Habermas in their attempt to argue that the bourgeois public sphere can offer no normative potential that is not always-already ideological. They argue, as Marx had done, that civil society premised on the rights of man is the expression of one class interest and involves the mystification, disorganization or recoding of others. Negt and Kluge develop this fundamental position in a myriad of directions, arriving at a comprehensive critique of the alienating and recoding structures of the bourgeois public sphere.

> The 'dictatorship of the bourgeoisie' articulates itself in compartmentalizations, the *forms* of the public sphere. Whereas the bourgeois revolution initially makes a thoroughgoing attempt to overcome the limits of the capitalist mode of production, the forms – for instance, the forced separation of powers, the division between public and private, between politics and production, between everyday language and authentic social expression, between education, science, and art on the one hand and the interests and expressions of the masses on the other – prevent even the mere expressions of social criticism, of a counterpublic sphere, and of the emancipation of the majority of the popula-

tion. There is no chance that the experiences and interests of the proletariat, in the broadest sense, will be able to organize themselves amid this splitting of all the interrelated qualitative elements of experience and social practice.

(*PSE*, p. xlvii)

The idea of the 'experiences and interests of the proletariat' is characteristically proleptic. It is marked by the very forces of alienation and reification that prevent its actual realization as a revolutionary political force. In this Negt and Kluge are faithful to their intellectual origins, as they themselves point out:

For Marx, the concept of 'the proletarian' resonates with a meaning content that is not reflected in sociological and political-economic definitions of the working class, although it constitutes their material foundation. In the proletariat there is concentrated the practical negation of the existing world that need only be conceptualized to become part of the history of the political emancipation of the working class.

(*PSE*, p. xlv, n. 3)

For Negt and Kluge the everyday experiences of the proletariat conceived empirically are prevented from achieving the clarity of 'proletarian experience' because they are mediated through the 'totality of the context of mystification', and thereby constituted in alienation from the real interests that motivate them.[38] Accordingly the worker 'would have to be a philosopher to understand how his experience is produced, an experience that is at once preorganized and unorganized and simultaneously moulds and merely accompanies his empirical life' (*PSE*, p. 6). The very social constitution of this experience thus presupposes its obstruction as an oppositional political force.

However, this does not mean that proletarian experience is impossible, but that its realization can only occur outside the mediating framework of the bourgeois public sphere, in which, even in the form of an extended franchise, or organized union and labour reform movements, it is compelled to assume a mystified form in which it reiterates itself through structures that are antithetical to non-propertied interests. Negt and Kluge argue that the solution to this bind resides in the formation of a proletarian public sphere – 'the autonomous, collective organization of the experience specific to workers' (*PSE*, p. 28). They again evoke Marx to pit authentic human need against the mystified, monadic subject – what Marx described in *On the Jewish Question* as 'egotistical man, man as a member of civil society, namely as an individual drawn into himself, his private interests and his private desires and separated from the community'.[39]

> Marx describes social wealth in this respect as the many-sided un-folding of the energies of the human species: **sociality – coopera-tion – freedom – awareness – universality – wealth of needs and of subjective human sensuality**. Each of these human modes of expression requires a public sphere for its development; each rep-resents an essential component of the proletarian public sphere.
>
> (*PSE*, p. 83)

Negt and Kluge then go on, in a manner that mimics that lexiconi-cal format of Marx's discussion of the terminology of the 1793 'Declaration of the Rights of Man and of the Citizen' in *On the Jewish Question*, to offer definitions of these terms that reveal their distance from mystified usages: '**Freedom** is understood as a material re-demption of the emphatic concept of freedom, a concept that the bourgeoisie coined but never put into practice; it embraces auto-nomy, identity, and production governed by the producers them-selves' (*PSE*, p. 83). This potential is redeemed, at the very least, as the basis of ideology critique.

> The category of true needs must, under existing circumstances, have something intangible about it, because the truth content of those needs could be verified only once they were developed; nevertheless they exist as that which is developing. Because they do exist, the following sentence has a substantive meaning: the question of true needs entails the concrete imperative to guard against false needs.
>
> (*PSE*, p. 84)

Where Negt and Kluge's text represents a significant advance beyond Habermas's is in its detailed and far-ranging discussion of the manners in which the bourgeois public sphere constitutes these false needs. Not only does the bourgeois public sphere block and fragment proletarian experience, but it composes itself of media that assimilate this experience, recode it, prepare substitute gratifications for the elements of social wealth it implies, and (dis)organize it such that it can be domesticated within prevailing forms of politics, consumption and privacy. The bourgeois public sphere, through these media, manufactures the appearance of a unified polity, a collective will, and a politically participatory constituency. It thus functions as the 'illusory synthesis of the totality of society' (*PSE*, p. 56). This synthesis is illusory because it constitutes a social order and modes of social and economic discipline around the essentially private bourgeois subject, and then retrospectively imagines these as if they were the products of the collective will. Once it is assumed that civic integration is linked to one's integration into the instrumentalized relations of emergent capitalism, that is to one's identity as a property owner even when this property amounts to one's own labour, then politics can proceed as the policing of elements that refuse these structures and the management of the body-politic conceived as an expansive and functionally integrated system of money and commodity flows. And all this amounts to no more than the implementation of the collective or public will. This illusory synthesis is equivalent to Hannah Arendt's notion of 'society' – the object of political economy – in which socialization necessitates the manipulation of behaviour, through precisely the kind of mechanisms that Negt and Kluge discuss, in order to maintain the functional integration of the social whole. 'Society', writes Arendt, 'always demands that its members act as though they were members of one enormous family which has only one opinion and one interest.'[40] As we will see in the following chapters, the image of the polity as a household, and of politics as a form of household management, is literalized in the sentimentalizing structures of reactionary politics in the 1790s, which conceptualize Jacobin politics in terms of a threat to the integrity of domestic space and to the women who reside there. In doing so these sentimentalizing strategies present domestic space both as an image of society, and as a bastion of the humanity that is supposed to inform it. Edmund Burke in particular will reveal the dependence of the social order on these ideological images, and the constructions of humanity and private space that they involve, in his commitment to their defense.

The media through which the bourgeois public sphere blocks, assimilates and disorganizes alien experience seem to include for Negt and Kluge (1) forms of political organization that assimilate their participants into bourgeois political institutions, (2) forms of education that alienate elements of the population from the linguistic and interpretive structures in which their experiences are phrased, (3) discourses that attempt to delegitimize, psychologize or criminalize elements that don't assimilate, and, most importantly for this study, (4) forms of culture equivalent to what I've described, after Marcuse, as affirmative culture. These media recreate the contours of the illusory public sphere in terms of imagined boundaries that imply a vision of integration and one of non- or disintegration. It is in this topography that concepts like politics, morality, status and pleasure are defined. The model that Negt and Kluge suggest can be imagined in the following way: the bourgeois public sphere is constituted within capitalism's mode of production as the latter's most central legitimizing component, as the largely imagined communal structure in which the experiences and interests of private subjects are harmonized and contained. This appearance of harmony is a result of discursive practices that undermine actual communal structures in the normalization of private interests and therefore limit the realization of proletarian politics, preventing it from moving beyond the institutions of the bourgeoisie. These discursive practices assume the monadic subject of what Marx refers to as civil society as their organizing principle. The public sphere takes on the illusion of collective will, despite its class-specific character, because interests and experiences outside its mystificatory structures are so fundamentally fragmented, disorganized and marginalized by these discursive apparatuses and the constitution of production generally, that they become spectral. Not existing through modes of legitimization they don't exist at all except as threatening, pathological variants of bourgeois behaviour increasingly defined as private and monadic in nature.

The relationship between affirmative culture and the public sphere is implicit in Negt and Kluge's crucial discussion of fantasy. Fantasy constitutes itself within proletarian production as 'a necessary compensation for the experience of the alienated labour process'. It is a 'defense mechanism' protecting the worker from the 'shock effects of an alienated reality' (*PSE*, p. 33). While fantasy is thus the condition if not of the worker's integration into the collective will of the bourgeois public sphere, then of his or her uneasy coexistence with it, it is also itself an alienated form of experience. Its mere existence, Negt and Kluge stress, has to constitute a critique of the alienating processes from which it protects the fantasizing subject. Fantasy, in other words, embodies the need to negate the everyday experience of life in an instrumentalized society. In this respect, as James Chandler points out, we might imagine Keats's 'Ode to a Nightingale' as a representation of fantasy in its relationship to the social reality, a turning away from a state of alienation to the imagined pleasures of reverie embodied in the nightingale's song.[41] Despite the merely escapist tendencies of fantasy, and the fact that the designation itself necessarily replicates the ideological allocation of non-reified impulses to a space which is private and individualized, fantasy is nevertheless a form of experience that, once recuperated in 'reality', could potentially transform the reality principle 'in opposition to which it exhausts itself' (*PSE*, p. 37, n. 57). Fantasy, it would seem, can thus take three possible forms: (1) it can be the raw expression of alienated experience implying, (2) its potential sublimation into reality in the form of organized proletarian experience, or (3) its incorporation into the public sphere and the world of valorized economic interactions through processes of commodification and consumerism which properly belong to the consciousness industry.

Marcuse, as we have seen, argues that art's apparent autonomy from the everyday world, which is its defining characteristic in bourgeois society, is ideologically mediated. On the one hand it embodies impulses that can find no tangible expression in the reified social and economic interactions of this society, while, on the other, it brackets these very possibilities in the sequestered space of aesthetic consumption such that they remain an aspect of one's private, internal world. The realm of art is thus constituted as one separate from the everyday (or from what Negt and Kluge refer to as the 'reality principle'), but this very separateness is the medium in which it replicates the alienated structures of what it apparently negates. In this contradiction resides literature's (or art's) 'affirmative' character, which articulates both aspects of its function. The absence of a discussion of literature in conjunction with fantasy in Negt and Kluge's text, given the obviousness of the connection and the precedent for making it, would seem to suggest the lengths to which they wanted to go in order to ensure that fantasy is not associated with the literary experience of bourgeois society in any definitional way. On the contrary literature, and affirmative culture generally, would be logically understood as one of the media that reifies fantasy beyond its merely alienated character, beyond its self-constitution as the negation of bourgeois society. The implication of Negt and Kluge's text is that, from the standpoint of proletarian experience, the distinction between literature, in the sense of affirmative culture, and the more obviously manipulative forms of the modern consciousness industry, is misleading. Both appropriate and domesticate fantasy, sublimating it into the act of consumption. This would mean that affirmative culture and the ideological manipulations of the consciousness industry, while not identical, are at least imbricated at the point at which fantasy is pacified and reintegrated into acceptable economies of discursive production and reception. Work done on spectatorship and cultural production in the late-eighteenth century already suggests this. Paula Backscheider's *Spectacular Politics*, for example, argues that Gothic theatrical productions of the 1780s and 1790s consolidated a public of culture-consumers, and that the public sphere was in fact never immune to, but actually contingent on these mass cultural forms.[42]

Negt and Kluge thus remove the possibility of reading the sensibility of literature as a locus for anything redemptive, and return to the more orthodox Marxist focus on the experience of the proletariat as the possibility of negating or sublating bourgeois society. But their view of the proletariat is not synonymous with an empirical working class by any means. The term stands for the possibility of needs in excess of the forms that needs can take in bourgeois society. To the extent to which one can experience one's everyday experience as alienating – in whatever localized or fragmented forms this would take, and fantasy seems to be one – the possibility of authentic needs beyond signification is graspable in this experience. Affirmative literature then does not simply fabricate a subject from nothing, but organizes subjectivity in a way that negates or pacifies the alienated experience of labour. It seizes on fantasy and links it to objects or spectacles such that the subject as consumer or spectator emerges alienated from the experience of alienation, into a world of ubiquitous communal responsiveness linked to a sensual-material experience that is both private and shared, and always contingent on affirmative media. This alienation from the experience of alienation I want to call surplus alienation. It eradicates the possibility of experience that, if organized, could be genuinely critical and oppositional because premised on the manifest injustice of wage-labour, and pacifies discontent with the pleasures of consumption. It is this aspect of the bourgeois public sphere that became increasingly pervasive in the late-eighteenth and early-nineteenth centuries, constituting an impediment to the realization of interests beyond the limits of bourgeois emancipation.

CULTURAL POLITICS IN THE 1790s

In the following chapters I discuss material from the last decade or so of the eighteenth century and position it with regard to the theoretical concepts that I have outlined above. The first chapter deals with Edmund Burke's speech at the impeachment of Warren Hastings in 1788, the last with the 1802 edition of Maria Edgeworth's *Belinda*. In the 14 years between these two points the milieu of radical corresponding societies and the mass distribution of radical publications render the ideological tensions of emerging capitalism more evident than at any other point in the century. The various complicities and antagonisms in the relationship between the bourgeois public sphere and proletarian political culture is what primarily defines this dynamic, at least for the purposes of this study. As Jon Klancher points out these two publics had a derivative and dependent relationship. On the one hand, the 'idea of a radical audience presupposed a dominant public' while, on the other hand, 'against a real or imagined radical antagonist, middle class writers and readers also helped produce a self-consciously dominant culture'.[43] Chapter 1 on Burke and Chapter 4 on the Gothic attempt to illustrate how, beyond models of sentimental humanism, different forms of discursive production consolidated the private subject and by extension an imagined community founded in some sense on the ubiquity of this privacy. In my discussion of Burke I argue that attempts to consolidate a normative sense of community, based on the moral culture of sensibility or empathy, repress the more perverse, unnameable pleasures of spectatorship inherent in the cult of sensibility. The affect of the sentimental spectacle and of voyeuristic sadomasochistic scenarios, linked explicitly to the sensationalism of culture-consumption, turn out to be codependent in a way that compromises the assumption of moral community cohering just through the solicitation of sympathy. By reading Burke's speech in this way we can see how the apparently normative component of an emerging bourgeois public sphere is complicit with consumer capitalism and the reproduction of the mode of production. Burke's speeches were not merely manipulative, persuasive or didactic in their avowal of a specific ideological position: the modes of reception and subject formation they implied actively formed the kind of public he saw as necessary to counter the dangerous publicity of Jacobin clubs, dissenting societies and popular mobilization. This public was one premised on the imagined collectivity of a monadic form of subjectivity. In this valorization of monadic subjectivity, more interactive publics oriented to forms of political intervention and activism were paradoxically stigmatized as synonymous with mass manipulation and indoctrination, such that figures like Richard Price, Thomas Paine, William Godwin, Thomas Spence and John Thelwall became the standard-bearers for a crass form of print-capitalism that could proceed without any regard for the welfare of society and the culture of sensibility which provided its apparently moral underpinnings. Burke's polarization of modes of cultural production and political thought figured prominently in the formation of a British national identity in which certain kinds of political philosophy and culture were marginalized and vilified.

The fourth chapter picks up this story, returning to the idea of culture-consumption as a basis for a subjectivity complicit with the structures of emerging capitalism. Examining anti-Jacobin and Romantic accounts of the relationship between culture-consumption (print-culture especially) and political populism, I argue that an insistent attempt to marginalize and repress the dangers of consumption imply what Foucault would call a regime of 'power-knowledge-pleasure' in which desire is finally rendered synonymous with practices circumscribed by these proscriptive discourses. The effect of repressing a consumer psychology, seen as common to libertinage and popular chaos, is actually to solicit this psychology and portray it as the basis of a natural, presocial subject. Transgression, liberation and freedom, in other words, inevitably become bound to a model of subjectivity deeply implicated in and complicit with market capitalism. In this way discourses explicitly critical of the market ultimately valorize it as the basis of authentic liberation. The culture of capitalism, in other words, effectively colonizes the very possibility of dissidence, circumscribing it within practices that consolidate the mode of production. What I call the discourse of 'Gothic consumption' deploys Gothic tropes simultaneously to repress and solicit the desire of the reader as consumer. In that Gothic texts were themselves understood as literary commodities, readers engaging with this process of repression and solicitation were themselves actually participating in the freedom of consumerism in the very act of reading. It is in this sense that one can talk about the discipline of reading – that is reading as a practice crucially implicated in the consolidation of emerging capitalism. Finally, in this chapter, I argue that Matthew Lewis's *The Monk* ironically foregrounds the discursive assumptions of Gothic consumption in its realization that readerly desire, populism and libertinage converge in the simultaneously sentimental and sadistic tableaux of the cult of sensibility.

The second and third chapters examine radical attempts to reimagine a public beyond the limits of the bourgeois model. The second chapter focuses on William Godwin's contradictory attempts to rethink the public sphere as the locus of political amelioration. I trace Godwin's simultaneous valorization of public interaction as the basis of rational social and political life, and his fear of it as a domain of mass manipulation. Continually running up against conceptual limits that compel him to read public interaction in terms of an emerging consciousness industry, Godwin finally embraces private life as a realm immune to the pathologies of public mediation. This defeatism is a failure to conceptualize structurally differentiated economies of cultural production and reception and is, I argue, analogous to contemporary theorizations of totalizing power that disallow the possibility of moral or epistemic privilege cohering in socially situated forms of interaction. In Godwin's case a misreading of the milieu of John Thelwall and the radical corresponding societies of the 1790s as symptomatic of pathological publicity closes down the organizational and institutional possibilities immanent in his initial, if very abstract, investment in the idea of public interaction. By mapping the institutional obstacles to his own communicative ideal, however, Godwin finally offers his readership an explication of the relationship between their own reading practices and bourgeois normativity, anticipating the kind of consciousness-raising practice that we can locate in the proletarian public sphere proper.

The third chapter examines the milieu Godwin rejected, in order to offer an account of how we might imagine a structurally differentiated proletarian public sphere emerging out of, but also moving beyond, bourgeois publicity. It details the career of the poet-activist John Thelwall, whose textual production and public oration throughout the 1790s moves from sentimental, proto-Romantic works to forms of oration, political philosophy and poetry that increasingly target the Burkean critique of radical publicity. Speaking at popular meetings and publishing in popular journals designed for an audience of artisans and workers, Thelwall deployed the same sentimental, affective images as Burke, but not as a defence of the social order, nor as affirmative artifacts, but as the medium through which social evils could be measured against the very ideals they transgressed. In his *Rights of Nature* the narrative of 'Gothic usurpation', similar to the narrative that Burke deployed at the impeachment of Warren Hastings, is the basis for a critique of emerging capitalism that clearly demonstrates the affinity between socialist thought and a certain demystificatory utilization of sentimental topoi. In contrast to the economy of affirmative culture, Thelwall demonstrates that sentimentality also functions as the medium in which capitalism first becomes intelligible as an object of critical cognition in the counterhegemonic space of London Corresponding Society meetings, lectures and rallies. Accordingly Thelwall's work opens up a dimension to both sentimental and Gothic textual production ignored by readings that see these only in terms of manipulation or mass culture. In his work we can discern the kind of radicalized aesthetic that Althusser found in the Piccolo Teatro, an aesthetic oriented to the 'production of a new consciousness in the spectator.'[44]

Yet the cultural politics of the 1790s were of course more complicated than the relationship between bourgeois and proletarian models of publicity suggests. The broad category of 'radicalism' has also come to include the feminism of writers like Mary Wollstonecraft and Mary Hays, which was seen by conservatives as broadly complicit with the so-called Jacobinism of figures like Thelwall, Spence and to a lesser degree Godwin. Yet it also seems clear that radical politics presented its own limitations and exclusions for women who might have been otherwise inclined to identify themselves with it. Radical publicity also reproduced the gendered connotations attending the distinction between public and private space. Alongside, then, the development of class tensions and alliances, we can also read the possibility of another kind of public not reducible to either bourgeois or proletarian interests. In the fifth chapter I discuss Mary Wollstonecraft's attempts to move beyond the heteronormative limits of radical discourse and culture-consumption in the formation of a specifically feminist public sphere oriented to the demystification of women's experience. Wollstonecraft, I argue, ultimately realizes that the possibility of a feminist critical practice is disabled by the material, spatial and discursive structures that enclose women within private space and limit critique (or liberation) to the consumption of escapist, sentimental literature. The centrality of textual production as an interpretive topos in her work, as paradoxically a supplement to both hegemony and critique, enables her to engage with the politics of affirmative culture more directly than perhaps any other writer in the period. In this chapter the theoretical assumptions under-pinning the book as a whole will, I hope, be unambiguous: critique is not a purely epistemic matter, but requires spatial and discursive infrastructures and practices which enact it not as a thought experi-ment, but as an active alteration of the discursive possibilities inher-ent in the mode of production.

It is perhaps appropriate to understand the cultural politics of the emerging bourgeois public sphere in terms of what has been called 'internal colonization'. That is to say that the public sphere, under-stood as the effect of an increasingly homogenous and homogen-izing economy of discursive production and reception, functioned as a way of integrating diverse communities into the infrastructures of both a national collective and a capitalist economy. When we discuss proletarian and feminist counterpublics we are thus trying to specify that way in which different sections of the population attempted to phrase their experience and their interests outside of this homogenizing system. Understanding the bourgeois public sphere in this way also lets us expand our account of its cultural politics to include a consideration of how the categories of bour-geois humanism and universalism functioned in the maintenance of power relations between the metropolitan centre and its colonies. While the drive towards a universal cosmopolitan public, implied by the cult of sensibility and high Romantic notions of aesthetics and sympathy, could be used to attack both racism in general and slavery in particular, it could also become the rationale for forms of imperial paternalism in which colonial power relations were reimagined in terms of wage-labour and contractual obligation between free individuals. In this shift, typical of the ways in which abolitionists imagined the future of the West Indian sugar planta-tions, anti-colonial insurgency was delegitimized as a form of dan-gerously revolutionary politics incompatible with the culture of capitalism. Chapter 6 develops this idea through a reading of Maria Edgeworth's 1802 *Belinda*. I argue that Edgeworth's vision of domestic relations beyond the disfiguring effects of slavery and racism also consolidated a particular social order in which the poss-ibilities of resistance to the encroachments of capital were marginal-ized and stigmatized as, alternately, atavistic and decadent. In Edgeworth's work, I argue, the fetish is defined as radically other to a modernity based on rational intercourse and domestic affection, and is used as the sign of those forms of non-identity that resist assimilation into the humanism of market capitalism and bourgeois privacy. Edgeworth's novel demonstrates the double thrust of bourgeois publicity, that its colonization of resistant communal structures works both internally and externally.

In this study I am using theories of the public sphere as a way of specifying very broad political and cultural processes typical of what critical theorists refer to as modernity. The critical utility of doing so is that it makes the potentials and dynamics of modernity, conceptualized as the Western drive towards regulated and disciplined sociability within the infrastructures of developing capitalism, intelligible in a way that they would not be were we simply to assume a series of disparate and local publics. When I began this project I imagined it as an attempt to contextualize literary production (and by extension the notion of 'Literature' itself) in terms of historically tangible forms of discursive practice and, relatedly, as an examination of the power relations inherent in these practices. As it has developed and become quite specifically a book about the 1790s my sense of the necessary exchange between critical theory and cultural history has become more emphatic. Theory remains vital insofar as it helps us describe, albeit in a necessarily heuristic manner, the processes and practices informing a history that is still, in many senses, whether we like it or not, our own. And it is only through the understanding that such accounts yield that we can hope to attain the critical agency that seems so elusive in an age when the instrumentalizing imperatives of modernity seem to be not just our present, but our past and our future as well.

1

Edmund Burke's Immortal Law: Reading the Impeachment of Warren Hastings, 1788

Edmund Burke's 1790 *Reflections on the Revolution in France* probably did more than any other single text or event to galvanize radical political culture in Britain. Thomas Paine and Mary Wollstonecraft, among many others, produced major responses to it, while journals like Daniel Isaac Eaton's *Politics for the People, or A Salmagundy for Swine* and Thomas Spence's *Pig's Meat: or Lessons for the Swinish Multitude* used what they read as Burke's euphemism for the people – 'a swinish multitude' (*RRF*, p. 173) – as the basis for their ironic addresses to the British working class. One of the things Burke's radical critics repeatedly pointed out was the performative, manipulative and distinctly literary quality of his writing and speeches and, relatedly, the ways in which these appealed to the sensibility, not the reason, of his audience. Paine's condemnation in *Rights of Man* is perhaps the best known of these critiques:

> As to the tragic paintings by which Mr Burke has outraged his own imagination, and seeks to work upon that of his readers, they are very well calculated for theatrical representation, where facts are manufactured for the sake of show, and accommodated to produce, through the weakness of sympathy, a weeping effect. But Mr Burke should recollect that he is writing History, and not Plays; and that his reader will expect truth, and not the spouting rant of high-toned exclamation.[1]

As Linda Zerilli has pointed out, Burke's use of figural language in the *Reflections* and indeed in his work more generally has led to the 'curious tendency in political theory scholarship to regard such prose as an almost inexplicable poetic digression'. As a result of treating Burke's hyperbolic rhetoric as 'imagination out of control', Zerilli writes, 'many informed critical readings of Burke see in his theatrical language and chivalric posturing little more than what Thomas Paine aptly coined a "dramatic performance".'[2] The point being made here is that Burke's use of literary conventions, figural digression and sentimental affect should be read as crucial to the ideological design of his work. Paine, of course, clearly saw this. The idea that Burke's manufactured facts were calculated to produce a 'weeping effect' suggests an acute awareness of how the *Reflections* exploited the cult of sensibility in order to legitimize its opposition to the French Revolution and its English supporters. The sense that Burke's digressions were central to his persuasiveness was actually quite generally acknowledged by his contemporary critics. Wollstonecraft, in *Vindication of the Rights of Man*, drew attention to Burke's 'sprightly sallies', 'theatrical attitudes' and 'sentimental exclamations' noting that 'Sensibility is the mania of the day, and compassion the virtue which is to cover a multitude of vices, whilst justice is left to mourn in sullen silence, and balance truth in vain.'[3] In a similar vein John Thelwall wrote, in 1795, that while Burke's 'combustible imagination fumes, and boils and bursts away ... apparently without design',

> the reader, who, on this account, should calculate upon the artlessness of Mr. Burke's mind, would do no credit to his own penetration. 'If this be madness, there is method in't.' In this excursive frenzy of composition, there is much deep design and insidious policy.
>
> (*RN*, p. 396)

By the mid-1790s Burke's writing had come to epitomize the imbrication of the political and the aesthetic. Not surprisingly then contemporary Burke scholars have been concerned with tracing the relationship between Burke's early aesthetic theories on the sublime and the beautiful and his later political thinking in order to come to the crux of what Tom Furniss calls his 'aesthetic ideology'.[4] *Reflections on the Revolution in France*, and its central tableau in which the Jacobin mob pursues Marie Antoinette at Versailles, have justifiably been the focus of this inquiry. In this chapter, however, I want to discuss the confluence of the aesthetic and the political by focusing on an earlier, often ignored moment in Burke's career, one that seems crucial to the development of his thinking in *Reflections*, and one that epitomizes his 'aesthetic ideology' more lucidly and emphatically than that work. Burke's 'Speech on Opening of the Impeachment of Warren Hastings', delivered to the House of Lords over four days in February 1788, is based on ideas about the sublimity and authority of the law that will be crucial to his defence of tradition, property and constitutionality in the *Reflections*, while critiques of its performativity clearly anticipate and inform those, quoted above, by Paine, Wollstonecraft and Thelwall. In the last phase of his career, in which he was obsessed with what he saw as the two great threats to the social fabric – Indianism and Jacobinism – Burke continually appeals to the law as a transcendental principle that underwrites the social order and forms the basis of the moral community he imagined steeled against the threat of revolution. Yet, in his speeches on India and on the revolution, this law – the 'immortal law' – is also a result of a kind of affect. It is a law 'engraved in our ordinances, and in our hearts' (*RRF*, p. 104). Because the law is also the law of the heart, because it must be felt, not simply obeyed, its palpability was also contingent on Burke's ability to present it in a manner that evoked strong feeling. As Burke well knew, a structure of aesthetic affect is central to his evocation of the law: 'public affections, combined with manners, are required sometimes as supplements, sometimes as correctives, always as aids to law' (*RRF*, p. 172). The process by which Burke's own writing and speeches make good his claim that the immortal law is not simply an abstraction, but a palpable, visceral reality integral to the constitution of the feeling citizen, is also the process by which he constructs certain kinds of communal identifications around the assumed ubiquity of sentimental affect. In this respect, I want to argue, Burke's literary and oratorical performances reveal not just the imbrication of the political and the aesthetic but, much more importantly, the ways in which the moral law as the basis of a certain kind of communal identification – or public – is mediated through a particular economy of discursive production. In this chapter my aim is to examine the 'deep design and insidious policy' informing Burke's impeachment speech, in order to show how it actually solicited the commitment to social order that Burke increasingly saw as crucial in the face of revolution abroad and popular political mobilization at home.

Warren Hastings had been Governor-General of Bengal between 1772 and 1785, during which time Burke had become increasingly interested in the conduct of the East India Company. In the two years before Hastings's trial for 'high crimes and misdemeanours' in India (which included the acceptance of bribes, the corrupt delega- tion of revenue collecting contracts and, most importantly, the usu- rious appropriation of capital in Oudh) Burke had been instrumental in leading the House of Commons to consolidate the articles of impeachment, urging closer parliamentary supervision of the Company's administrative practices.[5] The impeachment speech itself presented a bleak and deliberately impressionistic vision of extreme political and sexual violence, in a land ravaged by Company abuse, and peopled by Hastings's shadowy and sadistic Indian agents. What Burke called 'Indianism', however, involved more than just the rapid emergence of a morally bankrupt moneyed class, linked to the enormous gains of East India com- merce, and the threat to established property relations in India which it posed. The speech most explicitly evokes the threat posed by the lawless character of Company mercantilism under Hastings by drawing attention to the violence and cruelty of its assaults on the private space and, ultimately, the bodies of Indian women. The image of Marie Antoinette fleeing Jacobin daggers, for most readers the crux of the *Reflections*, is but an echo of the more exacting viol- ence Burke replayed at the impeachment as a way of illustrating the excesses of what might be called colonial libertinage.

Not surprisingly Burke's speeches on India established a senti- mental narrative frame that foregrounded the continuity and stabil- ity of the Indian propertied classes, the ritual purity of the women who resided within their estates, and, threatening both of these, the violent invasiveness of the East India administration.[6] This narrative frame drew upon images that his 1756 *A Vindication of Natural Society* had first deployed: images of a natural social order, based on the nuclear family and filial affection, systematically destroyed by forms of despotic government that are understood as usurpatory and artificial. Like the eighteenth-century cult of sensibility more gener- ally, Burke's evocation of the family and of the threatened female body as its emblem attempted to solicit a certain kind of public responsiveness. Public sympathy in the face of such images was implicitly understood to be a natural expression of an irreducibly human sensibility, in that it signified concern for the security and protection of filial communality based on 'natural Appetites and Instincts'.[7] Sympathy, in other words, was the visceral evidence of the humanity that one shared in common with other sympathetic respondents. The solicitation of sympathy thus also suggested an internalized code of moral conduct – a moral law inscribed within the sympathetic subject – as well as membership of a benevolent public devoted to the integrity of private space. The sentimentality of the impeachment speech allowed Burke to consolidate the idea of a universal moral law, engraved in the heart, through a structure of discursive affect. The affectivity of the speech, in other words, could mediate what Burke referred to as a 'moral community' united in its humane sympathy for the victims of Company abuse he presented. Burke's evocation of public sympathy, however, cannot be separated from his portrayal of the violence threatening Indian women. In his infamous descriptions of the torture accompanying Devi Singh's collection of revenue in Northern Bengal, Burke rehearsed the minute details of mercantile violence in a manner that his critics found shocking, obscene and excessive. In these descriptions, which importantly contained allegations not included in the formal charges laid against Hastings, the solicitation of sensibility is inseparable from the representation of sadistic agency violating the harmony of the sentimental tableau. In the impeachment speech what Claudia Johnson describes as 'Burke's lurid evocation of intense female suffering' not only attempted to incite pathos as a 'momentous national duty',[8] it also incited a prurient curiosity not only in excess of, but directly opposed to the moral responsiveness Burke attempted to solicit: a curiosity oriented to the consumption of sensationalized representations of sexual violence.

This duplicitous form of culture-consumption is structurally typical of late-eighteenth-century Gothic-pathetic literature, in which sympathy is usually predicated on witnessing some kind of suffering. Appropriated as public discourse in the impeachment speech, this structure was central to the consolidation of a metropolitan public complicit with the assumptions of paternalistic colonial authority, despite the speech's apparently anti-imperial leanings, and more broadly with what I have described as bourgeois individualism, in which the assumption of monadic interiority is the condition of communal solidarity. The speech performed a crucial double operation: in the face of Hastings's colonial libertinage it attempted to forge a public united in its moral outrage and ultimately assured of the universality of its moral norms as the basis of colonial management in India, while simultaneously enabling the individual members of this public to indulge in a form of spectatorship or culture-consumption oriented to the private abnegation of these norms. Insofar as it deployed aesthetic forms in which sentiment and suffering were not only coterminous, but mutually dependent, the speech implied the simultaneity of both community and monadic subjectivity, of both public law and private transgression. It could be experienced both as a political-judicial event soliciting a moral response in accordance with apparently universal laws of conduct, and as a form of spectacular entertainment soliciting more diverse and unnameable pleasures. This duplicity will force us to re-evaluate the affectivity of the speech, and by extension of the *Reflections*, from the perspective of the overdetermined, internally agonistic subject it fashioned – a subject that simultaneously introjects and refuses the authority of the law.

MORAL LAW AND THE GUILT OF EMPIRE

Burke begins the impeachment speech with an explication of the legal and moral obligations confronting the Lords. These obligations, as Burke presented them, were no ordinary matter of judicial procedure. On the contrary they have a significance that stems from Burke's understanding of the law he believed Hastings to have transgressed. In the speech, as in Burke's later writing and speeches, the law has two distinct but related meanings. On the one hand it is an objective, though geographically specific fact, a set of norms codified in legislative and judicial practice: the 'laws of the country'. On the other hand, however, it has a transcendental or suprasensible meaning: the 'eternal laws of justice', the 'one great, immutable, pre-existent law' (*W&S*, vol. 6, pp. 275, 350). Though the speech often deploys the word 'law' in a way that can conveniently elide these meanings, Burke also stresses the absolute priority given to the law as a transcendental fact understood as animating its specific constitutional manifestations:

> This great law does not arise from our conventions or compacts. On the contrary, it gives to our conventions and compacts all the force and sanction they can have. It does not arise from our vain institutions. Every good gift is of God; all power is of God; and He who has given the power and from whom it alone originates, will never suffer the exercise of it to be practised upon any less solid foundation than the power itself.
>
> (*W&S*, vol. 6, p. 350)

The relational distinction between the transcendental and empirical-historical senses of the law enables Burke to frame the impeachment as an attack on what he describes as 'geographical morality'. The moral problem epitomized by the Company under Hastings was that in the guise of mercantile autonomy from sovereign authority (whether British or Indian) it could act as if its interests were independent of a specific legal system and therefore accountable to neither legal nor public censure. In other words it lacked the discipline of the law, being animated by a self-directed 'corporate spirit' (*W&S*, vol. 6, p. 286). Transgressing the established laws of Indian political economy and especially of the Hindu caste system, which Burke describes as 'the fundamental part of the constitution' in India (*W&S*, vol. 6, p. 303), the Company, in its mercantile rapaciousness, had also transgressed the eternal law that breathes not only through the British legal system, but through constitutionality and codified systems of conduct generally, regardless of their local manifestations. This is why Burke goes to such lengths to expound upon the rigorous constitutionality of Indian society: 'in Asia as well as in Europe the same Law of Nations prevails, the same principles are continually resorted to, and the same maxims sacredly held and strenuously maintained ... Asia is enlightened in that respect as well as Europe' (*W&S*, vol. 6, p. 367). In contrast to this vision of enlightenment, Hastings had appealed to a version of moral relativism which Burke was quick to condemn:

he has told your Lordships in his defence, that actions in Asia do not bear the same moral qualities as the same actions would bear in Europe. My Lords, we positively deny the principle. I am authorized and called upon to deny it. And having stated at large what he means by saying that the same actions have not the same qualities in Asia and in Europe, we are to let your Lordships know that these Gentlemen have formed a plan of Geographical morality, by which the duties of men in public and in private situations are not to be governed by their relations to the great Governor of the Universe, or by their relations to men, but by climates, degrees of longitude and latitude, parallels not of life but of latitudes. As if, when you have crossed the equinoctial line all the virtues die, as they say some animals die when they cross the line, as if there were a kind of baptism, like that practised by seamen, by which they unbaptize themselves of all that they learned in Europe, and commence a new order and a new system of things.

(*W&S*, vol. 6, p. 346)

Burke's disquisition on the law and on geographical morality presents the relationship between Britain, India and British mercantilism in a light that might at a glance seem surprising were we to assume what, in recent critical discussions, have become the conventional dichotomies of colonial discourse: East/West, barbarity/civility, etc. In their adherence to the law both Britain and India could be understood as constitutional entities existing in enlightened subjugation to a moral code that transcends their cultural specificity. Hastings, in contrast, embodies an atavism that exercises its own will against the discipline of the law, recklessly usurping the time-honoured institutions of Indian society in his reordering of its property relations. Despite a moral universalism that embraces Britain and India, it is clear, however, that Burke was not advocating an end to the colonial presence in India, but a more thorough form of control and invigilation that would more firmly integrate India into the imperial fold by subjecting it to more thorough parliamentary oversight. Nevertheless, the quite specific ideological efficacy of the speech cannot be understood just in terms of this paternalism; that is, as part of the gradual supplanting of mercantile with sovereign British authority in India, supposedly to serve and protect indigenous interests. In order to grasp the speech as a form of discursive practice capable of soliciting actual communal identifications, we need to return to Burke's account of the law to examine exactly how it achieved its legitimacy and persuasiveness. How, in other words, might a transcendental notion of the law, apparently resting on the assertion of divine authority, have been introjected by the subject such that it could be experienced neither as a command nor as an imposition, but in the visceral form of sympathetic identification?

In Burke's speech the affectivity of the law worked through two related registers that we can schematize as abstraction and guilt. The idea of a moral state with universal validity promised the possibility of self-abstraction into a collective subject, a public potentially spanning Europe and Asia in which the principle of inclusion would simply be conformity to a law that embraced both and communal recognition of this similitude. The postulation of this community is the speech's most utopian gesture, indexing an enlightenment faith in universal norms, and by extension effacing the violence of bringing India under British jurisdiction. 'The sun in his beneficent progress round the world', says Burke, 'does not behold a more glorious sight than that of men, separated from a remote people by the material bounds and barriers of nature, united by the bond of a social and moral community, all the Commons of England resenting as their own, the indignities and cruelties that are offered to all the people of India' (*W&S*, vol. 6, p. 457–8). But if the speech addresses the Lords as potential members and legislators of this universal fold, it also phrases the impeachment as the test of their worthiness to be so. The outcome of the trial, Burke implied, would determine either the identity of the judiciary, and by implication the nation as a whole, with the law, or their guilty complicity with Hastings's mercantile excesses.

> my Lords, the credit and honour of the British nation will itself be decided by this decision. My Lords, they will stand or fall thereby. We are to decide by the case of this gentleman whether the crimes of individuals are to be turned into public guilt and national ignominy, or whether this nation will convert these offences, which have thrown a transient shade on its glory, into a judgement that will reflect a permanent lustre on the honour, justice and humanity of this Kingdom.
>
> (*W&S*, vol. 6, p. 271)

This passage not only suggests the possibility of guilt through judicial complicity with Hastings, but that this guilt pre-exists the impeachment and can only be expunged through a collective displacement of it to Hastings himself. The national benefits of Company mismanagement point to this prior corruption of the polity: 'It is well known that great wealth has poured into this country from India; and it is no derogation to us to suppose the possibility of being corrupted by that by which great Empires have been corrupted, and by which assemblies almost as respectable and as venerable as your Lordships' have been known to be indirectly shaken' (*W&S*, vol. 6, p. 277). The threat here is not just of bribery. The circulation of colonial wealth through Britain clearly suggests a national complicity that points to the absurdity of attempts to locate all the crimes of empire in one man. As Sara Suleri points out,

> The exercise of "arbitrary power" for which he [Burke] sought to impeach Hastings could not be so easily expunged from the

history of colonization; much of Burke's rhetorical extravagance suggests a subterranean admission that it was indeed too facile to assume Hastings alone could be held responsible for the exigencies of what it meant to colonize.[9]

If the speech implied the guilt of the British polity, it also offered the redeeming pleasure of self-abstraction into a moral community as a way of expunging this guilt. In doing so the speech implicated not only the Lords, but Burke's auditors and the more general public that read the impeachment proceedings as a printed text outside of Westminster Hall. The subject addressed by the speech could affirm cross-cultural unity with the Indian victims of colonization, under the aegis of the law common to both, in order to appease the guilt of having already transgressed the law as some passive accomplice to the economy of colonialism. The mechanics of this process are at moments startlingly evident in the speech. Recounting the initial consolidation of a British presence in Bengal (the acquisition of Calcutta) Burke himself must conceal certain facts lest they establish the fundamental unity of the colonial crime, and reveal what Suleri calls the lie of the impeachment proceedings, that is 'its failure to admit that Hastings's misdeeds were merely synecdochical of the colonial operation'.[10]

Many circumstances of this acquisition I pass by. There is a secret veil to be drawn over the beginnings of all governments. They had their origin, as the beginning of all such things have had, in some matters that had as good be covered by obscurity. Time in the origin of most governments has thrown the mysterious veil over them. Prudence and discretion make it necessary to throw something of that veil over a business in which otherwise the fortune, the genius, the talents and military virtue of this Nation never shone more conspicuously.

(*W&S*, vol. 6, pp. 316–17)

This passage resonates with Burke's insistence on the legitimacy of continuity in government and anticipates the image of the 'politic, well-wrought veil' that, in the *Reflections*, conceals all those historical circumstances that might undermine the rights and legitimacy of the monarchy (*RRF*, p. 103). As Terry Eagleton points out, and as the image of the veil suggests, the establishment of this legitimacy requires the effacement of what Eagleton calls the 'primordial trespass' informing all sociability. This notion of primordial crime is common to both psychoanalysis (in the form of parricide) and to Marxism (in the form of primitive accumulation).[11] In both the function of the law, much like the veil, is to repress the moment at which it was summoned into being – a moment which also inscribes its traumatic contingency. Two years later, attacking the *Reflections*, Paine will make exactly this point: 'A certain something forbids him to look back to a beginning, lest some robber or some Robin Hood should rise from the long obscurity of time, and say, *I am the origin!*'[12] In the above passage on the acquisition of Calcutta, Burke comes perilously close to announcing the primordial trespass at the origin of the British presence in India. Yet his virtual acknowledgment of the original sin of colonial power is matched by the rhetorical fervour of his attempts to displace liability to Hastings alone:

> we have brought before you the head, the chief, the captaingeneral in iniquity; one in whom all the frauds, all the peculations, all the violence, all the tyranny in India are embodied, disciplined and arrayed. ... if we have brought before you such a person, if you strike at him you will not have need of a great many more examples: you strike at the whole corps if you strike at the head.
>
> (*W&S*, vol. 6, pp. 275–6)

Hastings, in other words, must be sacrificed to the integrity of the imperial project. In order for the British nation to preserve its innocence, he alone must be cast as the great transgressor.

The pleasure of self-abstraction, then, is at least in part a release from the disfiguring stigmata of colonial power relations. In the possibility of universal sympathy uniting the subjects of Britain and India into one public administered by one law, the dichotomizing contingencies of colonial political economy apparently vanish, as if colonizer and colonized can come together in some providential realm simply as human beings. The community imagined by Burke depends on the idea that relations of production can be overcome in this way, and indeed his vision of sympathetic human beings bonded over the fact of their humanity has strong affinities with late-eighteenth-century images of the family as the model for a community comfortably beyond the exigencies of political and economic life. Jürgen Habermas, we've seen, has discussed the central role of the private in the consolidation of a subjectivity apparently unaffected by the relations of the marketplace. According to Habermas, the family secures a fiction of uncoerced communality between two spouses that also becomes a more general fiction of the 'human'. The moral community Burke entertains is based on the same fictitious idea that power relations can be suspended in the realization of a universal humanity – a family of man – as the principle of communal integration. In practice, however, the postulation of this community in his speech had the effect of consolidating imperial authority in India, at least in the eyes of the British public. By assuming a fundamental similitude between Britain and India the speech ratified the gradual shift to British sovereignty in India as an innocuous expression of a common humanity, allowing the project of empire to be carried on as enlightened benevolence once the state had effectively banished the corruption of mercantilism from its constitution. In this respect the ideological nature of the speech is clear. Yet this observation does not exhaust anything like its full performative resourcefulness. If identification with the law has its fundamental condition in the assumption of guilt, it will not do to leave this guilt in the form of an abstraction which would have meant little to a public that, in 1788, did not for the most part see itself as the direct beneficiary of East Indian mercantilism. Guilt, in other words, must also be introjected as a fundamental condition of the subject in order for the law to become palpable. And in order for this to happen the subject must also know the pleasure of transgression, the pleasure of having already refused the law. At the heart of the speech, in other words, is a kind of pleasure that must be disavowed as the condition of community.

PUBLIC TORTURE: SENTIMENT, SUFFERING, SPECTATORSHIP

The moral community that Burke imagined was, needless to say, not one of mutual recognition across cultures. The conduit of sympathetic identification ran one way. A British audience was encouraged to identify with Indian victims of exploitation. Michael Warner has suggested how the whole discourse of self-abstraction in the bourgeois public sphere denied the very specific and exclusive prerequisites that granted one the privilege of public identification:

> the ability to abstract oneself in public discussion has always been an unequally available resource. Individuals have to have specific

rhetorics of disincorporation; they are not simply rendered bodiless by exercising reason. And it is only possible to operate a discourse based on the claim of self-abstracting disinterestedness in a culture where such unmarked self-abstraction is a differential resource. The subject who could master this rhetoric in the bourgeois public sphere was implicitly – even explicitly – white, male, literate, and propertied. These traits could go unmarked, even grammatically, while other features of bodies could only be acknowledged in discourse as the humiliating positivity of the particular.[13]

Though the rhetoric of sympathy in the late-eighteenth century seems to predicate a largely female readership, through both the Gothic and the domestic novel, the appropriation of this rhetoric for explicitly juridical ends in the impeachment speech does bear out Warner's claim, predicating an abstract public, an imagined community based on 'unmarked' national and patriarchal identifications. In the speech, as in Burke's work more generally (most archetypically in the image of Marie Antoinette threatened by the Jacobin mob), sentimental tableaux built around images of threatened filial harmony solicit sympathetic identification and assume a kind of moral agency linked to the defence of the domestic idyll and in particular of the threatened women and children residing in it. In his 1756 *Vindication of Natural Society* Burke grounds the aesthetics of this representational strategy in an archaeology of the subject that finds the family at its origin: 'The mutual Desires of the Sexes uniting their Bodies and Affections, and the Children, which were the Results of these Intercourses, introduced first the Notion of Society, and taught its Conveniences. This Society, founded in natural Appetites and Instincts, and not in any positive Institution, I shall call Natural Society.'[14] In Burke's writings and speeches the family has a number of overlapping functions: it is the fundamental unit of society indistinguishable from the most basic components of the human subject; it is a model for community more generally; and, most importantly perhaps, it is the basis of affective spectacles intended to solicit communal affiliations through the ubiquity of sympathetic identification with it. Yet, as feminist readings of enlightenment culture have repeatedly pointed out, the assumption of this ubiquity, of the naturalness of the family and the sympathy it apparently solicits, masks the specificity of the male subject for whom the heteronormative family is experienced in neither political nor economic terms.[15] In Burke's work the image of the family is deployed in a way that stabilizes the structures of both patriarchy and capitalism around a series of mutually enforcing oppositions which assume the normalcy of male agency in the properly public world of politics and commerce, and the non-economic character of feminized labour, such as housework and child-rearing, in private. The family, and the female body as its sign, are established as anterior to the social, in order for them to retain their ability both to signify and solicit the sympathy integral to the process of self-abstraction for the male subject, a process in which the identity of *bourgeois* and *homme*, which Habermas discusses, is unproblematically established. As Anne McClintock writes, 'the family as an institution was figured as existing, naturally, beyond the commodity market, beyond politics and beyond history proper. The family thus became both the antithesis of history and history's organizing figure.'[16]

In the impeachment speech, as in the trial more generally, Burke represented Indian society in a manner that enabled it to occupy this imagined space, ideally beyond political and economic contingencies, for the male subject able to access and participate in the exclusive world of official political debate. As the speech circulated through the public sphere, reported in print, this subject remained 'unmarked' in direct proportion to the 'humiliating positivity' of what were presented as characteristically feminine responses to the speech, typified by reports of women fainting in the gallery, indicating the anomaly of women in official public spaces. The abstracted subject of the public sphere, by contrast, was assumed to be sympathetic, but emotionally unhistrionic in his responses to images of threatened conjugality, privacy, property and above all femininity in India. In the *Reflections* this fiction of male agency will be consolidated through constant appeals to the 'chivalry' that Burke found to be so deplorably lacking in a society that could level insult, not to mention violence, at its queen. In the impeachment speech the feminized domestic idyll itself assumed a universal significance: Burke used it to mark the point of contact between mercantilism and Indian society, and to efface the political specificity of this contact in the implied universality of a crime that was neither local, nor remote, but which, in violating the harmony of the idyll, violated the law itself. The domestic idyll, in other words, is positioned not as separate from the law, not as an object the law protects, but as its supplement. As a little constitution in its own right, the idyll both intimates and embodies the 'one great, immutable, pre-existent law' – a point that will be reiterated in the *Reflections* when Burke claims that the transmission of the crown and property from generation to generation demonstrates how the state and the family both embody a 'constitutional policy' which works 'after a pattern of nature':

> In this choice of inheritance we have given to our frame of polity the image of a relation in blood; binding up the constitution of our country with our dearest domestic ties; adopting our fundamental laws into the bosom of our family affections; keeping inseparable, and cherishing with the warmth of all their combined and mutually reflected charities, our state, our hearths, our sepulchres, and our altars.
>
> (*RRF*, p. 120)

Threats to the family, it turns out, are also threats to the law. Accordingly Frans De Bruyn rightly argues that Burke's speeches on India replicate the conventions of Gothic romance in which the narrative dynamic revolves around libertine threats to the female body and the specifically male prerogative to ward these off, comparing Hastings with Montoni, the villain of Ann Radcliffe's *The Mysteries of Udolpho*.[17] The ease with which Burke's speech can be read in these terms indexes the extent to which a narrative of colonial contact has been rewritten in terms of ubiquitous sentimental conventions for a British audience – conventions which also assume the gender specificity of their call to agency and community once they are reworked in official legal or parliamentry discourse. Burke either erases cultural and political difference, or recuperates it in the name of the law (as is the case in his discussion of the caste system) such that the European and Indian idylls have the same kind of affect, while Hastings emerges as an equally ubiquitous kind of antihero – the libertine violator of a hitherto vestal object. But because the idyll is the source of sympathy, of communal affection that bodies forth the law, it also resists the outlaw impulse of the libertine with its humanizing effects. Nevertheless, in the very act of this resistance, the idyll must also acknowledge its dangerous proximity to that which threatens it. The pathos of its affect is contingent on the insinuation, if not the brute immediacy, of its own violation. It is in this sense that sympathy and something akin to sadism can be read as co-dependent. The sentimental tableau always suggests its relationship to libertine

violence, a point borne out with monotonous brutality by Sade's
Justine, in which the eponymous heroine's innocence is a direct incitement to sexual violation. What is important here, however, is
that this co-dependency of sentiment and libertinage be grasped
not just as the textual form in which the ideas of law and criminality are represented, but as the form through which they are
experienced, in their introjection, as a very visceral kind of
responsiveness through which the law becomes palpable.

The climactic moments of the impeachment speech reveal this
structure. Burke was aware that the Devi Singh material would
have an impact on his audience. Writing to Philip Francis in 1788 he
noted that 'it has stuff in it, that will, if any thing, work upon the
popular Sense', though adding, in a moment of anxiety as to what
that impact would be, 'But how to do this without making a monstrous and disproportioned member, I know not.'[18] The scenes of
torture he describes were clearly intended to enlist public opinion
in the defence of the law as Burke had carefully framed it over the
first two days of his speech. Having been awarded the revenue
farm of Dinajpur, Rangpur and Idrakpur in Northern Bengal,
allegedly in exchange for a bribe that was paid through an interme-
diary to Hastings, Devi Singh and his agents were left to indulge in
acts of violence and rapine that, Burke claimed, typified Hastings's
misrule.[19] As Burke retells it (erroneously according to his contemporary critics), Devi Singh's authority as rent-farmer in the region
initiated a series of atrocities in which cruelty and tyranny were
indeed 'sublimed into madness'[20] as one atrocity exceeded the next
in its degree of savagery. Attempting to meet the increased revenue
demands of the Company while also preserving his own profit
margin, Devi Singh imprisoned 'all the landed Gentlemen and
nobility of that Country', in order to oblige them to sign a rent
agreement, imposed a series of new taxes and subsequently, according to Burke, effectively reduced the landed nobility to penury.
When they were unable to pay him, he took possession of their
property and auctioned it. Not surprisingly Burke recounts this
process in terms of the infiltration and violation of domestic space,
portrayed as the sanctified domain of women:

> There is a circumstance I may mention here that will call for your
> Lordships' pity. Most of the landholders or Zemindars in that
> country happened at that time to be women. The sex there is in a
> state certainly of imprisonment, but guarded as a sacred treasure

under all possible attention and respect. None of the coarse male hands of the law can reach them. But they have a custom, very cautiously and soberly used in all good Governments there, of sending female Bailiffs and Sergeants into their houses, but in this case persons of either sex of that occupation went into their houses and became masters of them, and the men and women Zemindars were obliged to fly the country.

(*W&S*, vol. 6, p. 415)

Under the brutal oppression of a tyranny described by Burke as 'more consuming than the funeral pile, more greedy than the grave, more harsh and inexorable than death itself', the 'gentry' was destroyed, lands confiscated, houses deserted and streets left to be 'over-grown with weeds' (*W&S*, vol. 6, pp. 415–16). But this is only a prelude to what Burke has to tell. The infiltration and destruction of domestic space extended to the poorer tenants (whom Burke refers to as 'yeomen' and 'husbandmen'), who were 'stripped of everything' and then 'dragged to their own miserable hovels or houses, and there they saw the last hope burnt to the ground before them' (*W&S*, vol. 6, p. 417). Under the pressure of poverty and famine, brought on by Devi Singh's usury, the filial loyalties and affections of the family were obliterated. With no property left to them,

there remained to the unhappy people of that country but two things, their families and their bodies. It is well known that men generally cling to domestic satisfactions in proportion as they are deprived of other advantages. My Lords, the most tender parents sold their children, the most jealously affectionate husbands sold their wives, and they thought that it was a tolerable escape from famine into servitude.

(*W&S*, vol. 6, p. 418)

With now only their bodies left to be violated Burke begins to move towards the horrifying crescendo of his account, heightening oratorical tension in a manner that mimics the mutilation of the tortured body itself. The way in which Burke registers his own embarrassment and uneasiness at having to rehearse these horrors suggests that his discursive agency has come perilously close to that of the mutilator of bodies he describes: that telling, the act of representation, is now no longer entirely innocent.

My Lords, I am obliged to make use of some apology for the horrid scenes that I am now going to open to you. You have had enough, you have had perhaps more than enough, of oppressions upon property and oppressions upon liberty, but here the skin was not touched.

(W&S, vol. 6, p. 418)

Needless to say the image of unmolested skin, depending on whether one reads it metaphorically or literally, can imply either Burke as the narrator of events, or the actual agent of violence he describes. The description that follows moves through a litany of tortures, culminating in the public rape and mutilation of peasant women who, Burke stresses, are also virgin daughters and wives. It is told with the rhetorical and descriptive intensity that typifies Burke's most excessive passages, foregrounding not only the violation of female chastity, but the symbolic destruction of the female body as the source of filial continuity, 'in order that nature might be violated in all those circumstances where the sympathies of nature are awakened, where the remembrances of our infancy and all our tender remembrances are combined' *(W&S*, vol. 6, p. 421). It is specifically the body of the mother that is destroyed (the breasts and uterus are the sites of mutilation) and again Burke must register his guilt and shame at having to narrate these events, as narrative agency pushes up against the limits of the law, threatening to exceed the bounds of sympathetic affect with its descriptions of extreme sexual violence:

they put the nipples of the women into sharp edges of split bamboos and tore them from their bodies. Grown from ferocity to ferocity, from cruelty to cruelty, they applied burning torches and cruel slow fires (My Lords, I am ashamed to go further); these infernal fiends, in defiance of everything divine and human, planted death in the source of life, and where that modesty which more distinguishes man even than his rational nature from the base creation, turns from the view and dare not meet the expression, dared those infernal fiends execute their cruel and nefarious tortures where the modesty of nature and the sanctity of justice dare not follow them or even describe their practices.

(W&S, vol. 6, p. 421)

The usurpation of an artificial and despotic system culminates in the very literal destruction of what Burke held to be the natural basis of filial continuity and social affection – the reproductive body. To the extent that these moments in the speech can generate sympathetic identification, they are also dependent on the solicitation of public curiosity that brings the subject of sympathy into dangerous proximity to a prurient voyeurism obsessed with the linguistically simulated spectacle of violation. And yet Burke's language is also very careful to avoid this sense, constantly apologizing for what ever might be compromising in the speech and constantly veiling its details in densely figurative language, as if to both solicit and frustrate this prurience. The ability of the speech to position a paternalistic subject, a chivalric hero outraged at the excesses of mercantile violence, is contingent on this undecidability. Precisely because Burke's language gives the impression that it is excluding prurient interest in the spectacle of torture, this subject can also appear to be excused from any accusation of voyeurism. The centrality of native intermediaries to Burke's portrayal of Hastings's guilt, moreover, had the unintended effect of displacing criminal agency from Hastings and re-establishing a more predictable and ideologically palatable writing of the colonial contact zone in terms of images of indigenous barbarity. The chivalric mode of masculine outrage and agency the speech attempts to solicit is nicely summarized in Gayatri Spivak's description of the fantasy of imperial paternalism: 'White men are saving brown women from brown men.'[21] But this is not the whole story. Burke's speech also points to the extreme instability of the subject predicated on the representation of sexual violence. This instability is indexed by Burke's own embarrassment at having to narrate torture – an embarrassment that, despite his best attempts, cannot conceal the possibility of a guilty pleasure undermining the assumption of communal sympathy. Burke well knew that the prospect of beholding violence is also the prospect of positive pleasure in the subject. 'The idea of bodily pain', writes Burke in his *A Philosophical Enquiry into the Origin of our Ideas of the Sublime and the Beautiful*, 'in all the modes and degrees of labour, pain, anguish, torment, is productive of the sublime.'[22]

I am convinced we have a degree of delight, and that no small one, in the real misfortunes and pains of others; for let the affection be what it will in appearance, if it does not make us shun such objects, if on the contrary it induces us to approach them, if it makes us dwell upon them, in this case I conceive we must have a delight or pleasure of some species or other in contemplating objects of this kind.[23]

Prurient interest in representations of suffering, in the case of Burke's speech what we could call simulated voyeurism, and sympathetic identification are not sequentially opposed, but simultaneous in the duplicitous and undecidable structure of the sentimental idyll.

Burke's speech, we might say, implies two poles of pleasure: identification with the law or sympathy, on the one hand, and passive, disincorporated distance or voyeurism before the scene of transgression, on the other. The latter implies a state unconditioned by and unresponsive to the law's demands.[24] Because introjection and refusal of the law are simultaneous, the subject of the law is also always guilty before it. This guilt is not simply referable to the impotence of the witness before the scene of violation. As Slavoj Žižek points out, the impotence of the witness in the face of unspeakable horror arises because 'desire is split, divided between fascination with enjoyment and repulsion at it'.[25] Žižek phrases this enjoyment in terms of a suspension of the authority of the father that he elsewhere identifies with public law:

> the unbearable, traumatic element witnessed by the gaze is ultimately the feminine enjoyment whose presence suspends the authority of the big Other, of the Name-of-the-Father, and fantasy (the fantasy of the "threat" woman is to be "rescued" from) is a scenario we construct in order to elude feminine enjoyment. Freud's "A child is being beaten" is to be supplemented by what is perhaps a more elementary example of fantasy scene : "A woman is being tortured-coited."[26]

This passage complements Spivak's analogous phrasing of the fantasy scene, bringing to light what is absolutely repressed in the sentence 'white men are saving brown women from brown men' – that is, the prurience and passivity of cognition itself, the risk of bearing witness to the traumatic element that Žižek names 'feminine enjoyment' (by which he means enjoyment that refuses or transgresses the limits of a patriarchal, and hence masculine law) and of becoming fixated by it. The colonial mission can be presented as an extension of sympathetic identification in Spivak's sentence precisely because the transgressive character of voyeurism is repressed by it, a gesture that Burke enacts in his embarrassed and artful inability to confront the scene he nevertheless vividly conveys: 'My Lords, I am ashamed to go further', modesty 'turns from the view and dare not meet the expression' (*W&S*, vol. 6, p. 421). Burke constantly draws attention to his faltering ability to narrate the Devi Singh affair, simultaneously summoning and effacing its violence. The speech is both an act of disclosure and foreclosure, bringing the auditor into proximity to the event he/she is to be made conscious of, only to veer away from the lure of representation and spectacularity, and into a rhetoric of unspeakability and disavowal. Yet this gesture itself was so overtly performative that it remained largely transparent, and certainly Burke's critics were quick to accuse him of a lurid interest in the whole affair, in the course of registering their own equally performative inability to confront the moment of violation. It is at the point of this uneasy consensual refusal to be fully cognizant of representational violence that moral community is affirmed in what amounts to a comedy of disavowal.

Accordingly critiques of Burke's speech shift their focus from the allegations themselves to insinuate that Burke was some how guilty of representation. Typically these critiques make veiled reference to the details of the speech, while refusing to overtly recount them. John Scott's open letter to Fox epitomizes this style:

> In every public street of London you may see a print of the High Court in Westminster Hall, in which the great orator appears, detailing those detestable stories, that I have too much respect for decency, to mention; next Mr Fox and the managers, with grief and horror upon their countenances; a peeress fainting (which, by the by, was not the fact), and the whole Court, Commons, Spectators, and Judges, are faithfully represented, with such an expression in the appearance of each, as the relation of such horrible cruelties would naturally produce.[27]

In this passage Burke himself emerges as the source of horror, as in breach of the decency that prevents Scott from being explicit on the subject of 'those detestable stories'. In a series of doggerel letters attacking Burke, Ralph Broome does something very similar. Broome is more explicit than Scott, and indeed turns what he describes as Burke's 'language obscene' to comic effect, but the process of disavowal is still evident in the comic trivialization of sexual violence.

> The cruelties here, which the *Orator* stated,
> Are more than in verse can be justly related.
> He describ'd to the audience in language obscene,
> New *sockets* for *candles*, and *glasses unclean*;
> From these *filthy cups*, some were drinking waters,
> While others were ravishing mothers and daughters;
> For tearing off nipples, a *Bamboo* was clift,
> And the suffering female was stripp'd to her shift:
> Whilst Edmund these cruelties horribly painted,
> Some ladies took salts, others wept, and one fainted.
> And indeed, my dear brother, I'm free to confess,
> As Edmund described it, they could not do less.
> Some people, however, who perfectly knew
> The true state of the case, said 'twas mostly untrue;
> On this subject farther, I've only to add,
> The surprising effect which his eloquence had,
> Not only on those, *who ne'er heard it before*,
> But on Burke, who had read *it a hundred times o'er*.
> In the annals of painting, *'tis certainly new*,
> For the *artist* to faint, *at the picture he drew*;
> But Burke was so touch'd that he fainted away,
> Like Siddons, the tragedy Queen in a play.[28]

The terms of Broome's critique of Burkean prurience and theatricality certainly inform those later critiques of the *Reflections* with which I started this chapter. In the case of Broome, however, it seems clear that the ribald element reproduces exactly the prurience and the lack of delicacy that also, at least in part, seem to motivate the passage. Communal identifications based on appeals to moral decency, in other words, require either the implicit or explicit solicitation of prurience, and thus guilt, as part of the process of self-definition. This is perhaps what Žižek has in mind when he discusses the 'solidarity-in-guilt induced by participation in common transgression': 'What "holds together" a community most deeply is not so much identification with the Law that regulates the community's "normal" everyday circuit, but rather identification with a specific form of transgression of the Law, of the Law's sus-

pension (in psychoanalytic terms, with a specific form of enjoyment).'[29] Burke's speech consolidates an imagined community precisely in these terms: by rendering guilt a consequence of
voyeurism his speech also makes it palpable for his auditors. The
disavowal of both guilt and voyeurism is then the process by which
moral community is realized as identification with a law not just
immortal, but also engraved in the heart.

CONCLUSION: *REFLECTIONS ON THE REVOLUTION IN FRANCE*

Two years after the impeachment speech, while the trial of Hastings
was still going on, Burke redeployed its principal arguments and
rhetorical strategies as the basis of *Reflections on the Revolution in
France*. As numerous critics have pointed out, *Reflections*, while
ostensibly concerned with events in France, is first and foremost an
attack on the emergence of radical counterpublics within Britain, as
the full title of the text suggests. Burke frames the *Reflections* as an
attack on the Revolution Society and in particular on Richard Price's
'Discourse on the Love of Our Country', delivered at the Old Jewry
in November 1789. Burke saw Price's claim that monarchy is under-
written by popular support as constituting a serious threat to the
social fabric – one that portended the political upheavals of France
in Britain itself. Reiterating the appeals to the law that formed the
basis of the impeachment speech, Burke represents the claims of
Price and the Revolution Society as a refusal of the 'immortal law' in
favour of what he saw as a spurious and abstract political philosophy. What remains implicit in the impeachment speech becomes
explicit in the *Reflections*: the internalization of the law as the basis
of communal identifications also presupposes a commitment to the
preservation of existing social inequalities and property relations.
The kind of polity Burke imagines is one in which disparate class
interests are contained within one vast functionally integrated
structure amounting to what Negt and Kluge describe as the
'illusory synthesis of the totality of society', which they associate
with the infrastructures of the bourgeois public sphere. Adherence
to the 'old common law of Europe', Burke claimed, might have led
the French to a 'free constitution; a potent monarchy; a disciplined
army; a reformed and venerated clergy; a mitigated but spirited
nobility ... a liberal order of commons, to emulate and recruit that

nobility' and , finally, 'a protected, satisfied, laborious, and obedient people, taught to seek and to recognise the happiness that is to be found by virtue in all conditions' (*RRF*, p. 124). The harmonious integration of Burke's ideal polity, it becomes clear, is dependent on the maintenance of a hierarchy in which each section of society knows and accepts its place. The 'monstrous fiction' of revolutionary culture, on the contrary, is designed to disturb this integration 'by inspiring false ideas and vain expectations into men destined to travel in the obscure walk of laborious life', and thus serves only to 'aggravate and imbitter the real inequality, which it can never remove; and which the order of civil life establishes as much for the benefit of those whom it must leave in a humble state, as those whom it is able to exalt to a condition more splendid, but not more happy' (*RRF*, p. 124). The community bound together under the aegis of the law is one based on intractable class differences.

As Frans De Bruyn has pointed out, the communicative forms privileged by Burke imply the exclusive public that Thelwall and other radicals denounced. Parliamentary speeches and personal letters suggest the 'privileged, exclusive ambit of eighteenth-century politics'.[30] While Burke's writing and speeches do address an exclusive, highly literate demographic centred on but not limited to institutions of official power and policy, they also can be read as actively creating their public, as consolidating communal identifications that worked against other forms of communal interaction, like those embodied in the emerging milieu of radical corresponding and debating societies that prompted the *Reflections* in the first place. We have seen how the impeachment speech used the Devi Singh affair to translate the immortal law into a felt reality and in doing so attempted to realize a particular kind of community. The *Reflections* uses the events of the 6th of October 1789 at Versaille to the same ends. Numerous contemporary critics have examined the bed chamber scene in order to demonstrate how Burke's politics hinges on the image of Marie Antoinette assaulted by the Jacobin mob.[31] The point I want to make regarding this moment is that it too, like its analogous moment in the impeachment speech, is premised on a degree of enjoyment that is also necessarily disavowed as the condition of identification with the law. The rhetorical excess of the *Reflections* leaves us in no doubt. Burke renders the violation of the private as a violation of the law in the most hyperbolic and Gothic terms imaginable: the 'most splendid palace in the world' is left 'swimming in blood, polluted by massacre, and strewed with scattered limbs and mutilated carcasses' (*RRF*, p. 164). To ignore the pleasure-content in Burke's account of 'the Theban and Thracian orgies, acted in France' (*RRF*, p. 165) is to ignore precisely what makes the *Reflections* such an effective vehicle for the moral law and the kinds of communal identifications that Burke pitted against the threat posed by radical political culture. Both the impeachment speech and the *Reflections* turn on the mutually sustaining relationship between private pleasure and public morality. The ideological effectiveness of a text like the *Reflections*, we might say, resides in the fact that it is able to reconcile private, antisocial pleasure with community, public order and morality. A form of dissidence that otherwise might be dangerous or destructive (desire in excess of the law) is appropriately sublimated in the act of reception. In this way Burke's work – public discourse in the most literal sense – also implied an economy of discursive production that could consolidate social order because it bracketed anti-social forms of pleasure in the sequestered space of culture-consumption. We might rephrase this by suggesting that Burke attempted to defuse revolutionary potential in Britain by offering his readers a simulacrum of the revolution in France, a kind of textual panorama that foregrounded the grotesque and carnivalesque while containing this disruptive potential in the act of reading. Note the slippage between image and actuality in the following passage:

> Plots, massacres, assassinations, seem to some people a trivial price for obtaining a revolution. A cheap, bloodless reformation, a guiltless liberty, appear flat and vapid to their taste. There must be a great change of scene; there must be a magnificent stage effect; there must be a grand spectacle to rouze the imagination, grown torpid with the lazy enjoyment of sixty years security, and the still unanimating repose of public prosperity.
>
> (*RRF*, p. 156)

The 'grand spectacle' might just as readily refer to the *Reflections* itself as to the revolution. So long as revolution is simply a matter of consumption, the 'sullen resistance to innovation' (*RRF*, p. 18) that Burke saw as a laudable national characteristic could be preserved. In the *Reflections* Burke is very explicit about how the maintenance of civic order requires the management of the passions in the interests of 'sullen resistence'.

Government is a contrivance of human wisdom to provide for human *wants*. Men have a right that these wants should be provided for by this wisdom. Among these wants is to be reckoned the want, out of civil society, of a sufficient restraint upon the passions. Society requires not only that the passions of individuals should be subjected, but that even in the mass and body as well as in individuals, the inclinations of men should frequently be thwarted, their will controlled, and their passions brought into subjection. This can only be done *by a power out of themselves*; and not, in the exercise of its function, subject to that will and to those passions which it is its office to bridle and subdue. In this sense the restraints on men, as well as their liberties, are to be reckoned among their rights.

(*RRF*, p. 151)

As we have seen this 'power out of themselves' – the law – is also an effect of discursive affect, such that culture itself becomes crucial to the whole project of management and order. In the *Reflections* Burke has much to say about this process in which aesthetic spectacles, evoking 'melancholy sentiments', mediate morality for the public good (*RRF*, p. 175). But what he does not say is just as important. The economy of discursive production and reception his work embodies is dependent on the transmission of an affirmative pleasure that, like the 'abominations' of the revolution itself, must remain 'unutterable'.

2

William Godwin and the Pathological Public Sphere: Theorizing Communicative Action in the 1790s

William Godwin's *Enquiry Concerning Political Justice* was published in February 1793, the same month in which France and England declared war on each other, and only a matter of weeks after Louis XVI was beheaded. Three years after its commencement the French Revolution had demonstrated to the English ruling classes the precariousness of their privilege, and the need to police attempts within Britain to mobilize non-propertied classes in support of an extended franchise and parliamentary reform. By this time Edmund Burke's histrionic representation of the Revolution and of the British reformers sympathetic to it seemed vindicated in the eyes of the Pitt administration, which saw organizations like the London Corresponding Society (LCS) as potentially violent threats to property and domestic stability.[1] In a climate marked by increasing violence in France, and official repression of so-called Jacobin political culture in Britain, Godwin's *Enquiry* maintains a faith in the possibility of political enlightenment that seems at odds with the realities of its day. This faith, moreover, sits oddly with Godwin's own pessimism in the midst of forces on both sides of the political spectrum that seemed to portend growing class polarization and escalating conflict. Confronted with what he perceived as the dangerous populism of radical corresponding and debating societies, and the legislative assaults on freedom of the press and freedom of speech launched by the Pitt government, Godwin was at pains to map out the foundations of a moral and rational society in which both official invigilation and populist mobilization would be left in the wake of enlightened progress. At the heart of his 'rational anarchism' is a conflict between, on the one hand, uncensored public

59

discussion and interaction, in which subjects discover and rehearse their rationality and intellectual independence, and, on the other, an array of political and economic infrastructures that threaten this rational potential with various forms of coercion and deception. These forms of coercion range from formal law and demagogic manipulation, to modes of behaviour premised on the monadic and egocentric subjectivity of the marketplace. Godwin locates all socially ameliorative potential in the possibility of uncoerced public interaction directed to the pursuit of truth and the rational exposition of individual interests which, in the spirit of late-eighteenth-century radical-reformist discourse, will turn out to be inseparable from a broader communal interest. Because the public exposition of these interests in a public argumentative exchange has the compulsion of truth, the 'unforced force' of the better argument, even the tenuous dawn of public interaction and discussion in the early 1790s implies a teleology in which the coercive institutions of state and economy gradually wane in direct correlation to the emergence of a self-directed community of rational individuals. In this future society the rule of formal legal structures and of populist demagogues, regardless of what political positions they represent, would be an unnecessary imposition. Godwin was no revolutionary – he advocated not the overthrow of established authority, but its withering away in keeping with a process of reform facilitating the development and maturation of public opinion, which he describes as 'the most potent engine that can be brought within the sphere of political society' (*EPJ*, p. 580). Anticipating the importance of communicative interaction in contemporary theories of the public sphere, and of modernity more generally, his intent was to protect the integrity of public opinion from the corrosive effects of state political power until it could become the real locus of communal decision making processes in a direct democracy. 'The legitimate instrument of effecting political reformation is knowledge', he writes:

> Let truth be incessantly studied, illustrated and propagated, and the effect is inevitable. Let us not vainly endeavour, by laws and regulations, to anticipate the future dictates of the general mind, but calmly wait till the harvest of opinion is ripe. Let no new prac-tice in politics be introduced, and no old one anxiously super-seded, till the alteration is called for by the public voice. The task

which, for the present, should occupy the first rank in the thoughts of the friend of man is enquiry, communication, discussion.

(*EPJ*, p. 565)

The opposition between unmediated public opinion and the coercive effects of political and legal institutions is, however, one that Godwin can only maintain so long as the public sphere is understood in abstract terms; that is, as embodying the ideal of communicative interaction independently of tangible communicative infrastructures. Whenever he discusses what were the actual institutions of counterhegemonic public interaction – working class organizations like the London Corresponding Society, or popular presses producing cheap editions of libertarian political tracts – the public itself becomes a pathological variant of this ideal, precisely because of the extent to which it is mediated through both popular oration (which Godwin understands as demagogic) and print media (which he understands as manipulative). In other words, the actual institutions of public communication compromise Godwin's ideal even when they could be readily understood as fortifying the integrity of public opinion against the legalistic and explicitly anti-democratic incursions of the Pitt government. In the *Enquiry* the public can, in an instant, become the multitude, rational communicative exchange can become a form of administered consciousness, and public opinion (the engine of amelioration and enlightenment) can imply the political atavism and mindless uniformity of the mob. This dynamic suggests a problem that typifies both political philosophy and sentimental literary production at the end of the eighteenth century. On the one hand, the importance of public communicative practices to the process of social amelioration was broadly acknowledged. On the other, however, the extent to which existing modes of public interaction and opinion formation were seen as complicit with popular violence, mass indoctrination and forms of government-sponsored repression encouraged a paranoid retreat from the public sphere and a corresponding valorization of private space as the site of uncoerced communality and the ideal speech community. Kristen Leaver has described this in terms of Godwin's retreat into 'a distinctly "romantic" vision of literature as a private inner world'.[2] But because the sentimental texts that valorize the private space of the family or domestic idyll were themselves public documents, this recoil from the public sphere remained a very public gesture. The rejection of public life, in other words, became the exemplary form of affective public presentation across a range of discursive contexts: from the domestic idylls of William Wordsworth's *Lyrical Ballads* and Ann Radcliffe's Gothic novels, to Edmund Burke's writing of the French Revolution as an Oedipal drama premised on the destruction of filial harmony. Godwin's work, I want to suggest, enacts this paradox and ultimately reveals the impasse it implies. Texts that rejected the public sphere in order to propagate an image of sympathetic interaction in private both circulated in public and allowed the practices of textual consumption in which they were implicated to mediate a public of readers united by the affect of the idyll. Through the medium of print-culture the private was transformed into a sentimentalized tableau that stabilized a specific mythology of rational, harmonious communal existence. In this way the sentimental retreat from the public sphere was in fact fundamental to the actual formation of a public. This retreat, it turns out, was premised on moments of textual or rhetorical affect implicated not only in explicit forms of political indoctrination, but in the ideological manipulation of readerly sentiment more broadly conceived. We are thus confronted with the apparent impossibility of conceptualizing a space or a form of communicative practice uncompromised by the power relations of a public sphere that was seen as structurally antithetical to the ideal of rational interaction. The *Enquiry* and *Caleb Williams*, I want to argue, contain important explications of what Habermas calls the bourgeois public sphere and its relationship to the practices of culture-consumption, print-capitalism and ultimately ideological control. Nevertheless we can only move beyond the impasse they enact by suggesting their affinity with forms of discursive praxis that they are unable to imagine in any tangible or substantive way. Godwin's own theorization of the opposition between the 'moral' and the 'tendency' of a text can help us make this connection, enabling us to recast the contradictions of a work like *Caleb Williams* in terms of a more open-ended form of critical reception and interaction, to which the novel itself seems oblivious. In publicly explicating the structural impediments to an institutional or activist practice capable of realizing the ameliorative potential of his communicative ideal, Godwin's work finally made its most concrete contribution to the formulation of counterhegemonic interactive practices.

PRIVACY AND THE IDEAL OF PUBLIC INTERACTION

The *Enquiry* constantly enacts the switch from idealized and abstract to tangible but administered forms of public interaction and reception. Godwin, for example, valorizes the printing press as both the icon and progenitor of enlightenment. Through the art of printing, he writes,

> we seem to be secured against the future perishing of human improvement. Knowledge is communicated to too many individuals to afford its adversaries a chance of suppressing it. ... By the easy multiplication of copies, and the cheapness of books, everyone has access to them. The extreme inequality of information among different members of the same community, which existed in ancient times, is diminished. A class of men is become numerous which was then comparatively unknown, and we see vast multitudes who, though condemned to labour for the perpetual acquisition of the means of subsistence, have yet a superficial knowledge of most of the discoveries and topics which are investigated by the learned. The consequence is that the possessors of knowledge being more, its influence is more certain.
>
> (*EPJ*, p. 280)

On the other hand, however, the printed text is also a dangerous means of manipulation and seduction, particularly when it is used as a source of political education. Political publications are perused, he writes, 'not to see whether what they contain is true or false, but that the reader may learn from them how he is to think upon the subjects of which they treat. A sect is generated, and upon grounds not less irrational than those of the worst superstition that ever infested mankind' (*EPJ*, p. 284). This will to blind uniformity is also the logic of political associations. Godwin is referring to the milieu of the LCS and the public oration of the radical activist-poet John Thelwall (whose mobilizing strategies he rejected), as much as to reactionary associations committed to the protection of property distinctions,[3] when he describes the homogeneity and erosion of critically reflective faculties that characterize the constituency of political organizations:[4]

> in political associations, the object of each man is to identify his creed with that of his neighbour. We learn the Shibboleth of a

party. We dare not leave our minds at large in the field of enquiry, lest we should arrive at some tenet disrelished by our party. We have no temptation to enquire. Party has a more powerful tendency than perhaps any other circumstance in human affairs to render the mind quiescent and stationary. Instead of making each man an individual, which the interest of the whole requires, it resolves all understandings into one common mass, and subtracts from each the varieties that could alone distinguish him from a brute machine. Having learned the creed of our party, we have no longer any employment for those faculties which might lead us to detect its errors. We have arrived, in our own opinion, at the last page of the volume of truth.

(*EPJ*, pp. 284-5)

The tendency to reduce associational organizations to the status of political parties is symptomatic of the extent to which the public sphere is suspect for Godwin, because its structures faithfully replicate the logic of a state political apparatus antithetical to enlightened public interaction. The rhetoricity and performativity of popular oration, moreover, necessarily occlude rational cognitive and critical faculties precisely because they function as forms of mass indoctrination designed to seduce opinion and provoke prerational responses linked to the affect of public spectacle and group identification.

The memory of the hearer is crowded with pompous nothings, with images and not arguments. He is never permitted to be sober enough to weigh things with an unshaken hand. It would be inconsistent with the art of eloquence to strip the subject of every meretricious ornament. Instead of informing the understanding of the hearer by a flow and regular progression, the orator must beware of detail, must render everything rapid, and from time to time work up the passions of his hearers to a tempest of applause. Truth can scarcely be acquired in crowded halls and amidst noisy debates. Where hope and fear, triumph and resentment, are perpetually afloat, the severer faculties of investigation are compelled to quit the field. Truth dwells with contemplation. We can seldom make much progress in the business of disentangling error and delusion but in sequestered privacy, or in the tranquil interchange of sentiments that takes place between two persons.

(*EPJ*, pp. 285–6)

In a curious turn the ideal of public interaction can only occur in 'sequestered privacy' because public spaces are unable to facilitate unmediated interaction once the interactive community extends beyond a face to face exchange between, ideally, two participants. The crowded hall and the noisy public debate imply manipulative authority figures and passive, malleable audiences characterized by the mindless uniformity of the mass, into which the discerning individual sinks and vanishes. The institutions of political interaction and communication, in fact, are themselves now the principal danger to the formation of enlightened opinion, and the principal agent of an emerging consciousness industry. Caught in this web of coercive and manipulative influences, public opinion loses its ameliorative potential and becomes a dangerous contagion portending violent populist eruptions. No doubt the French Revolution, the 1780 Gordon riots and the 1791 Birmingham riots linger close to the surface of Godwin's attempt to delegitimize political mobilization and represent it as political violence: 'While the sympathy of opinion catches from man to man, especially among persons whose passions have been little used to the curb of judgment, actions may be determined on which the solitary reflection of all would have rejected. There is nothing more barbarous, blood-thirsty and unfeeling than the triumph of the mob' (*EPJ*, p. 288). Again the private becomes the refuge of rationality as pathologized opinion, catching from man to man like a disease, spreading through the crowd in a way that reconstitutes it as the mob, leaves only the quarantined individual capable of sober judgement.

These arguments were emphatically reiterated by Godwin in his 1795 *Considerations on Lord Grenville's and Mr. Pitt's Bills, Concerning Treasonable and Seditious Practices, and Unlawful Assemblies*. Here he discusses the LCS and the 'political lecturer in Beaufort Buildings', that is John Thelwall, directly, implying that both index the extent to which the processes of public discussion and opinion formation have been degraded by their integration into the world of spectacular identification and culture-consumptions in which the demagogue essentially markets a political or philosophical creed before an audience of consumers.[5] 'It almost universally happens to public speakers', Godwin writes, 'that, though they may begin with the intention of communicating to their auditors the tone of their own minds, they finish with the reality of bartering this tone for the tone of the auditors.'[6] Accordingly, the viability of a public speech becomes entirely linked to its ability to provoke popular applause.

Again it is only at a safe distance from 'collected multitudes', in the 'domestic tranquillity' of the fire-side, that rational interaction can take place,[7] precisely because the public sphere, unlike the hearth, is imagined as continuous with the marketplace in which the citizen as consumer, immersed in the practices of monadic, hedonistic subjectivity, indulges in the pleasures of demagogic solicitation and group identification. This reading of radical political culture is precariously close to the anti-Jacobin propaganda that portrayed Richard Price, Joseph Priestley, Thomas Paine, Thomas Spence, Thelwall and Godwin himself as the emissaries of a fraudulent print-capitalism peddling words and ideas before a public of ill-educated labourers easily deceived by shrewd marketing strategies.[8] But Pitt and Grenville, whose so-called 'two acts' attempted to effectively dismantle the infrastructures of the public sphere – freedom of speech, of the press and of association – are similarly understood by Godwin as implicated in the massified realm of the spectacle and consumerism. They also consult 'not the coolness of philosophy, but the madness of passion'.[9] 'They have laid aside the robes and insignia of authority; and leaped, like a common wrestler, upon the stage. They have been loudest in increasing the broil; they have urged on the animosity of the combatants; they have called for blood.'[10] The image of combatants wrestling on a public stage indicates Godwin's attempt to place Pitt and Grenville, along with the populist Jacobin demagogue, in the world of massified spectacle production, in which incitement and sensationalism, rather than reason, are the principles of public presentation.

But if the ideal of public interaction is here banished to private space, Godwin elsewhere in the *Enquiry* acknowledges that its actual ameliorative ability is contingent on the very structures of public mediation and dissemination that, we have just seen, are so dangerous. And to be sure he seems unaware, at such moments, that he is replicating what he most wants to reject, right down to the metaphor of contagion as a way of understanding the formation of opinion:

show to mankind, by an adequate example, the advantages of political disquisition, undebauched by political enmity and vehemence, and the beauty of the spectacle will soon render it contagious. Every man will commune with his neighbour. Every man will be eager to tell, and to hear, what the interests of all require them to know. The bolts and fortifications of the temple of truth will be removed. The craggy steep of science, which it was before difficult to ascend, will be levelled. Knowledge will be generally accessible.

(EPJ, p. 290)

In this oversight Godwin, it would seem, refuses to accept the conclusion so emphatically implied by his own text – that the ideal of public interaction is itself a public impossibility because the production and reception of knowledge, information and text simply do not allow individuals to interact outside of specific interpretive contexts that ultimately constitute the public and public opinion as always, in some sense, dependent on the authority of demagogic oration or of printed texts presenting affective spectacles. *Caleb Williams*, we will see, confronts the apparent irreducibility of a problem that Godwin is here unwilling to acknowledge. The institutions of the public sphere imply powerful and pervasive forms of mediation, and public opinion, Godwin has apparently shown, cannot tangibly exist independently of these except as the negation of publicity, that is in sequestered privacy. This problem is external to the actual content of interaction. It is a formal or structural one: even the ideal of public interaction must be mediated by spectacles that render it contagious, before it can even exist as an object of cognition.

Godwin's declaration of the importance of the 'beauty of the spectacle' to the moment of political enlightenment was by no means an eccentric or contextually unfounded one. On the contrary we find that, throughout the 1790s, Gothic and sentimental narrative structures, both affective and spectacular, organize the public dissemination of a vision of modernity similar to Godwin's. Political discourse at the end of the eighteenth century, moreover, was as dependent on the 'beauty of the spectacle' as the most pathetic literary forms. Thelwall, for example, characterized his own work as 'politico-sentimental'.[11] As Claudia Johnson points out, 'Gothic-pathetic literature' and public political expression were largely continuous in their use of sentimental images and affective language.[12] It is also no coincidence that sentimental narratives of the coming enlightenment are extremely distrustful of mediated publicity, which they variously understand as economic exchange and culture-consumption. In the work of writers as diverse as Radcliffe and Thelwall, the ideal of an interactive, self-directing community finds its realization not in or through the pathologized realm of public interaction, but in the mythic space of pastoral domesticity that exists either before or beyond the public. In a virtual pantisocracy that is itself thoroughly spectacular – a product of Gothic-sentimental literary conventions – the heteronormative family becomes an ideal communal structure always threatened by the Gothic incursions of corrupting economic interests, egocentric libertines or the deceptive allurements of aesthetic spectacles. Accordingly, the family itself becomes the embodiment of the form of communal interaction that Godwin sought in the ideal of public opinion and discussion. As Habermas has pointed out, this valorization of the family, pervasive in the 1790s, is ideological to the extent to which it recodes gender-based power relations as natural, uncoerced relations between equals. The space of the family, he argues, becomes the imaginative abode of the communality and subjectivity that will constitute the basic ideological fiction of a bourgeois society convinced of its moral authority and of its role as arbiter of universal human values: 'In the intimate sphere of the conjugal family privatized individuals viewed themselves as independent even from the private sphere of their economic activity – as persons capable of entering into "purely human" relations with one another' (*ST*, p. 48). It is equally important to grasp the related point, however, that images of the family, of sequestered privacy and of conjugal love, are themselves public ones, in the sense that they are entirely mediated by the very practices of public presentation, dissemination, exchange and consumption that are so toxic to them in the plot of the sentimental narrative.

The paradox here is that the valorization of the private sphere takes place in a public medium, and is thereby implicated in the very problematic it addresses. The circulation of sentimental textual artifacts celebrating the private and revealing the forces that threaten this, becomes the infrastructural basis for an imagined communality – a public – consolidated around the collective reception of these texts. This form of discursive praxis and the kind of communality it makes available is what Habermas describes as a literary public sphere. Habermas is intent on reading this public, and its developed form in the bourgeois public sphere proper, as the embodiment of rational communicative norms similar to those defended by Godwin. In the literary public sphere, Habermas argues, individuals could come together in disinterested and free discussion over the fact of their common humanity as it was bodied forth in sentimental texts like Richardson's *Pamela* or Goethe's *The*

Sorrows of Young Werther. The forums for public interaction in which such literary texts were discussed needed only to be extended to include political and economic issues for this public of readers to become the politicized public intent on defending its own integrity and autonomy from forms of state control and intervention (see *ST*, pp. 27–57).

But it is also clear from Habermas's analysis that the literary public sphere must have been mediated by textual objects read, at least initially, in private by people with sufficient leisure time to consume and sufficient means to purchase these objects. The communality of the literary public sphere, in other words, was premised on the collective character of private consumption. The forms of pleasurable affect that the individual reader experiences become, in their imagined ubiquity, the basis for identification with a wider community of readers. In this way individualized, serialized subjects experience a form of collectivity that is in fact contingent on their very separation as individual consumers, on privacy as the enforced absence of communicative interaction. The sentimental text both positions readers as isolated individuals and, insofar as these readers all entertain the same relationship to the sentimental text, as members of a community. The 'beauty of the spectacle', the affect of sentimental textual production, mediates this complex interpenetration of private and communal identities; it positions monadic subjects oriented to the pleasures of the text, but allows these subjects to experience the act of private textual consumption as a form of communal solidarity. In this way subjects consuming sentimental tableaux could experience a form of communal existence otherwise occluded by the atomizing relations of production and exchange in emerging capitalism. This experience, however, is still always contained by the economy of culture-consumption and thus ultimately reproduces the monadic subjectivity of the marketplace at the very moment that this has apparently disappeared into the harmony of uncoerced communal empathy. The ultimate political complicity of the sentimental text is thus dependent on its ability to create an imaginative release from atomizing social and economic relations. This is the sense in which the production of sentimental aesthetic artifacts is most emphatically ideological. Virtually regardless of their content such artifacts participate in and reinforce an economy of discursive production and reception in which the monadic subject of emergent capitalism can experience the normative component of readerly sympathy – the fiction of universal, ethical, human responsiveness – in the sequestered space of private consumption. The subject of the bourgeois public sphere, by this reckoning, was essentially a culture-consumer whose experience of his or her identity, insofar as it had a communal dimension, was entirely contingent on and contained within the act of consumption. In this sense the public sphere was merely the aggregation of private individuals assured of their integrity as both property owners and consumers.

According to this reading notions of individual autonomy and of the communal solidarity based on it are, like the group solidarity resulting from populist oration, contingent on the mediation of a public discursive praxis – the circulation of printed texts. Godwin's vision of communality mediated by the 'beauty of the spectacle' both underscores and evades this problem: it indicates the deep affinity of the *Enquiry*'s account of redemptive public opinion with sentimental narrative conventions and the public affect of responsiveness to them, but refuses to acknowledge that this affinity means that the 'beauty of the spectacle' might be structurally indistinct from the equally sentimental and affective modes of public interaction embodied in populist oration and official invective – in, for example, Edmund Burke's public speeches and the slew of pamphleteers who imitated his performative, sentimentalizing excesses, or in the 'politico-sentimentality' of Thelwall's public lectures. All, it would seem, deploy representational and rhetorical strategies that solicit passionate, intuitive or sympathetic responses, and allow the assumed ubiquity of these responses to become the basis of communal solidarity and identification. The fact that the abstract ideal of interactive, uncoerced publicity is mediated by the 'beauty of the spectacle' would suggest, moreover, that it is itself contingent on a historical context permeated by the steady dissemination and circulation of textual objects; on spectacles that both represent community and actively form it in the fact of empathetic readership. With culture-consumption in the eighteenth century no longer confined to specific locations like the theatre or court, but becoming increasingly pervasive through the rise of mass literacy and mass production, sentimental, affective literature can be read as anticipating the forms of mass mediation that, for Horkheimer and Adorno, constitute the modern culture industry. According to this scenario, the very idea that public interaction could be a mechanism of social amelioration and rational autonomy would itself be a function of a discursive praxis inseparable from the consolidation of market capitalism, and involving the dominance of sentimental textual forms, the spread of literacy, the development of print-technology, and of increasingly expansive modes of textual dissemination. Normativity, in other words, would also be normalization mediated by the consumption of textual objects, and what Godwin believes to be the ideal of public interaction would be phenomenologically dependent on the very structures that threaten its integrity.

CALEB WILLIAMS, PUBLIC SURVEILLANCE AND THE CIRCULATION OF CRITIQUE

Godwin's 1794 'political-Gothic' *Things as They Are, or The Adventures of Caleb Williams*, is both engaged with and, as a circulating textual object, implicated in this problematic. If the novel is a fictional embodiment of the opposition, initially present in the *Enquiry*, between public opinion and the institutions of political power and authority, it is also a faithful replication of the further split between the ideal of unmediated opinion and its pathological, administered variant in the public sphere itself. The novel's eponymous protagonist discovers, in his relationship with his aristocratic patron Falkland, that public opinion mediated through the dissemination of textual objects and the formation of a national reading public synonymous with the boundaries of the emerging nation-state, far from facilitating the bright dawn of political justice, is in fact emptied of all capacity for independent thought and thoroughly integrated into a regime of administered consciousness. This regime, moreover, is not simply the result of elite conspiracy: it is ultimately no more nor less than a formal effect of the public sphere and its structures of authority.

The novel is initially based on conventional sentimental images of Gothic surveillance and aristocratic persecution. Caleb, after the death of his parents, finds himself in the service and residence of Falkland, whose inexplicable behaviour arouses his curiosity. Caleb's own maniacal pursuit of the truth at the bottom of Falkland's behaviour leads to the embedded narrative of the servant Collins, which relates Falkland's past. This narrative, itself a rehearsal of Gothic-sentimental conventions, reveals that Falkland, a self-conscious embodiment of aristocratic virtue and honour (a Charles Grandison figure, but also a parody of Edmund Burke's chivalric pretence) had been publicly assaulted and humiliated by his nemesis Tyrrel, an aristocratic savage responsible for the Clarissaesque persecution and death of his own niece, whom he had suspected of falling in love with Falkland.[13] When, soon after this public assault, Tyrrel is found murdered, Falkland is suspected, but quickly cleared of the crime. His public image in tatters and all hopes of chivalric redemption gone with the death of his assailant, Falkland has become a depressive recluse still clinging to the pathetic remnants of his former authority as a public figure. Naturally enough the inquisitive Caleb suspects his master of the murder and engages him in a series of verbal jousts designed to solicit a confession. Finally admitting his guilt, yet still protective of his public reputation, Falkland declares his undying hatred of Caleb, solicits a promise of eternal secrecy, and vows never to let him out of his control. Caleb becomes a virtual prisoner on Falkland's estate. The manor house, now a version of the Gothic castle, becomes the centre of a Gothic-sentimental topography and seems to Caleb like 'one of those fortresses, famed in the history of despotism, from which the wretched victim is never known to come forth alive' (*CW*, p. 157). 'I was a prisoner', he laments, 'and what a prisoner! All my actions observed; all my gestures marked. I could move neither to the right nor the left, but the eye of my keeper was upon me. He watched me; and his vigilance was a sickness to my heart. For me there was no more freedom, no more of hilarity, of thoughtlessness, or of youth' (*CW*, p. 149). Falkland, on the other hand, is overtaken by a paranoid and panoptic will to power that seizes on its object with relentlessness and an apparent omniscience. 'You little suspect the extent of my power', he warns; 'At this moment you are enclosed with the snares of my vengeance unseen by you, and, at the instant that you flatter yourself you are already beyond their reach, they will close upon you. You might as well think of escaping from the power of the omnipresent God, as from mine!' (*CW*, p. 150). In a typically sentimental reversal of affective agency, common to both Gothic literature and radical-reformist discourse in the 1790s, the scene of incarceration ceases to be the object of panoptic surveillance and now positions the observer as the subject of compassionate responsiveness.[14] Presented with the tableau of the suffering, isolated prisoner, the reader-observer's sympathy for the prisoner becomes an indication of his or her humanity, while the now displaced eye of power – Falkland as the police in Godwin's novel – becomes an aberrant transgression of sentimental propriety.

But when Caleb eventually escapes these confines, the authority initially invested in Falkland extends itself to include an ever widening object domain, moving through more expansive forms of incarceration, from the manor house, to a legal-judicial system, to the whole land mass of England, Scotland and Wales. Soon after Caleb's escape Falkland fabricates a charge of theft against the object of his hatred. At this point an entire policing apparatus seems to become an extension of Falkland's authority and panoptic omniscience. The later circulation of an erroneous criminal biography, *The Most Wonderful and Surprising History and Miraculous Adventures of Caleb Williams*, moreover, enlists public outrage and invigilation as a crucial component of this apparatus. Critics are right to read this aspect of the novel in Foucauldian terms. As James Thompson points out, *Caleb Williams* is a political novel primarily because it excavates the formation of the new bourgeois state in terms of the panoptic disciplinary mechanisms that Foucault describes in *Discipline and Punish*.[15] This is indeed how Caleb imagines the agency inspiring the circulation of his own biography, which seems to follow him and destroy his reputation at the moment that he seems to have found a refuge beyond the persecuting hand of textual dissemination: 'It was like what has been described of the eye of omniscience pursuing the guilty sinner, and darting a ray that awakens him to a new sensibility at the very moment that, otherwise, exhausted nature would lull him into a temporary oblivion of the reproaches of his conscience' (*CW*, p. 316). In this formulation the panopticon of Falkland's manor house is replaced by the panopticon of the state policing apparatus and of the public opinion that it co-opts as its greatest resource. We would do well to note, however, that the latter is only panoptic in a metaphorical sense. The apparatus that pursues Caleb beyond the bounds of the manor house is in fact based on modes of organization that, in their very expansiveness, so fundamentally eradicate the possibility of centralized agency – the eye of power – that we can only imagine them in precisely the terms that they deny; that is, as omniscient or supernaturally inspired, which is how they appear to Caleb. What Foucault describes as the lowered threshold of describable individuality that characterizes modern policing practices, in which the criminal is an individual case constituted by textual data and assembled by administrative specialists, implies a mechanism that 'must be coextensive with the entire social body and not only by the extreme limits that it embraces, but by the minuteness of the details it is concerned with'.[16] This system is dependent on the circulation of textual materials such as newspapers and flyers that report crime, describe suspects and offer rewards, on the collection and dissemination of such information and, centrally, on the constitution of a national reading public that can receive information in textual form, internalize the civic burden of police work, and play its part as an agent of civic authority. We get an indication of the centrality of this process to the novel very early on. Falkland's mansion is going to become a Gothicized space of tyrannical authority and surveillance, but before it has any of these sinister connotations it is introduced to the reader as a place that collects texts. Caleb is employed by Falkland as a kind of librarian, and as he imagines his master as the eye of omniscience, he is ironically unaware of his proximity to the banal, innocuous and decentralized mechanisms of disciplinary power.

My point here is that what Caleb imagines as panoptic – a form of administrative expertise that applies a panoptic structure to a greater area and number of bodies – is actually a more varied and complex deployment of power inseparable from the infrastructures of the public sphere. And this point is entirely compatible with Foucault's work, much of which seeks to demonstrate how something analogous to public space is coterminous with disciplinary practices that lurk behind, or more accurately in a normative facade of freedom, rights and civic responsibility. In *Caleb Williams* the public that consumes and discusses textual objects is both formed and functionalized by the circulation of texts through it. The erroneous criminal biography of the infamous Caleb Williams, circulated by Falkland, galvanizes a public of readers around the imperatives of property, and the common responsibility of all citizens to protect it: communal fidelity to formal legal imperatives, the objectification of criminals and the sentimental presentation of their victims are presented as mutually enforcing. But this process does not happen simply because the biography is a manipulative representation of an apparent criminal. The very idea of community as an embodiment of moral and civic authority is itself a function of the media available for the production and transmission of knowledge and information in the eighteenth century. Accordingly, it is perhaps misleading to suggest, for example, that the text-based policing schemes of Henry and John Fielding, so faithfully captured in Godwin's novel, sought to co-opt textual production and dissemination in the interests of law enforcement. On the contrary, the developments in print technology, in modes of national distribution, and in mass literacy themselves constitute the conditions of possibility for the modern policing practices writers like the Fieldings imagined, precisely because they also made possible the notion of community (the aggregation of possessive, private individuals) that was the basis of these policing schemes. John Fielding's 1772 circulars, for example, articulate a text-based system of public invigilation intended to realize 'the vigorous Circulation of Civil Power' flowing in a 'rapid Stream throughout every Jurisdiction'.[17] Through the national distribution of newspapers and flyers detailing crimes and suspects, the fact of readership enacted a community inseparable now from civic responsibility, the protection of property, and the identification of those outcasts who threatened both of these. In this way we can read the public sphere as a disciplinary formation that regulates its members at the very moments that it produces 'community', 'opinion' and 'access to information' as the conceptual underpinnings of an enlightened culture. It is no coincidence that sensationalized criminal biographies have such currency and popularity throughout the eighteenth century and beyond. These biographies, the 'histories of celebrated robbers' which Caleb himself produces in the novel (*CW*, p. 268), enabled the experience of private readers to become the basis of a community that could function not just as a check on state authority, as Habermas claims, but also as its agent. This reading of the public sphere and public opinion as inseparable from the exercise of state power and the consolidation of policing practices committed to the defence of private property is emphatically thematized in Godwin's novel.

But in *Caleb Williams* the penetration of public opinion by administrative and legalistic imperatives apparently external to it still allows the novel's victimized protagonist to have faith in the ideal of public interaction undistorted by power relations. Indeed it is through unhindered and rational communication that Caleb hopes to end his plight as a fugitive and have the charges against him dropped. At a fundamental level then the novel is based on the opposition between undistorted communication and the invasiveness of state authority, on the hope that the ideal speech community of the private sphere can be publicly realized. But just as in the *Enquiry*, this opposition belies the extent to which the public sphere itself and its institutions are structurally antithetical to this ideal. When Falkland voluntarily withdraws the charges against Caleb, but leaves opinion to run its own course via the mediation of the criminal biography, it becomes clear that the protestations of a mere individual cannot compete with the authority assumed by a printed text. If a form of discursive praxis constructs community, it also deploys authority for this community in an authoritarian and monological manner, through the printed text itself as a virtual fetish object – 'the last page of the volume of truth', as Godwin writes in the *Enquiry*. When Caleb ostensibly retreats from contact with the public sphere into a small Welsh town 'remote from the bustle of human life' (*CW*, p. 300), the invasiveness of textual production is emphatically demonstrated. The town and in particular the family of Laura Denison, into which Caleb is initially embraced, seems to foreshadow the ideal speech community of private subjects engaged in uncoerced and undistorted communication. Laura is herself a maternal figure for Caleb and the confluence of familial and romantic idylls in which he is now positioned both constitutes a sentimentalized tableau for the reader, and promises Caleb himself the sympathy he has hitherto been denied.[18] But when Caleb's biography finally appears in this midst the idyll is shattered. While the authority of the biography is unquestioned, even by Laura, Caleb's increasingly hysterical proclamations of innocence force him into what seems to her an overtly performative style of self-presentation. Caleb's language, as it does throughout his narration, becomes excessively affective and thus seems to announce its own artificiality. Ironically Laura suspects Caleb of using language as a method of deception and manipulation. 'True virtue refuses the drudgery of explanation and apology', she warns; 'True virtue shines by its own light, and needs no art to set it off. You have the first principles of morality as yet to learn' (*CW*, p. 310).

The crisis enacted at this moment is, however, not simply reducible to the corruption of a hitherto inviolable idyll. On the contrary, the familial idyll over which Laura Denison presides is so receptive to the public account of Caleb's life because it is already founded on the reception of publicly circulated, sentimental texts. At the most fundamental level the community of sympathetic subjects presented by the idyll is mediated by texts conveying an affective image of chivalric, paternal virtue. The text of Falkland's Italian adventures, narrated to Caleb by Collins, is the founding mythology of Laura's family, in which it has the authority of scripture. Upon hearing Laura repeat the 'all-dreadful name', Caleb discovers that,

> ... Mr Falkland had been known to the father of Laura: that he had been acquainted with the story of Count Malvesi, and with a number of other transactions redounding in the highest degree to

the credit of the gallant Englishman. The Neopolitan had left letters in which these transactions were recorded, and which spoke of Mr Falkland in the highest terms of panegyric. Laura had been used to regard every relic of her father with a sort of religious veneration; and, by this accident, the name of Falkland was connected in her mind with the sentiments of unbounded esteem.

(CW, p. 304)

The centrality of epistolary documents to the perpetuation of Falkland's reputation highlights the undecidability that characterizes the epistolary form. The letter is at once an apparently private and therefore uncoerced communiqué, a transparent medium in which sympathetic subjectivity can communicate itself, but also the basic device for sentimental texts, like Richardson's, oriented to the public performance of this subjectivity. The name of Falkland, Laura tells Caleb, 'had been a denomination, as far back as my memory can reach, for the most exalted of mortals, the wisest and most generous of men' (*CW*, p. 311). Rehearsing the superlatives that are the unmistakable sign of Richardsonian fiction, Laura's own language suggests an uncritically devotional relationship to the sentimental text and its chivalric, Grandisonian fictions. At the origin of the idyll then, is an image that has the power of divine revelation, but which is also continuous with the circulation of other affective textual objects. At this point a sympathetic community distinct from the public is not only compromised, it is shown to be always already coterminous with the forms of textual production and reception that characterize the public sphere. This problematization of the opposition between an unmediated form of community and the pathological public emphatically states the paradox that remained unacknowledged in the *Enquiry*'s account of community mediated by the 'beauty of the spectacle': if sympathetic communities are necessarily mediated by tableaux that convey norms of communal life and, in their affectivity, position individual subjects as ubiquitously human in the sensibility of their responses, it becomes impossible to imagine a form of communal existence not compromised by the infrastructures of the public sphere. Caleb, it would seem, finally realizes and confronts this problem. Already an experienced criminal biographer, he would seem to have no choice but to exonerate himself in public through the very modes of presentation and dissemination which have hitherto cancelled the possibility of rational public interaction. Hence he writes the novel we are in fact reading, a sentimental presentation of his own victimization that deployed itself, for the actual reader of the period, in public.

If, as John Bender has argued in *Imagining the Penitentiary*, the novel form replicates the structure of the panopticon in its construction of an omniscient third-person narrator who then presents a carefully ordered and moralized object domain to the reader, Falkland's fabrication of Caleb's criminality and the production of the erroneous biography, literalizes narratological authority in the public objectification of the criminal body.[19] Falkland's manipulation of events constructs Caleb's life as a narrative in which the latter is totally alienated and, one might say, disembodied. As a conscious subject, Caleb becomes irrelevant to the story of which his physical body, as a criminal body, is part. He has been literally constructed in a way that he has no control over, and as he circulates through the land mass he is trapped in, accompanied by his textually objectified shadow, what he experiences is the inability to refashion himself in sentimental terms for anyone – anyone, that is, except the actual reader of the novel. While the reading community represented in the text is totally administered by and contingent on the authority of the biography, such that all possibilities for sentimental identification are quickly replaced by conditioned responses, the presentation of this alienation positions the reader beyond the text, alone, as a sentimentally engaged subject. In so doing the novel establishes disciplinary modes of object constitution and consciousness, integrated into the exercise of power, as its subject matter, while sentimental identification is the way in which the actual reader of the novel can distinguish him/herself from these practices. In other words, if sentimental identification appears to resist disciplinary power, reconstituting the object body of disciplinarity (the criminal) as the object of readerly compassion (the prisoner or victim), it also replicates the administered, mediated character of the reader-responsiveness portrayed in the novel itself. Caleb has essentially displaced his own criminal biography with another monologically authoritative, compulsively sentimentalizing text, and the respective truth claims of these texts would seem to be irrelevant to the fact that both cancel the possibility of unmediated public interaction. Both index modes of textual production, dissemination and reception that mediate the experience of community for otherwise private subjects and deploy authority monologically in the printed artifact.

The realization of this apparently irreducible problem accounts, I think, for the extreme pessimism of the novel's conclusion. In the original version of the ending Caleb finishes his manuscript on the verge of insanity, abdicating his claim to humanity, declaring 'True happiness lies in being like a stone – Nobody can complain of me – all day long I do nothing – am a stone – a GRAVE STONE! – an obelisk to tell you, HERE LIES WHAT WAS ONCE A MAN!' (*CW*, p. 346). This passage revealingly echoes one that appears in the earlier *Enquiry*: 'Reserve, deceitfulness, and an artful exhibition of ourselves take from the human form its soul, and leave us the unanimated semblance of what man might have been; of what he would have been, were not every impulse of the mind thus stunted and destroyed' (*EPJ*, p. 317). In the revised ending to the novel, in which Caleb is ultimately vindicated, the implicit connection between vacant or denigrated subjectivity and narrative performativity is explicitly consolidated in what Gary Handwerk describes as Caleb's 'obsessive identification' with Falkland.[20] Caleb's attempt to exonerate himself has indeed culminated, or so he believes, in an artful exhibition (involving the kinds of affect, performativity and authority I have discussed), enabling him to believe that he has merely repeated the very structures of power that Falkland has so expertly exploited. If we accept this conclusion we must also surmise that the possibility of enlightened communicative interaction, imagined at moments in both the *Enquiry* and *Caleb Williams*, is not only deeply problematic, but always constitutes its own negation because it is inseparable from the very structures that are hostile to it: Caleb's narration, it turns out, is no less performative and manipulative than the oration of the demagogue or the text of the criminal biography. The very act of narration brings with it a guilty complicity with ideological structures. In this respect Godwin seems to write the possibility of public enlightenment not so much as a history of decline, but as a deconstructive subversion of itself in which the compulsion of truth in a rational communicative exchange always gives way to the compulsion of textual affect.

To conclude I want to argue that this negation hinges on the rather undifferentiated, ahistorical and abstract notion of public interaction that the *Enquiry* initially valorizes, and the ensuing consolidation of a theory/praxis opposition that is too readily dismissive of contingent forms of communication. By rethinking this notion of the public we can, I believe, avoid the defeatism of a theoretical position which cancels the possibility of actual public interaction as a politically redemptive force. This move is important not least because the totalizing character of Godwin's pathologization of public life remains a standard critical posture today in critiques of modernity from Adorno to Foucault. In such critiques apparently ameliorative potential located in the public sphere is either an extension of the command structures of capitalism, or a function of hidden power relations. The crucial question here has to be how experience (or subjectivity) is mediated, formed through, or articulated in the institutions of public interaction. For critiques that read modernity as inevitably functionalized or instrumentalized, experience is entirely a product of mediating strategies, and subjectivity is tied inextricably to a model of interpellation or administered consciousness. As it is for the readers of the fabricated biography in *Caleb Williams*, subjectivity is merely the interiorization of programmed responses that reproduce relations of production. Hitherto I've wanted to demonstrate, with Godwin, how the public sphere can be read in these terms: that is as a form of discursive praxis in which notions of subjecthood and community, and the forms of civic responsibility, interaction and equality based on them, are manufactured and normalized so that they appear to be the inevitable extension of an indubitably 'human' nature. One would then read the literary public sphere, for Habermas the space from which the rational and politically redemptive content of bourgeois publicity arises, as either predicating a society of culture-consumers, in which consumption rather than humanity is the principle of membership, or as synonymous with disciplinary structures summoning and consolidating norms of conduct linked to the integrity of individual readers as property owners.

But we can read the relationship between experience and publicity very differently if we historicize it in a more varied way, suggesting the possibility of forms of public interaction not reducible to those presented in *Caleb Williams* as the limit of public life. In the next chapter I will argue that the milieu of radical corresponding societies that Godwin was proximate to, but ultimately critical of, suggests the possibility of a structurally differentiated economy of cultural production and reception very different from that which occupied Godwin in the *Enquiry* and *Caleb Williams*. While Godwin's dismissal of these infrastructures demonstrates the difficulty involved in imagining forms of communicative action resistant to the ideological closure of a totalized and homogenized model of pathologized publicity, his own work can still be read as participating in a form of counterhegemonic interaction. In the distinction between what he referred to as the 'moral' and the 'tendency' of a literary work, Godwin suggests that the full import of a text cannot be grasped just in terms of its own properties, whether these be a matter of form or content, but should more properly be sought in the text's reception. In an essay entitled 'Of Choice in Reading', published in *The Enquirer* in 1797, he writes 'The moral of any work may be defined to be that ethical sentence to the illustration of which the work may be most aptly applied. The tendency is the actual effect it is calculated to produce upon the readers, and cannot be completely ascertained but by the experiment'.[21] In prioritizing tendency as the principle of meaning, Godwin suggests a reader-response oriented method of interpretation: the public reception and use of texts is the basis upon which they must be explicated as social documents. But the apparently open-ended nature of this formulation need not lead to a post-structuralist valorization of the interpretive process as a potentially endless series of rejoinders to a text that would have as many tendencies as it does readers. On the contrary, *Caleb Williams* rehearses the conventions and topoi of both the popular sentimental novel and subliterary sentimental forms like the criminal biography, in order to demonstrate how these forms compel a certain form of subjectivity and arrest the critical powers of the reader with their own affectivity. While Godwin's novel performs the constraints that sentimental texts place on their readership, it does so as an explicitly sentimental narrative. At least part of its tendency, then, is not arbitrary at all: the novel forces its readers to become aware of the conditioned nature of their own apparently spontaneous responses to it. It thus raises fundamental questions about the very assumptions of individual and communal identity its own conventions otherwise encourage. It attempts to demystify the process of its own public reception, bringing the source of bourgeois normativity – public solidarity mediated by increasingly massified, yet essentially private reading practices – to public consciousness, revealing the relationship between power, discipline and the interpenetration of private and public spheres.

For a 1790s audience caught in the grip of rapidly consolidating juridical and ideological structures intent on the disorganization of critical facilities in the name of private property and national security, this excavation would have been genuinely and urgently demystifying, revealing the contingency of forms of social life that, in their apparent inevitability, remained immune to criticism. Explicating the infrastructural obstacles to counterhegemonic communicative practices, the novel itself initiated another structure of communication which did not mediate subjectivity as such, but examined a prior structure of mediation and its ultimately alienating consequences. By communicating to its readers the ideologically inflected character of their own reading practices, it anticipated a resistant public premised on a collective understanding of the alienation experienced in common by subjects integrated into the structures of bourgeois publicity. Despite the apparent defeatism of Caleb's narrative, Godwin's efforts to clarify and articulate relations and structures simultaneously conditioning and mystifying communal experience were thus not limited to a moment of negative critique. On the contrary, they placed him in a political milieu concerned with the theorization and radical reinvention of public space and interactive practices. That Caleb himself cannot acknowledge the genuinely enlightening content of his own narration remains a pertinent index to the kinds of ideological mystifications the novel is revealing: the pathological public sphere that Godwin strove to escape finally breeds pathology itself, embodied in Caleb's guilt, as a symptom of the closure enacted by a unitary model of public space in which the administered public of sentimental culture-consumption is imagined as the limit of possible experience. Succumbing to this defeatism not only forces one to ignore the very real possibilities of counterhegemonic public mobilization and communicative interaction evident at the end of the eighteenth century, but portrays the historically contingent forms of bourgeois life as timeless, totalizing and intransigent structures, and thereby participates in their ideological validation.

3

Politico-Sentimentality: John Thelwall, Literary Production and the Critique of Capital in the 1790s

In E. P. Thompson's *The Making of the English Working Class*, John Thelwall embodies the pathos of thwarted heroism that typifies the radical milieu of the 1790s in the imaginings of the British left. 'Thelwall took Jacobinism to the borders of Socialism; he also took it to the borders of revolutionism', writes Thompson eulogistically.[1] As one of the London Corresponding Society members prosecuted for treason in 1794, and as the orator who addressed an estimated crowd of one hundred and fifty thousand in Copenhagen Fields in 1795, Thelwall has at least a consistent profile in histories of the labour movement and in materialist social histories of the 1790s. Besides political philosophy and public activism, however, Thelwall also published several collections of poetry, though as a figure in the development of Romantic literary forms and as an inheritor of the eighteenth-century cult of sensibility, he is marginal at best, typically warranting a dismissive footnote, or at most figuring in the background of studies on Coleridge, Wordsworth or early Romanticism more generally. I do not want to claim that Thelwall too demands the adulation reserved for those poets central to the imagining of an English literary culture, though I do want to suggest that the imagining of this culture is also the occasion for an ideologically mediated amnesia that has consigned writers like Thelwall and the possibilities they stood for to the margins of cultural history. What is compelling about Thelwall is that, as both a Romantic poet (albeit a minor one) and a radical political leader, he was forced to work through issues surrounding the political efficacy of sentimental and Romantic literary production against the context of activism and populist mobilization. His career tangibly demonstrates how affective sentimental discourse, which through the figures of Richardson and Goethe takes on such singular importance in Habermas's account of the bourgeois public sphere, could be appropriated for radical political ends and become crucial in the formation of what Oskar Negt and Alexander Kluge call a 'proletarian public sphere', or what Günther Lottes, discussing late-eighteenth-century British radicalism specifically, calls a 'plebeian public'. Thelwall's work – both his literary production and his political writings and speeches, in their complementarity and antagonisms – makes available to us the possibility of a genuinely activist economy of cultural production and reception very different to those economies we identify with either canonical Romanticism or its apparent antithesis, an emerging culture industry. It is in these terms that Thelwall remains a little explored resource not only for materialist accounts of the late-eighteenth century, but for theorists interested in articulating what counterhegemonic public spaces and practices, resistant to culture-consumption, national identification and the reproduction of capital, might look like in this century.

POLITICIZING THE LITERARY: RADICALISM AND THE CULTURE OF SENTIMENTALITY

In 1793 John Thelwall published, in three volumes, *The Peripatetic*, subtitled *Sketches of the Heart, of Nature and Society; in a Series of Politico-Sentimental Journals*. Modeled after Sterne's *A Sentimental Journey* it recounts the adventures of its travelling protagonist, Sylvanus Theophrastus, as he moves through a series of sentimental encounters and tableaux. Thelwall was indeed anxious to avoid accusations that his work had simply appropriated the stock gestures of sentimental literature so prevalent at the time, and in the preface to the text in fact pays specific deference to Sterne, as well as Johnson, in order to shore up his own claims to originality. 'The author', writes Thelwall, 'therefore, presumes to hope, that no resemblances will be found, in the course of the ensuing volumes, to the modes of composition of any of his literary predecessors, but such as are the involuntary result of an occasional similarity in the bias of sentiment and reflection' (*PP*, I, p. iv). Indeed the similarities that do exist between *The Peripatetic* and *A Sentimental Journey* are both intentional and superficial. While Yorick's passionate responses to the spectacles and interactions he experiences mark the realm of sentiment as the indeterminate and inexplicable space between conscious and preconscious thought, Sylvanus's sentimental effusions index a nascent but still critical awareness of the processes that for Marx will define capitalist production: accumulation and monopolization of the means of production, and the corresponding creation of a population released from the bonds of feudalism into the freedom of the market as 'sellers of themselves'.[2] For Thelwall the material capable of evoking sentimental responsiveness on the part of the reader was inseparable from the social and economic relations that increasingly characterized the 1790s as a decade of growing class polarization. 'The subject of our political abuses', writes Thelwall in the preface, 'is so interwoven with the scenes of distress so perpetually recurring to the feeling observer, that it were impossible to be silent in this respect, without suppressing almost every reflection that ought to awaken the tender sympathies of the soul' (*PP*, I, p. viii).

It is through the image of the rural idyll that *The Peripatetic* most explicitly attempts to evoke sentimental responsiveness as a form of political awareness and critique. Cottagers, rural families, ruddy-faced children and gypsies recur throughout Sylvanus's travels, yet so too do the relations of ownership that threaten these innocent, idyllic communities: 'not among the least cruel of the practices by which the higher orders of society among us wantonly, and with impunity, oppress the poor, is the modern tyranny of exterminating, from the vicinity of each proud mansion, the inhabitants of these humble sheds' (*PP*, I, p. 133). As it was in Goldsmith's 'The Deserted Village', which clearly informs Thelwall's writings, and in Wordsworth's 'Salisbury Plain', written in the same years as *The Peripatetic* was published, the displacement of the peasantry is conceived as an assault on the integrity of the hearth and the family unit. Once the owner of a large estate decides to remove the inhabitants of the surrounding area as part of a programme of 'projected improvements', the former inhabitants are displaced from 'the spot, dear to them, perhaps, from the embrace of their own infantile sports, or from the comforts it has afforded to their little families' (*PP*, I, pp. 133–4). The family idyll is directly contrasted with what replaces it – the life of an urban proletariat which embodies the violation and destruction of filial prosperity and of a now effaced rustic plenitude.

Whatever be the cause, the poor inhabitant is driven from his cottage, from his little garden, and his bubbling spring, to seek, perhaps, a miserable habitation within the smoky confines of some increasing town; where, among narrow lanes, house crouding upon house, and every floor, every room containing its separate family, he is doomed to see the once cleanly partner of his joys and cares, who had used by her industry to assist his own, compelled to dedicate her whole incessant labour to fruitless efforts for the preservation of a sufficient degree of cleanliness in her family to prevent contagious approaches of disease: – he is doomed, in all probability, to behold those infants who, with health and cheerfulness painted on their cheeks, could stretch their little limbs in harmless gambols among the field-flowers with which they loved to decorate their sun-burnt bosoms, now drooping and inactive, confined within a narrow smoky room, and tied, perhaps, (for dread of accident) to a chair; there to languish into decrepitude, leaning the palid, wasted cheek upon the shoulder, till friendly death relieves them from the gloomy prospect of helpless manhood.

(*PP*, I, pp. 135–6)

In writing the family idyll as the utopian space threatened by increasing urbanization, Thelwall is, to be sure, implicated in the ideological work of Gothic-sentimental literature obsessed with the private, intimate space of the family as a model of unmediated communality free from the distorting effects of power relations. As is the case, for example, in Ann Radcliffe's novels, heterosexual love is the basis of a relationship between two equal parties such that, in the private space of the hearth, husband and wife come together simply as human beings unmarked by the hierarchical structures that, elsewhere in these novels, typify a world of Gothic intrigue and exploitation. The family, in other words, becomes the site of a subjectivity and a form of communal solidarity outside of and unmediated by relations of ownership and exchange. Thelwall never seriously questioned the heteronormative love idyll, nor ceased to employ it as the basis of his critique of capital. If sentimentality could be the medium of political critique it was also a form of cultural expression central to the public dissemination of an image of private life assumed to be both natural and universal. This valorization and mystification of the family, moreover, involved a constant disavowal of housework, child-rearing and other historically feminized forms of labour inseparable from and crucially implicated in the mode of production.

Thelwall, however, was also aware that spectacularized, sentimental tableaux were a seriously limited medium of political consciousness-raising and cognition, and indeed the real interest of *The Peripatetic* lies in those moments at which the work seems to grasp the ideological character not just of specific images, but of the medium itself, that is the form of discursive praxis in which the sentimental tableau was available as a material fact. Sylvanus, for example, knows that he appreciates the sight of gypsies around an open camp fire in exactly the same way that he appreciates a work of art. Gypsies add 'embellishment' to 'rural scenery', inspire 'a thousand romantic visions' and solicit a kind of spectacular enthusiasm that merges quickly into an aesthetic appreciation of 'fancy-stirring scenery':

> When among the ruins of some antique castle, or the ivyed fragments of some prostrate abbey, or (what they are more attached to) the shelter of some wood or thicket by the road side, you see them flocking around their crackling fire, or dispersed in little cheerful groups, basking in the sun, or indulging their eternal propensity for conversation, tell me, do you not feel that if these idle wanderers were exterminated, the landscape painter would be robbed of one of his most agreeable sources of embellishment, and the poet of an object well calculated to give variety to his descriptions?
>
> (*PP*, II, p. 47)

If images of undisturbed, harmonious sociability, embodied in cottagers and gypsies, can measure the disruptions of rural displacement and property monopoly, their political efficacy as such is also threatened by their absorption into the practices of culture-consumption, in which the moment of sentimental responsiveness merely allows the reader momentary release from the functionalized subjectivity of everyday production and exchange. Without some experiential correlative anteceding the moment of readerly sympathy, Thelwall's evocation of the idyll can only have a fleetingly gratifying influence on the reader, who approaches it simply as a consumer of aesthetic artifacts. The tableau, in other words, becomes a form of escapism, insofar as sympathetic identification yields private pleasure to the reader.

This was indeed the basis of Thelwall's attack on what he called the 'modern sophists', whose evocation of '*fancied grievances*' and even 'animated remonstrations against *real oppression*' were unable to 'excite serious discontent in the popular mind, till the enormity of the evil has *brought home the consequent suffering to every man's business and bosom*':

> Remove but the *real causes of complaint;* nay, keep them but at such a distance, that they may not *goad the bosoms* of those who have the capacity to act, and whatever may be the transient influence of poets and orators on the heated fancies of a few, everyone will quickly find, ... some *personal feeling,* some *individual interest* to overpower the *sympathies of imagination,* and restore the momentary wanderer to *himself.*
>
> (*PP*, II, p. 103)

This is a difficult passage unless we grasp the valence of 'himself' in radical-libertarian writing of the period. As in William Godwin's *Enquiry Concerning Political Justice,* popularized in Thelwall's speeches, the self to which the wanderer returns is not an authentic origin, but the isolated, monadic subjectivity of property ownership, incapable of thinking in terms of communal interests and solidarity, yet prepared to experience and indulge in moments of apparent sympathy in order to satisfy the individual quest for pleasure and sensation. Here *The Peripatetic* begins to raise some quite vexed questions concerning the political efficacy of sentimental textual production. The text's presentation of sentimental spectacles is, by Sylvanus's own admission, implicated in the production of consumable aesthetic objects. If the practices of culture-consumption appropriate images of suffering and exploitation as the basis not of a politicized, popular awareness, but as an avenue of individual pleasure similar to the ambiguous pleasure Burke's spectator feels in the face of the sublime, then Thelwall must be confronted with the potential neutralization of his own political aims by the circulation of his text through the marketplace, and the ensuing creation of a public of readers who are in fact merely individualized, serialized subjects experiencing their collectivity – their humanity – in the assumed ubiquity of their responses to the affect of the tableau. In this sense we can argue that the sentimental tableau facilitates only the momentary, imaginative experience of a form of communal existence occluded by atomizing relations of production. This experience, however, is still always contained by the economy of culture-consumption and thus ultimately reproduces the monadic subjectivity of property ownership, in so far as the experience of readerly sympathy remains subservient to the needs of private pleasure and thus sustains an ideology of possessive individualism. We are again running up against the limits of what Herbert Marcuse refers to as the 'affirmative character of culture': 'the assertion of a universally obligatory, eternally better and more valuable world that must be unconditionally affirmed: a world essentially different from the factual world of the daily struggle for existence, yet realizable by every individual for himself "from within", without any transformation of the state of fact.'[3]

In Thelwall's career the limitations of this kind of literary sensibility as a form of political consiousness led not to a refusal of Gothic-sentimental narrative frames and topoi, but to a structural alteration in the forms of production and reception in which his work was implicated. By 1794 Thelwall had become active as a key member of the London Corresponding Society, and the movement's most powerful and articulate public orator, speaking on behalf of an extended franchise and against the equation of legitimate political agency with the distinctions of property ownership. The transformation of the sentimental poet of the late 1780s and early 1790s into the radical activist and theorist was one that Thelwall himself enacted in his political lectures. He begins his first lecture *On the Moral Tendency of a System of Spies and Informers* with a decidedly ambiguous call to the renunciation of 'idle phantoms of pastime and frivolity', in order to secure the 'sedateness of character', 'the improvement in knowledge and true wisdom', and the 'advancement towards the perfection of truth and fortitude' necessary for public activism and political consciousness. 1794 was, for Thelwall, 'no season for indulging the idle sallies of the imagination', as the forces of state police and censorship gathered around the growing radical infrastructure, threatening corresponding societies and printers with prosecution and imprisonment for treason and sedition (p. 1). The 1794 arrest and trial of LCS members including Thelwall himself, the trial and deportation of the 'Scottish martyrs' (Joseph Gerrald, Maurice Margarot, Thomas Fyshe Palmer and William Skirving) and the separate prosecutions of Daniel Isaac Eaton and Thomas Spence for publishing and selling Paine's *Rights of Man*, amply testify to this climate of increasing official invigilation and repression. It was in this atmosphere that Thelwall signaled his arrival as an activist intent on fostering public discussion, association and investigation into the rights that state policing, legislation and invective were in the process of refuting.

aware of the precipice upon which we stand, and to the very verge of which the persecuting violence of an overbearing and desperate faction is endeavouring, so precipitately, to urge a half-awakened nation, I have renounced myself those pursuits of taste and literature to which, from my boyish days, I have been so fondly devoted, as to sacrifice to them the flattering prospects of affluence and worldly ambition, which a lucrative profession pre-sented before me; and have devoted myself, whole and entire, to the service of the public; a sense of whose injuries is the only stimulus of my conduct, and whose happiness alone I look forward to, as my dearest, and my ultimate reward.

(PL, p. 2)

But, predictably enough, the renunciation of literature is itself a suitably literary topic, such that Thelwall, marking the poetic au-thority that underlines his own assumption of oratorical authority, produces this renunciation in verse:

> Sportive lyre! whose artless strings,
> Brush'd by young Affection's wings,
> Playful Fancy hov'ring round,
> Whipser'd oft the varied sound –
> Sportive lyre! from hence adieu:
> Nobler thoughts my soul employ:
> Nobler objects rise in view, –
> TRUTH and glorious LIBERTY.
> Rous'd by these, my glowing soul,
> Pants a nobler height to gain;
> Pants for glory's patriot goal,
> Where the daring Virtues reign;
> Pants to hear the graver muse,
> Wake the loud enthusiast shell,
> Whose notes heroic pride infuse,
> And bid the soul with ardour swell.

(PL, pp. 2–3)

While the medium of poetry turns out to be an appropriate way to renounce literary pursuits, it is momentarily unclear as to whether Thelwall is offering his own literary career as an example of 'amuse-ment', or whether he is claiming for poetic sensibility a constitutive role in popular political enlightenment. The ambiguity is revealing in that it suggests an anxiety regarding the limitations of literature and a concurrent need to preserve the redeeming effects of literary sensibility in order to urge the members of his working-class audience away from the amusements that had hitherto limited their ability to foster the requisite virtues for engaged and articulate political life.

But Thelwall's continual appeal to the sensibility of poetry underscores the radical difference between sentimental text and public oration as communicative media, and points us to the specific utility of sensibility as an oratorical strategy. In his first lecture Thelwall offers the sensibility conveyed in 'serious objects of mental exertion' as the basis of enlightened community and political life.

It is, however, a fortunate circumstance in the constitution of man, that, flattering as those pursuits may at first appear which are to be considered merely as amusive, the more serious objects of mental exertion furnish, in reality, a fund of more lasting and genuine satisfaction; and that happiness is never so perfectly attained, as when, careless of the mere impressions of pleasure, we pursue, with ardour and perseverance, the path of duty, and seek for Wisdom, where, wedded with eternal Truth, she sheds her mingled radiance through the regions of the intellectual paradise.

(*PL*, p. 3)

Thelwall's account of this satisfaction, a deeper and more substantive kind of pleasure linked to the evocation of a muse figure, a 'graver muse' to be sure, and to the practice of mental rigour and discipline, reads like an attempt to diffuse the sensibility of his own Romantic, sentimental writing into the everyday experience of ordinary people.

It is mind alone, the bold and active exertion of the rational faculty, that opens the living fountains of genuine and lasting happiness, and pours the continuous tide of felicity through the heart of man. To trace these fountains to their sources, to shew their immediate connection with wisdom and virtue, and diffuse (as far as I have the power) their fertilizing streams through the little paddock of every man's private feelings and capacities, and thus nourish the neglected blossoms of social kindness and universal benevolence (the natural productions of a genuine system of enlightened politics) is a talk, I believe, not ignoble in its nature; and which, if properly executed, will have a tendency to render you better members, not of the community only of which you constitute a part, but of the world at large, which it is your duty also to love and benefit, whatever State Hypocrites may preach to you, from selfish motives, about hostile interests, patriotism, and natural enmity.

(*PL*, pp. 3–4)

The process of sentimental consciousness-raising evokes the rural idyll – 'the little paddock of every man's private feelings' – as the irreducible basis of both subjectivity and communality continually threatened by the attacks of 'State Hypocrites'. Thelwall, to be sure, is deploying a sentimentalized vision of communality. Yet, crucially, he is doing so for an audience whose access to such images had been hitherto blocked by the absence of an economy of cultural production and reception capable of disseminating the benevolence of sympathy beyond individualized reading practices that presupposed a level of literacy and leisure indicative of class privilege. By continually foregrounding that fact of official prohibition directed against popular associations, moreover, Thelwall was also able to foreground a form of subaltern identity and communality premised not on the mediations of sentimental spectacles, nor on the mysteries of sympathy, but on his audiences' awareness that they were in violation of the limits ascribed to them by official forms of political discourse and textual production. The public meeting itself, in other words, was constructed as a limit case demonstrating the extent to which the absence of sufficient economic and social distinction could problematize one's legal freedom to associate, express one's views and enjoy the educational benefits of Thelwallian sensibility. For this reason the meeting embodied a kind of public space and interactive practice very different from the practices of culture-consumption that mediated the bourgeois public sphere and harmonized the mode of production by integrating subjects into the imagined community of literary sensibility. Radical associational organizations, debating societies and public lectures, such as those given by Thelwall, effectively formed a space oriented to an articulation of the experience of economic, political and cultural disenfranchisement, which could then become the basis not only of community, but of activism rationally engaged with the structures limiting the political and intellectual life of this community.

If Thelwall's speeches appeal to the redemptive sensibility of poetry, it is still, nevertheless, a species of literary production that he identifies as the agent of social degradation and polarization: it is 'Mr. Burke's sentimental romance', in conjunction with a ragamuffin entourage of ideologues, that deploy a language of mystification and artifice in which popular associations are stigmatized as dangerous threats to political order and stability. '*Ye state jugglers! ye sanguinary hypocrites! ye fur-clad priests of Chaos and Devastation!* who abuse our intellects, and inflame our passions, by your unintelligible jargon! can ye not perceive the absurdity of your doctrines?' (*PL*, pp. 4–5). With the bardic 'ye' Thelwall attempts to establish his authority as the bearer of an authentic and substantive voice – the voice of literary antiquity and tradition, the voice of nature and natural law – that towers over the petty deceptions of Burkean rhetoric revealed as a degraded and ideologically motivated series of textual tricks. But Burke is not only a constant and logical object of critique for Thelwall, he is also a spectral presence motivating and inhabiting the performative excesses of Thelwall's own language. Like Burke's representation of Jacobinism in, say, *Reflections on the Revolution in France*, Thelwall's accounts of Burke and the policing mechanisms of the Pitt government rely on a notion of textual deception, and relatedly conspiracy, which Thelwall worked into a Gothic narrative of darkness and enlightenment linked to both the legal mechanisms of repression and to reactionary, anti-Jacobin literary production. In his first political lecture Thelwall's language in fact ironically rehearses the oratorical histrionics for which Burke was famous. Thelwall accusingly refers to the forces rallying against radical association as 'INQUISITORIAL ASSOCIATIONS', 'ILLEGAL CONSPIRACY *and cabal*, (wrapped in the flimsy veil of *pretended* veneration for *monopolized property* and *obsolete institutions*, but revealing, through the thin disguise, the clenched hand and thirsting dagger of POLITICAL ASSASSINATION)' (*PL*, p. 8). There can be little doubt that the dramatic revelation of the 'thirsting dagger' was intended to evoke Burke's 1792 speech on the Alien Bill, at the climax of which he brandished a dagger claiming 'This is what you are to gain with an alliance with France.'[4]

This strategy of ironic mimicry is evident much more generally in radical culture throughout the 1790s. Daniel Isaac Eaton's journal *Politics for the People: or, a Salmagundy for Swine*, for example, which published excerpts from Thelwall's speeches and writings, abounds

with Gothicized accounts of political oppression and sentimentalized scenes not only of rural innocence, but also of public association threatened by government invigilation, invective and
legislation. Because Thelwall deployed the opposition between
popular association and Gothicized government in the context of a
public lecture in constant danger of infiltration by government
spies, this Gothic imagery specularly represented the experience of
an audience itself in danger of arrest. Thelwall's lectures were most
often about the legal precariousness of their own attempts to establish a site of counterhegemonic public discussion – a precariousness
in which all present were simultaneously implicated. Though his
rhetoric is no less hyperbolic than Burke's, in its representation of
dark threats to rational political intercourse, this self-reflexiveness
located the possibility of enlightenment in socially-situated interactive contexts, rather than in the sequestered space of private
reading or culture-consumption. As Thelwall constantly pointed
out, public interaction and communal opinion formation constituted the basis of political amelioration. By merely being present at
the public lecture his auditors were not only participating in this
process, they were also being made to confront the legal structures
antithetical to their communicative freedom. In Thelwall's speeches
these structures are figured through the seemingly uncontrollable
eruption of Gothic-sentimental imagery, marking the projects of
populist mobilization and rational political disquisition with the
conditions of their own impossibility. The forces of political oppression, in other words, are registered in the affective histrionics of
Thelwall's own language.

> Come then from your lurking corners, ye tools of perjured treach-
> ery – ye spies, ye dark assassins, ye venal associators for the most
> detestable of purposes – come forth, I say, if in your dark retreats
> the voice of manly indignation can reach your ears – come forth.
> Bring all the terrors of your chains and dungeons, and all the
> malice of your *inquisitorial* inventions: ye shall not daunt the soul
> that virtue fortifies, nor prevent me from uttering the truths
> which conscience tells me are important for man to know.
>
> (*PL*, pp. 9–10)

Thelwall rehearses the rhetorical excesses of Burke's language as a
displacement and appropriation, but also as an ironic, even comic
revelation of its rhetorical and performative affect. In this repetition

Thelwall's auditors were reminded of the ways in which they were represented by forces opposed to political reform and popular mobilization. They were reminded of the rhetorical excess – embodied in phrases like 'the swinish multitude' – that constituted them as dangerous and anarchic threats to national security and stability. In so doing radical culture implicitly foregrounded and demystified the forms of public discourse that were complicit with official attempts to limit oppositional public discussion and interaction.[5]

RADICAL THEORY: THELWALL'S *RIGHTS OF NATURE*

It is possible perhaps to understand the structural differentiation Thelwall's speeches involved as a kind of mimesis. Rather than being presented with a sentimental tableau, with regard to which the reader is a detached spectator/consumer, the auditor experiences himself as an actual participant in the tableau. Which is to say that the tableau is no longer a tableau, it is the actual political life of the auditor whose access to the redemptive possibilities of public association, in which the sensibility of poetry is diffused, is directly and immediately under threat. The experience of labour, of political disenfranchisement, of alienation from official public discourse and notions of civic identity, otherwise lost in the minutia of production and accordingly experienced in local, fragmented and individualized intuitions of injustice, here reaches a communal clarity. This is a very different economy of cultural production and reception from that implied by the practices of private consumption. It constructs communal identity, and accordingly deploys socially situated knowledge, in a way that privatized reading practices alone could not. The public meeting itself becomes a mediating context making articulate oppositional knowledge possible in a way that does not manipulate isolated subjects in violation of their individual integrity, but that demonstrates the socially contingent nature of the isolated, monadic subject in the first place, and its relationship to forms of hegemony, exploitation and repression specifically designed to contain experience within the bounds of individuated subjectivity and hence to efface the possibility of collectively articulating the common experience of political disenfranchisement.

Thelwall's *The Rights of Nature*, a series of letters attacking Burke specifically, published in two parts over 1795 and 1796, theorizes the relationship between the accumulation of capital, the experience of labour, and public association as the medium in which this kind of cognitive mapping could be carried out. Here the overcoming of individualism is central to the counterhegemonic, associational spaces he imagines. The manifesto-like character of Thelwall's first letter enacts the overcoming of this alienation, the overcoming of a structure that 'considers the great mass of the people as mere brute machines; mere instruments of physical force; deprived of all *power*, and destitute of all *right* of information' (*RN*, p. 407), as a twofold enlightenment. On the one hand, the formation of working-class communities or publics, via radical literary dissemination and organizations like the LCS, empowers disparate groups and over-comes the heterodoxy and individualism that threatened the reform movement with the prospect of assimilation into the structures of capitalism: 'while the friends of liberty, instead of considering themselves as one common family, cherish their private jealousies, and forget their common interests, so long will fresh projects of usurpation be formed and executed with impunity, and mankind be treated like a herd of cattle' (*RN*, pp. 394–5). On the other hand, but relatedly, it is the formation of such associational bonds that create the conditions for discussion and debate in which working-class interests can express themselves, present the 'living body' of their complaints to their oppressors, and reach a level of self-awareness blocked by the misleading rhetoric of reactionary textual production – the 'idle jargon' of Burke, or Pitt's 'charms and spells of pretended negotiation' (*RN*, p. 404). Against the erroneous assumptions of possessive individualism which, as Marx will show, provide the philosophical and metaphysical legitimization of capi-talism, Thelwall wanted to demonstrate how the constitution of the dispossessed labourer as an individual property owner, and relat-edly as an individual consumer, was a historical process dependent on the monopolization of capital. If his work posits a mythologized image of 'natural man' ensconced in a communal plenitude – a primitive communism – this image is only meaningful as the means of making the impoverishment of alienated, monadic subjects intel-ligible. It is in opposition to man 'laboriously employed ... so poor, so lost, so abject, and so vile – so gross in appetite, so bankrupt in happiness, so unshaped in intellect, and so dead to generous and expansive morality', that Thelwall evokes 'natural man' defined by the realization of his sensuous potential, his 'vast funds of moral, physical, and intellectual wealth which the elements of nature lay open to his exertions', as the possibility denied by the present

(*RN*, p. 458). The obstruction of this ideal is clearly referable for Thelwall to the institution of property and state concern for its security over and against the most immediate form that the rights of man can take – the 'franchise of popular discussion' (*RN*, p. 460).

Thelwall's third letter develops this critique of property distribution and monopoly as the basis of a theoretical model in which labour is ultimately extolled as the principle by which natural rights can be reintroduced into a society structured around their usurpation.[6] In civil society, as Thelwall experienced it, liberty and property, 'so frequently joined together, in popular exclamations', turn out to be antithetical: 'the very basis of the latter, by a sad necessity, furnishes the foundation of an altar upon which the former is too frequently sacrificed' (*RN*, p. 466). With the development of agricultural societies, property increasingly ceased to be a communal right, becoming subject to private ownership, accumulation and monopoly. This process can be historically verified through an examination of legislative innovations facilitating the enclosure and seizure of common lands, as Marx shows in his examination of 'primitive accumulation'.[7] Rather than protecting the right of communal access to property as a collective resource, legal innovations in fact encouraged the inequality of distribution, and indeed as late as the final decades of the eighteenth century the complicity of legislation not just in the maintenance of accumulated property, but in the actual seizure of common property was evident[8]: 'laws upon laws have invaded the equal rights of man, and annulled the common claims of relative and private justice' (*RN*, p. 474). The increasingly unequal distribution of property and the ensuing creation of a dispossessed population culminates in the distinction between 'Proprietor and Labourer':

> The cultivator, whose farm was too small for the support of himself and family, or who had been obliged to supply some temporary want by bartering away his penurious inheritance, was necessitated, for subsistence, to become the hireling labourer of him whose possessions had encreased beyond the limits of individual culture.
>
> (*RN*, p. 474)

This is the '*Tyranny of Property:* that is to say – *the power and disposition of the wealthy few, to oppress and plunder the indigent and unprotected many*' (*RN*, p. 475). The distinction between the proprietor as the owner of property and the labourer, Thelwall argues, leads to the institution of what Marxism will theorize as wage-labour and surplus-value.

Does the employer reject the decision of nature? Does he plead some recent compact between himself and the labourer? *I agreed with you for so much; and I pay you what I agreed!* I answer, that an unjust agreement, extorted by the power of an oppressor, is, morally, and politically, void. Yet such, in a variety of instances, are the compacts between the labourer and the employer. The territorial monopolist dictates the terms upon which he will condescend to employ the disfranchised labourer, from morn to night, in the cultivation of his fields, and the repair of his hedges and ditches.

(*RN*, p. 477)

The market itself, the structures of supply and demand in which labour is caught, and foregoing these the police as a disciplinary organization, perpetuate this process. Should the labourer dispute his wages the proprietor may reply, '*Fellow! there are many labourers and few employers. If you do not choose to drudge through the whole day for half a meal, go home to your family, and starve there altogether. If you will not work for half a loaf, there are others that will: and if you conspire together to get a whole one, we will send you to the house of correction!!!*' (*RN*, p. 477).

The institution of wage-labour, according to Thelwall, conceals the fact that labour is in fact the basis of value mistakenly located in property by the structures of capital: 'Let the proprietor reflect upon the nature of his possession – let him reflect upon the genuine basis of property. What is it, after all, but human labour? And who is the proprietor of that labour? – Who, but the individual who labours?' (*RN*, p. 475). This being the case Thelwall argues that a just and reasonable estimation of the relationship between labour and property would compel the distribution of profit on the basis of labour: the labourer would have 'a right to a share of the produce, not merely equal to his support, but, proportionate to the profits of the employer' (*RN*, p. 477). Property as the basis of value, and wage-labour as symptomatic of surplus-value and accumulation for the proprietor, thus represent a violation of communality, for Thelwall the irreducible principle of human sociability, while labour itself, grasped as the basis of value, embodies the realization of a social structure premised on communal solidarity, cooperation, and harmonization of interests, rather than on increasing class polarization and antagonism:

> if accumulation is not only encouraged, but enforced, and if the labourer, the *real cultivator*, is insulted with such wages as are totally insufficient for the decent and comfortable subsistence of himself and family, then (I repeat it – and I will abide by the text in all the courts of law to which I can possibly be summoned) that which is miscalled landed property, is the worst of usurpation and plunder.
>
> (*RN*, p. 476)

The rights of man as an irreducibly communal being and the rights of labour are thus synonymous, both being 'grounded on the triple basis of *nature*, of *implied compact*, and *the principles of civil association*' (*RN*, p. 476). What Thelwall refers to as the usurpation of 'Gothic customary', which secures the rights of property ownership and accumulation as the basis of a notion of social order and harmony, is thus understood as alienation from nature.

This alienation is the horizon of working-class experience, an experience which Thelwall's activist programme sought to galvanize into a collective consciousness. Yet the associational mediation of this collective consciousness was also imagined by Thelwall as already immanent in the mode of production. The structures of monopoly and the collectivizing processes of industrial production themselves facilitate the formation of pockets of communicative interaction outside of hegemonic public spaces and interactive practices.

> The fact is, that the hideous accumulation of capital in a few hands, like all diseases not absolutely mortal, carries, in its own enormity, the seeds of cure. Man is, by his very nature, social and communicative – proud to display the little knowledge he possesses, and eager, as opportunity presents, to encrease his store. Whatever presses men together, therefore, though it may generate vices, is favourable to the diffusion of knowledge, and ultimately promotive of human liberty. Hence every large workshop and manufactory is a sort of political society, which no act of parliament can silence, and no magistrate disperse.
>
> (*RN*, p. 400)

In this formulation the power relations of emergent capitalism actively enable another kind of power capable of engaging with and reforming the modes of subjectivity on which capital is premised. If capitalism imagines itself as monadic subjects negotiating in the marketplace, in what Marx ironically refers to as that Eden of 'Freedom, Equality, Property and Bentham',[9] it also collectivizes these subjects in the momentum of mass production, and thus threatens its own stability. In association, writes Thelwall, a 'multitude of individuals can be melted and organized into one harmonious mass' (*RN*, p. 461), as a form of collective resistance. In moments of oratorical enthusiasm, Thelwall imagined the possibility of this collective being synonymous with the whole nation – 'one grand political Association, or Corresponding Society, from the Orkney's to the Thames, from the Cliffs of Dover to the Land's End'.[10]

POETRY AND THE FATE OF THE POLITICAL

By the late 1790s, however, Thelwall had all but retired from public political life to become a farmer in Llyswen, Wales, where he had moved with his family. After his 1794 acquittal, by which time England was at war with France, the bloody aftermath of the French Revolution had effectively stigmatized English radicalism, and so-called Jacobin doctrines of equality were repudiated by even moderate Whigs, the legal pressure on the LCS and Thelwall in particular only increased. This pressure ultimately resulted in the dispersal and disorganization of mobilizing associational societies after the 1795 passing of what were known as the 'Two Acts' (36 Geo III, c. 7 and 8), which expanded the definition of treason in a way that specifically targeted radical associations and public meetings. Thelwall, at this point, left the LCS, but continued to lecture, avoiding censorship and prosecution by disguising his speeches as a series on classical political history. Actual physical harassment, however, and what Thompson argues was an attempt to kidnap and impress Thelwall at Yarmouth, ultimately led to his total withdrawal from political life.[11] Thelwall seems to have left public life marginalized and stigmatized for his relentless adherence to the ideas expounded in *The Rights of Nature* and his public lectures. He saw himself as a victim forced into exile in order to avoid the barbs of public persecution and vilification, which had reduced him and his family to the brink of financial ruin. His 'Prefatory Memoir' to the 1801 *Poems Chiefly Written in Retirement* constructs the rustic idyll, the 'obscure and romantic village of Llys-Wen', as a refuge from the torments of public life in which, he writes, (referring to himself in the third person) he had been hunted by 'a proscription more ferocious than if assassination ... had been proved against him': 'The ordinary transactions of life have been interrupted – the intercourse of the closest relationship violated and impeded, and the recesses of the utmost obscurity have been disturbed – even magistracy, that should have protected, has been the insidious prompter of hostility and insult' (*Poems*, pp. xxxiii–iv). Under such pressure, Thelwall relates in his memoir, he renounced politics, believing that the idyllic world of Llyswen could become a space in which a rustic, private utopia could be created as the antithesis of political life. He imagined his retreat as an 'enchanted dormitory' in which 'the agitations of political feeling might be cradled to forget-fulness, and the delicious day dreams of poesy might be renewed', where agriculture and the 'visitations of the Muse' could 'secure that humble sort of subsistence to which he had determined to accommodate his desires' (*Poems*, p. xxxvi). While Thelwall under-stands his move to Llyswen as a renunciation of politics and an attempt to recover an Edenic world untainted by what now must have appeared as an irrevocably corrupt and oppressive society, his memoir is similarly concerned with reconstructing its author not as a public figure, but as a man beyond any kind of social and political contingency: 'It is The Man, and not The Politician, that is here delineated. The disciple of the Muses; not The Lecturer and Leader of Popular Societies now no more' (*Poems*, p. i).

What is abundantly clear, however, is that Thelwall's writing of his renunciation of politics is also itself a thoroughly politicized statement. If his 'enchanted dormitory' is intended as the occasion for political amnesia, the lingering, melancholic traces of loss and defeat continue as both a validation and a subversion of the idea of renunciation. As a result his memoir and his 1801 poetry, to the extent that they fail to forget, become a strangely demystificatory rehearsal of the Romantic-sentimental renunciation narrative, in which the poet moves away from the public into a world of solitary experience and literary production. Thelwall's text effectively reveals the intensely political character and, more importantly, the historical and social contingency of 'the retreat from politics' as an intellectual and literary posture. In other words the affirmative character of Romantic renunciation is thoroughly foregrounded and its ideological content readable: poetry, and the pastoral imaginary that inspires it, compensate for real political isolation, powerlessness and exhaustion, offering a space beyond the impoverished experience of the alienated individual at the very moment that they replicate the limits of this experience, writing the heightened sensitivity of pastoral seclusion as the principle of transcendence. Thelwall had adapted sentimental and Romantic aesthetics in the context of a social movement, but the movement back to private aesthetic production and consumption was equally social. Like the 'Prefatory Memoir', the 1801 poems, in their desperate but futile attempt to become amnesic, to remove themselves from the political, do not simply efface their political or historical context in their valorization of a privatized world of poetic experience, but on the contrary reveal the historical contingency of this experience. Though they may attempt to transport the reader into the realm of epiphanic and sentimental aesthetic gratification, they also constantly present traces of political disillusionment that stand as the real against which the pastoral fantasy scenario is constructed and problematized. If Thelwall's *The Rights of Nature* and public lectures, like radical culture more generally, attempted to re-member or put together the fragmented collective subject of resistance as a kind of consciousness-raising, his 1801 poetry remembers in quite a different way – as an explication of the process of forgetting.

Poems like 'Lines, Written at Bridgewater' and 'To the Infant Hampden' rehearse the construction of the rustic idyll as the antithesis of political persecution and frustration, but do so in ways that continually foreground the latter. In 'Lines, Written at Bridgewater', composed in 1797 after visiting Coleridge at Nether Stowey,[12] Thelwall typically equates the idyll with domesticity, his wife and family, but finds the occasion for the poem in his temporary separation from these as he walks in pensive solitude, chiding the hours that keep him 'from her arms – / Her's and our smiling babes'. It is in the space of this truancy, the absence of domesticity and the poet's distance from the hearth, that the traces of the political intrude as the possibility of a corruption against which the family idyll dissolves.

> – Eventful Day!
> How shall I regret thee now, at thy return,
> So often mark'd with sadness? Art thou, say,
> Once more arriv'd a harbinger of woes,

> Precursor of a Year of miseries,
> Of storms and persecutions, of the pangs
> Of disappointed hope, and keen regrets,
> Wrung from the bosom by a sordid World
> That kindness pays with hatred, and returns
> Evil for good? – a World most scorpion-like,
> That stings what warms it, and the ardent glow
> Of blest Benevolence too oft transmutes
> To sullen gloom and sour misanthropy,
> Wounding, with venom'd tooth, the fostering breast
> That her milk turns to gall.

(*Poems*, p. 127)

The image of maternal breast-feeding polluted by the vile incursions of misanthropy and its serpent-like 'venom'd tooth' suggests a fall narrative taking place not in spatial or geographic terms, as the fall from Eden, but on or in the female body itself, which succumbs to a kind of pollution and as a result undergoes physiological change. Milk turns to gall, as the pure bodies that had hitherto inhabited the hearth are overcome by the sordidness of a world that spawns 'storms and persecutions', 'pangs of disappointed hope' and 'keen regrets'. It is in opposition to such possibilities that Thelwall goes on to reinvent the pastoral world of seclusion, healthy fertility and reproductivity as the material of poetic production and sentimental experience. 'Sweet retirement', 'friendship', 'love', 'studious ease', 'philosophical thought' and 'poetic dreams' accompany a sylvan landscape of dells, brooks, woods, mountains and caves. It is in such an environment that Meonides and Milton found their inspiration and in which Shakespeare, in the private space of sexual and poetic procreation,

> Pierc'd the dark womb of Nature, with keen glance,
> Tracing the embrio Passions ere their birth,
> And every mystic movement of the soul
> Baring to public ken.

(*Poems*, p. 128)

Thelwall imagines the poet interacting with nature as both lover and child, positing a sublime and omniscient femininity as the embodiment of a utopia beyond persecution. The poet's mind flows in 'tides of generous ardour, scattering wide/ Smiling fertility, fresh fruits and flowers/ of intellectual worth', but is also 'cradled in the solitary haunts', cherished by nature and protected from the 'throng/ Of cites, or of courts' (*Poems*, p. 128). But, needless to say, Thelwall cannot sustain his pastoral enthusiasm without casting a backward glance which dramatizes and foregrounds the contingency of his paradise regained.

> – For my soul
> Is sick of public turmoil – ah, most sick
> Of the vain effort to redeem a Race
> Enslav'd, because degenerate; lost to Hope,
> Because to Virtue lost – wrapp'd up in Self,
> In sordid avarice, luxurious pomp,
> And profligate intemperance – a Race
> Fierce without courage; abject, and yet proud;
> And more licentious, tho' most far from free.
> Ah! let me then, far from the strifeful scenes
> Of public life (where Reason's warning voice
> Is heard no longer, and the trump of Truth
> Who blows but wakes The Ruffian Crew of Power
> To deeds of maddest anarchy and blood)
> Ah! let me, far in some sequester'd dell,
> Build my low cot; most happy might it prove.

(*Poems*, p. 129)

Try as Thelwall might to establish a distance between politics and his regained world of retirement and creativity, between the sordidness of power and manipulation and the purity of his own endeavours, it is impossible for him to disassociate the latter from the former or to conceal the causal connection between them. The multitude, the 'Ruffian Crew', is now a source of revulsion as it remains unredeemed by organization and didactic radicalism. It is the helpless tool of power, 'wrapp'd up in self', and rendered amenable to the kind of amusement (intemperance) that Thelwall's political lecturers had firmly condemned.[13]

The contingency of renunciation is more subtly figured in the series of ten 'effusions' entitled 'Paternal Tears'. Here Thelwall constructs the hearth and family as a lost plenitude, lamenting the death of his daughter Maria, who becomes the occasion for both epiphanic and intensely melancholic poetic memorials. But what is revealing about the poem is the dedication of the first effusion to J– G–, Joseph Gerrald, an LCS delegate arrested and convicted of sedition in 1794 and subsequently deported to Australia, where he died in 1796. In 1795 Thelwall had given a public lecture on Gerrald's 'superior excellence' in which he recounted the scene of the latter's incarceration as one indeed worthy of paternal tears: 'Gerrald goes down upon the summons, and is immediately double-ironed, like the vilest felon, and dragged away without even permission to go back again to his room, and kiss the little lips of his sweet babe, that kept him company in prison.'[14] The first effusion opens with a memorial to Gerrald, whose constancy and commitment is compared to that of the 'changeling multitude'. But while Thelwall himself is no longer tormented by the 'insensate howl' of the 'demon Persecution', 'remorseless Destiny' has still taken its toll as the poetic voice imagines itself languishing on the brink of death as if dying of extreme sensibility:

> So the chords
> Of this frail being (sensitive too much
> To every touch of passion) sad, reply
> With dissonance responsive. Yes they jar:
> Each nerve and fibre feels the untuning touch
> Of most assur'd decay.

> (*Poems*, p. 146)

In this state of increasing morbidity, in which 'Hope's vital lamp, benighted, droops, appall'd,/ Amid the horrors of sepulchral gloom' (*Poems*, pp. 146–7), Thelwall appeals to Gerrald for a sympathetic reader as a preface to his own lament: 'to you/ Seeking the balm of sympathy, I ope/ My bosom's inmost anguish' (*Poems*, pp. 148–9).

In summoning Gerrald the first effusion performs a revealing substitution: the loss of Maria and the possibility of expressing this loss in poetry necessitate the conjuring of political affiliations that Thelwall's 'Prefatory Memoir' had already established as 'now no more'. Accordingly the opposition between political life and the private sphere, which the 'Prefatory Memoir' had emphatically stated, is problematized, and the continuities between the political and the personal become apparent. Just as the private pleasures of

the family, the hearth and poetry compensate for political defeat,
so too can a model of political virtue, embodied in the memory of
Gerrald, be summoned to console for the death of Maria and bear
witness to the melancholy in which Thelwall is immersed. The effusion establishes a congruence between paternal and political sensibility, but also asserts the identity of Maria and Gerrald as objects
of both lament and address. Both are the occasion for memory that
now understands hope as unattainably deferred by the signifiers of
its very absence – the sylvan landscape that echoes Maria's name
and the tomb that bears it. It is with the dead that Thelwall imagines redemption, over tombs and sepulchres that his thoughts
linger as if dwelling endlessly on the possibilities lost to him,
possibilities both political and personal.

> Why, on the mouldering tomb of other Times,
> Sits my lorn wanderer, in the muffled robe,
> Veiling her pensive brow, and to the winds
> Giving, on such bleak height, the unshelter'd form
> Of feminine softness! Broods her thoughtful mind
> Some legendary fiction? or some tale
> Of Tragic record, pregnant with the woes
> Of virtue vainly brave? Or does she mourn
> Time's changeful progress, thro' these desolate Realms
> Too sadly mark'd?

> (*Poems*, p. 161)

It is against this typically romantic image of brooding melancholia –
'the mouldering tomb of other Times' – that Marx's euphemism for
the role of tradition and memory in revolution might resonate:
Totenerwechung, the resurrection of the dead, which, he reminds us,
should attempt 'to recover the spirit of revolution, rather than to set
its ghost walking again'.[15]

4

Gothic Consumption: Populism, Consumerism and the Discipline of Reading

Anti-Jacobin writers in the 1790s were extremely suspicious of the market for cultural commodities. They saw the public consumption of literary texts, political pamphlets, popular journals and philosophical tracts as the means by which a gullible and manipulable audience could be swayed from passivity to the violence and atavism of revolution. In anti-Jacobin discourse the image of the ragged crowd, an aggregation of individualized, serialized subjects, typically signifies a demographic that is impressionable, malleable, fickle in its affiliations, easily distracted, and motivated by the hedonistic laws of monadic pleasure. This crowd, lacking any stable commitment to moral norms, is also a collection of potential consumers awaiting writers, hacks or demagogues prepared to empower or gratify it. Far from embodying any genuine sense of unified and rationally considered political purpose, the crowd is the form in which anti-social individualized desire becomes available to cognition: multiplied by that indeterminate number, the multitude, individual desire takes on its visible manifestation in cataclysmic outbreaks of popular violence. The spectre of the atavistic mob, which haunts and motivates textual practice across a variety of discursive sites at the end of the eighteenth century, thus embodies the mass eruption of a series of hitherto repressed subjects. It is for this reason that Gothic literature can enact such a fluid movement between individualized desires and collective violence. In novels like Matthew Lewis's *The Monk* or, later, Charles Maturin's *Melmoth the Wanderer*, repressive, Bastille-like structures seize upon individuals and impose, as Peter Brooks suggests, 'mental constraints ostensibly devoted to chastity and discipline'. These dark, 'claustral'

107

spaces, Brooks continues, contain 'the product of erotic drives gone berserk, perverted and deviated, a figuration of the price of repression'.[1] In Lewis's novel, for example, excessive mob violence is both lexically and figuratively associated with Ambrosio's rape of Antonia in the crypt under St Clare. As David Punter writes, the novel connects '"public" activity and more overt sexual violation'.[2] In anti-Jacobin discourse popular violence similarly originates from, or at least is evoked by specific sites within a typically Gothicized topography, by which I mean a topography that embodies a refusal of bourgeois normalcy – what Foucault calls 'unreason'. Unlike the Gothic fortress, however, these sites do not embody official forms of political and religious discipline; they are the dark, equally claustral sites in which treasonable political factions and cabals form through the poisonous and perverting dissemination of Jacobin texts and conspiracies. The dungeon and the crypt as spaces that embody the repressed underside of official power relations – a kind of energy that, like Orc in Blake's 'America', threatens an eruption of both political and sexual violence – are replaced by, quite literally, sites of textual production and reception: the alehouse in which political pamphlets were communally read, popular presses and corresponding and debating societies. Accordingly, the repressed, forbidden, but incessantly visualized terrain in which transgression and excess ferment, inevitably came to be centred around the act of reading and the mechanisms of print-capitalism, rather than institutions of official repression and state power. Radical political culture, in other words, imagined as continuous with the marketplace, is also imagined as a Gothicized site causally implicated in the atavism of collective violence.

The reactionary critique of popular politics in the 1790s was also, then, a critique of print-culture, consumerism and what conservative writers saw as their morally baneful effects. In a rehearsal of the prototypal Gothic-sentimental narrative, the forces of Jacobin textual production and doctrine, construed as a form of libertinage, fatally intrude upon the domestic stability of the family and threaten what were understood as the natural bonds of filial loyalty and conjugal love. This frame, of course, is abundantly evident in the writings of Edmund Burke, whose representations of Jacobinism hinge on the intrusion of a transgressive libertine desire, at times individualized, at others collective, threatening the intimate space not only of Marie Antoinette, but of sequestered females more generally. The libertinage of Hastings and the East India Company becomes, for Burke, the form in which radical political culture is also imagined. Yet, in producing this typically Gothic scenario, anti-Jacobin discourse also extended its critique of print-culture to Gothic romances themselves, suggesting, as Thomas James Mathias did, that the textual representation of popular violence bursting repressive fetters was somehow complicit with the threat of actual popular violence. In such readings the Gothic novel, Matthew Lewis's *The Monk* in Mathias's text, is understood as a textual commodity appealing to the passions of its readers, addressing a public of dangerously manipulable consumers. Ronald Paulson is of course correct in arguing that Gothic conventions functioned as a way of making revolutionary politics intelligible, but in a text like Mathias's the Gothic was also much more than this.[3] Lewis's novel, Mathias suggests, was actually analogous to Jacobin texts attempting to sell political transgression. It is at this point that anti-Jacobin discourse overlaps with Romantic critiques of mass culture, forming an over-determined representation of the connections between print-culture, mass entertainment and dangerous political populism antithetical to the sentimental idyll in all its possible Romantic variations: Burke's 'natural society', Wordsworth's cottagers and even William Godwin's ideal speech community all deploy images of sanctified domestic space antithetical to the pathologies of a public sphere given over to market forces and mass cultural forms. In Wordsworth's depiction of London in Book VII of *The Prelude*, for example, Burkean anxieties about popular politics and a recognizably Romantic anxiety about popular culture come together in an archetypical representation of the threatening volatility of public space. In the 1790s the popular Gothic novel seems to have become a sign of this threatening confluence. As E. J. Clery has argued 'the creeping democratization of the republic of letters represented by the success of the popular novel was not unrelated to the threat of political democracy in the eyes of the British anti-Jacobins'. Popular politics and popular culture, in other words, represented 'the unmistakable victory of popular demand and market forces over the legislation of writing from above'.[4] In anti-Jacobin discourse in particular, however, threats to the social order are often represented, marginalized and stigmatized by replaying, in some form, the constitutive elements of Gothic literature: transgressive, corrupting forces, often linked to the consumption of mass culture, threaten a hitherto unadulterated domestic space usually embodied in sentimentalized female figures. If the Gothic text is understood as an object to be consumed, the locus of a variously dangerous and degraded kind of popularism, its topoi and narrative frames are also needed to render the culture of popular consumption palpable. The very forces that opposed the popularization of political and literary expression, in other words, were also forced to exploit popular Gothic conventions in order to represent their object. Looked at in this way the Gothic itself becomes an intensely undecidable category: it is both an object and an agent of critique, indicating a kind of performative contradiction that will force us to rethink the political function of Gothic conventions altogether.

Texts that use Gothic representational strategies to contain and marginalize the monadic, hedonistic subjectivity of the libertine-consumer, whether in the name of sensibility, filial integrity or political order, also dwelt upon the excesses of this subjectivity as they intruded upon and violated the harmony of the sentimental-ized domestic idyll. The affect of the sentimental tableau, it would seem, is always contingent on the affect of representing the vari-ously transgressive, libidinalized, sometimes sadistic forces swarm-ing around it and precipitating its destruction. If the explicitly moral or proscriptive intent of Gothic representation resides in the mar-ginalization and stigmatization of transgressive desire, these repre-sentational strategies also depict this desire with morbid fascination. As I argued with regard to Burke's impeachment speech, the spec-tacle of desire released from its fetters, seizing upon and violating a hitherto unadulterated or vestal object, presents itself to the reader as both the occasion of moral sympathy and of more unnameable pleasures. The slippage between sympathetic identification, evoked by the pathos of the sentimental idyll, and voyeuristic pleasure at the violence attending its adulteration means that anti-Jacobin cri-tiques of political libertinage and its consumerist rapaciousness are only possible on the condition of their own participation in the pro-duction of polymorphously pleasurable spectacles of precisely the forms of transgression they sought to outlaw. For such critiques to circulate as proscriptive documents they must themselves be founded on a kind of repression: the repression of their status as variously sensationalized textual objects, and the disavowal of the spectacular pleasures they yield. The forbidden pleasure of textual consumption is always the hidden agenda of texts that are otherwise explicitly critical of the enjoyment they evoke.

We can read what Michel Foucault has called a 'regime of power-knowledge-pleasure' at work here, by which he means a discursive structure in which notions of pleasure and freedom are mediated in such a way as to reinforce certain power relations. The constitution of a pleasure that needs to be disciplined or renounced in the interests of the status quo also invites one to imagine 'liberation' as the negation of discipline – the negation of a negation. The process of circumscribing certain actions, insofar as it attempts to position subjects within the boundaries of the moral law, also produces these outlawed actions as indexes of a desire at once immanent and laboriously visualized, articulated and classified in the process of its prohibition. This simultaneously repressed but incessantly represented desire is finally understood, in accordance with Hobbsian images of natural man, as simply what we are, what we would be if left to ourselves, unrestrained by social conventions, moral impositions and legal imperatives. The circumscribing of transgression, in other words, has the effect of mandating desire, of soliciting and arousing it in terms of very specific manifestations.[5]

If, as I'm arguing here, late-eighteenth-century uses of the Gothic are oriented to the simultaneous marginalization and representation of a consumer psychology, then the monadic desire of the consumer in the marketplace would be that discursively produced fact that summons both the necessity of disciplinary control and the promise of absolute freedom. Liberation, by this reckoning, would be liberation into the practices of consumption, and the most threatening, dangerous and delicious of transgressions would be to affirm the subjectivity of emerging capitalism. What the Gothic scenario constitutes as repressed desire, then, is simply the everyday dynamic of object-cathexis that typifies the experience of consumerism. But because the proscriptive Gothic-sentimental text is, despite itself, already an object integrated into the market for cultural commodities, it allows its readers to exercise (and exorcise) this desire in a very specific act of consumption – the act of reading, or of spectatorship more broadly conceived. The text is already the medium through which liberation into the practices of consumerism occurs. It is in this sense that one can talk about reading as a disciplinary practice that solicits a form of desire wholly compatible with its containment in the sequestered space of textual consumption. The deployment of Gothic tropes, in other words, effectively constitutes the forbidden pleasures of liberation as synonymous with the consumption of Gothic texts. In this way the culture of emerging capitalism manages to colonize the very idea of transgression, ensuring that notions of freedom, liberation and pleasure, far from being actually disruptive, consolidate its own material organization. We have seen how Burke's *Reflections*, in offering the textualized spectacle of revolution in place of revolution itself, functions in this way.

In this chapter I want to examine some anti-Jacobin and Romantic accounts of the relationship between libertinage, textual consumption and populism, in order finally to suggest that Matthew Lewis's *The Monk* both reveals and celebrates the paradoxes inherent in these discourses. Lewis's novel dramatizes itself as both the unfolding of repressed, transgressive desire into sentimental scenarios, and the bracketing of this desire in discrete representational practices. In consuming the Gothic text as an itinerary of otherwise repressed desire, the reader is in fact exercising that desire freely and openly, as a consumer seeking a voyeuristic pleasure analogous to the pleasure of the libertine. Because *The Monk* constantly and self-consciously rehearses the simultaneity of libertine and readerly desire (which, in fact, turn out to have an allegorical relationship to each other), foregrounding the extent to which variously libidinal, sadistic and voyeuristic tendencies are evoked by the sentimental tableau, its rehearsal of Gothic conventions dramatizes the extent to which desire and consumerist object-cathexis are inseparable in the language of Gothic textual production. What I'm calling 'Gothic consumption' in the late-eighteenth century is discourses encompassing anti-Jacobin, Romantic and more explicitly Gothic-sentimental textual forms, in which desire turns out to be coterminous with the practices of consumer capitalism, producing a version of liberation that never transgresses the forms of monadic subjectivity on which the reproduction of capital is based. It is yet another face of Marcuse's affirmative culture.

THE REPRESSED OF ANTI-JACOBIN DISCOURSE

Anti-Jacobin writers represented radical textual dissemination as a manipulative mode of indoctrination that, by flattering the egos of hitherto disempowered subjects, ushered them to the precipice of revolutionary violence. Because of the large circulation, low price and lack of Latin erudition that characterized radical publications, the imagery of Grub Street, of mercenary literary commercialism, was an easy one for anti-Jacobin writers to deploy in their attacks on Thomas Paine, John Thelwall, Thomas Spence and others. In such attacks the radical pamphleteer becomes the image of crass, manipulative print-capitalism, a desperate pedlar of shoddy ideas and texts, a literary harlot selling political seduction. In this discourse print capitalism and popular politics similarly imply a dangerous kind of democratization in which political equality is also equality in the marketplace. The anonymous author of 'The Rise, Progress and Effects of Jacobinism', serialized in *The Anti-Jacobin Review*, typically summarizes the metaphysical character of 'democratical and anti-hierarchical doctrines' as consisting in the postulation of a freedom that refuses to take into account man's inability to govern himself and conform to moral codes independently of legal directives. The dissenters Joseph Priestley and Richard Price are the two principal objects of attack here. The former, 'by defining liberty to consist in such an exemption from restraint as was totally incompatible with every purpose of government ... mislead many to believe that ours was not a free constitution'. The latter, according to the author, in propounding the 'abstract theory of the rights of man', essentially pleaded for the anarchic state in which every man would be his own legislator, such that '*thieves and pickpockets have a right to make laws for themselves*'.[6] The efficacy and popularity of such doctrines resided in their appeal to 'vulgar and undistinguishing minds'. Thomas Paine's *Rights of Man* epitomizes the popular articulation of 'levelling systems' and 'metaphysical disquisitions' for the anti-Jacobin intelligentsia, appealing to the vanity of labouring classes and flattering them into political affiliations based on their own empowerment.

The plain perspicuity of his language, the force of his expressions, the directness of his efforts, wore so much the appearance of clear and strong reasoning, (to those that judge from manner more than matter,) that numbers, borne down by his bold assertions, supposed themselves convinced by his arguments. The substance of his doctrine was peculiarly pleasing to the lower ranks. When mechanics and peasants were told that they were as fit for governing the country as any man in the parliament, the notion flattered their vanity, pride, and ambition. While he had for the ignorant these notions of equality, so agreeable to the populace, he had additional charms, in metaphysical distinctions and definitions, to delight the half-learned with the idea, that when they were repeating his words, they were pouring forth philosophy.[7]

The mode of textual production and circulation that character-ized Paine's *Rights of Man* is referred to as 'dissemination' by the writers of *The Anti-Jacobin*. Dissemination, as Jon Klancher has argued, signifies a pathological and socially destructive circulation of ideas that deviates from legitimized flows of acceptable textual or cultural commodities. Because these ideas had the ability to cloak themselves in the rhetoric of respectability, dissemination was tan-tamount to a form of intellectual counterfeiting. Hence Paine's text had only the appearance of reasoning, while in reality the appeal of Jacobinism was of the nature of seduction, not logic. Writers like Paine, Price and Priestley could communicate their principles and gain popular support for them precisely because of the extent to which their terminology defied rationality and appealed to a desire outside of and immune to logical argument. A 1799 satirical 'Essay on the Use of Polysyllables', by a pseudonymous Abracadabra, maintains that the principles of the Jacobins were 'closely analogous to the principles of music': 'A wild and capricious overture rouzes our attention by the rattling sounds of *philosophy, reason, and the Rights of Man*; an enlivening *minuette* then paints to our imagination the *energies of mankind, and the desire of universal freedom*.'[8] As Klancher points out, discussing Arthur Young's *Travels in France*, the distinction between dissemination as political seduction, and the circulation of legitimate, substantive meaning, also implied a topography of reading in which the sites of dissemination – the alehouse for instance – became part of the vilified nether world of lower-class depravity, imagined in James Gillray's 1798 caricature of a London Corresponding Society meeting. While the middle-class reader 'gravitates to sunlit coffeehouses and breathes their air of freely ventilated opinions', radical writing 'festers in dark moist places – among "assemblies in alehouse kitchens, clubbing their pence to have the *Rights of Man* read to them"'. Accordingly 'Alehouse kitchens become hidden, dangerous folds in the social fabric, the site of illegitimate reading, as though radical disseminat-ing discourse itself were intoxicating, bypassing the carefully pre-pared channels of middle-class circulatory patterns to put in place the fermenting of radical subculture.'[9]

The world of political conspiracy and textual dissemination, however, did not just imply concealment within the secret enclaves of Jacobin societies. Because conspiracy was also seen to exist behind the facade of constitutional procedure and the rhetoric of rationality, it was the very innocuousness of English radicalism that

James Gillray, 'London Corresponding Society Alarmed'

constituted the uniqueness of its threat and bolstered its seductive and insidious ability to gain converts and assume the guise of public legitimacy. Radical literary societies, 'originally established as a bond of union among men combined for the detestable purpose of disseminating atheistical, immoral, and seditious principles; poisoning and corrupting the minds of their fellow creatures', ultimately lead to the erosion of civil society and culminate in the production of that which is most antithetical to government and social order – the 'philosophical savage', who represents a Hobbsian state of anarchy.[10] 'Here lies our danger in the present moment', wrote Arthur Young in 1793, 'it is not the rank Jacobin with bare and bloody arms, pike in hand, and ready for your throat: it is his gentleman usher, your modest reformer, who, meaning a great deal, asks a little, and knows how to make that little much.'[11] The tropes of invisibility, of concealment, of spectral presences emerging out of dark places, constitute the violent Jacobin as the repressed lurking behind images of quite commonplace respectability. In this way anti-Jacobin discourse attempted to render the otherwise everyday processes of textual production and reception as uncanny deviations from themselves. Print-culture, in other words, embodies conspiracy. In 1794 William Atkinson described the centrality of print-culture to a conspiracy of rational dissenters in these terms: 'the principals in the plot had been busily employed in disseminating the seeds of dissension by their writings. They had secured the two principal Reviews, had established circulating Libraries, and had expended amazing sums of money in propagating liberty and rational Christianity; for these were the *cant* terms made use of to conceal their seditious purposes.'[12]

But if this threat is invisible, it is also, as Young's image of the 'rank Jacobin' indicates, incessantly visualized, in its collective, cataclysmic form – revolutionary violence. It is no surprise then that English critiques of English radicalism are just as much about the French Revolution as they are about dissenters, corresponding societies or parliamentary reform. This is not just because the French example was seen as a precedent for a possible domestic insurrection, but also because it could be produced as an image of what lay hidden behind a political culture that, in Britain at least, was tending towards constitutional avenues, not rebellion. This is, needless to say, the basis of Edmund Burke's Gothic recasting of the French Revolution, which is, at the same time, a critique of Richard Price, the radical dissenting tradition and the reform-oriented debating societies of the 1780s. In his *Reflections on the Revolution in France* philosophical justifications for revolution – 'in proportion as they are metaphysically true, they are morally and politically false' (*RRF*, p. 153) – lead to the perpetual night of apocalyptic savagery in which the triumphal march is a 'spectacle more resembling a procession of American savages, entering into Onondaga, after some of their murders called victories' (*RRF*, p. 159). Between 1789 and his death in 1797 Burke became obsessed with visualizing the atavistic character of Jacobinism, in the process producing the political terrain of the 1790s as a series of Gothic-sentimental narrative possibilities that revolve around the sanctity and potential violability of the family. The mob that bursts into the bedchamber of Marie Antoinette and which Burke imagines as a sexual violation of the sentimentalized female figure, is thus integral to his evocation of the domestic idyll. The aggressive virility of the regicidal eruption is also the moment at which French Chevaliers no less than the king himself reveal their inadequacy as protectors of female virtue and of domestic space. Not only is domestic space violated, but it is sullied with 'promiscuous slaughter' that literally turns the domestic into its spatial and poetic antithesis, a realm tainted by corporal refuse: the 'sanctuary of the most splendid palace in the world' is left 'swimming in blood, polluted by massacre, and strewed with scattered limbs and mutilated carcasses' (*RRF*, p. 164). This dismemberment is not only a signifier of revolutionary violence. The revolutionaries themselves embody the 'grossness' (Burke's word) of carnage, which merges into the grotesque and abject realm of anal/oral regression that for Burke characterizes the world of the Jacobin.[13] In recent critical discussions the image of Marie Antoinette has become emblematic of the manner in which Burke's production of Jacobinism attempted to produce political affiliations by provoking emotional responses to highly stylized aesthetic spectacles. Christopher Reid, for example, discusses Burke's Marie Antoinette as a sentimental image deriving from the 'she-tragedies' of Otway, Rowe and Lillo, and epitomized by the performances of Sarah Siddons as a suffering, virtuous object of compassion. By 'highlighting the distress of a woman of high rank and its elevation of the family as a symbol of the attachments and obligations of civil society' the *Reflections* enacts a 'mode of performance which, by positing the reader in a situation of spectacle, works on the sympathies in order to produce intense emotional effects'.[14] In anti-Jacobin writing of the period the style Burke developed is constantly reiterated in texts that deploy a level of detail untempered by Burke's often densely figurative language. Thomas Moore's *Address to the Inhabitants of Great Britain on the Dangerous and Destructive Tendency of the French System of Liberty and Equality*, for example, recounts the horror of Jacobin violence in terms that, while clearly indebted to Burke, are precariously similar to the deliberately sensationalized scenes of mob violence that we encounter in novels like *The Monk* and *Melmoth the Wanderer*:

> The Princess de LAMBALLE, the most beautiful and accomplished woman in France, (who was a particular favourite of the Queen) was dragged from her prison; in vain she implored on her knees, while the pearly tears trickled down her beautiful cheeks, a remission of her fate only of one hour, to prepare her soul for that great and awful change she was about to experience; but her murderers were deaf to her cries, and her tears, which would have melted a heart of stone, had no effect on these savages. – After cutting her thighs across, and offering such indignities to her as decency will not permit me to relate – they deliberately cut off her head, combed out her fine hair, and, fixing the head on a pole, carried it through the streets; – and to insult the feelings of the unfortunate Queen, presented the head of her favourite to her prison window: – Her naked body was afterwards exposed to the multitude.[15]

In this passage the public display of the naked body implicates the 'multitude' in a kind of voyeurism that places it beyond the limits of a moral society. Yet the passage itself also relies on a dynamic of disclosure that is at least analogous. It too makes the naked body of the Princess de Lamballe public. A similar dynamic is recognizable in texts that implicate individual members of the radical intelligentsia in a kind of libertine violence. Biographies of Thomas Paine, for example, delighted in replaying his private life as one of depravity and domestic violence that again have distinctly Burkean resonances. Charles Elliot, for example, drawing on Francis Oldys, describes the 'unnatural husband' in a manner that establishes a correspondence between radicalism and sadistic sexuality:

> One night, on his return from the coarse revelry of a tap room, exhaling the sweet redolence of beer, gin, and tobacco, he compelled his *maiden* wife to rise out of bed, and sit by him, undressed and

shivering in the midnight cold. With ghastly grin he surveyed un-
covered charms, while silent nature blushed at his obscene
cruelty, and the inefficacy of her own boasted, baffled, instinct in
the breast of man. Had he rested even there, human depravity
might perhaps have been able to furnish a parallel. But in this, as
in other fable traits of his character, there appears a depth of delin-
eation which must stamp an infamous originality on his name.
While the tyrant and his fair vassal *enjoyed* this pleasurable tête-à-
tête, the cat, apparently drawn by the congenial ferocity of its
master, came and purred sympathy with the gloating sage. Not
more ingenious in the invention, than quick in the exercise of mis-
chief, he took up *grimalkin*, and forced the resisting animal where
the reader must guess, for indignant modesty cannot be more explicit. The two kindred agents of this inhumanity, *Puss* and *Paine*,
left the bleeding sufferer to dry her tears and a crimson stream for
every fang with which nature had furnished the former.[16]

In both these passages moments of violence that push against the
limits of representational possibilities are used to reinforce a particular kind of moral economy in which the feminine, as the sign of
filial sympathy, is pitted against a sadistic rapaciousness common
to both the mob and the political philosopher.

In attempting to solicit sympathy as the basis of collective opposition to radicalism, Burke and his followers were not only concerned
with explicit violence as a threat to the sanctity of the domestic. As
Ronald Paulson points out, the seduction of political doctrines was
also imagined as a threat to the domestic. When Burke discusses
Rousseau as the icon of Jacobin metaphysics, political seduction is
quite directly related to the seduction of virtuous daughters, portending the usurpation of paternal authority and an invasion of the
sanctity of the domestic realm.[17] The Jacobins, according to Burke in
his *Letter to a Member of the National Assembly*, had established
Rousseau in the place of the paternal authority they usurped. Yet
Rousseau travesties paternal functions not only because he was an
'unnatural' father who 'without one natural pang, casts away, as a
sort of offal and excrement, the spawn of his disgustful amours, and
sends his children to the hospital of foundlings' (*W&S*, vol. 8,
pp. 314–15), but also because, in the guise of the tutor, the peda-
gogue who is supposed to be 'sober and venerable' and 'allied to
the parental', he stands for an infiltration into domestic space and a
sanctioned corruption of malleable young minds:

In this age of light they teach the people, that preceptors ought to be in the place of gallants. ... They teach the people, that the debauchers of virgins, almost in the arms of their parents, may be safe inmates in their house, and even fit guardians of the honour of those husbands who succeed legally to the office which young literators had pre-occupied, without asking leave of law or conscience.

(*W&S*, vol. 8, p. 316)

Rousseau stands for a 'philosophical gallantry' at odds with the masculine virtue of authentic chivalric gallantry oriented to the protection of the domestic and its sentimentalized female inhabitants. By elevating Rousseau to the status of paternal icon the revolution infuses into youth 'an unfashioned, indelicate, sour, gloomy, ferocious medley of pedantry and lewdness; of metaphysical speculations, blended with the coarsest sensuality. Such is the general morality of the passions to be found in their famous philosopher, in his famous philosophic gallantry, the *Nouvelle Eloise*' (*W&S*, vol. 8, p. 317). Echoing Burke's tone William Hamilton Reid, a one time member of the London Corresponding Society, examines the effects of radical culture on the domestic spaces of its adherents, charting the breakdown of what he calls 'domestic economy' that comes from the 'effusions of some superficial or political pamphleteer'. This breakdown is predictably seen as the enervation of the paternal figure, around which the general descent into domestic chaos ensues. Rehearsing the anti-Jacobin writing of Gothic consumption, Reid foregrounds the presence of textual objects in the domestic sphere:

I have observed, that the heads of many industrious families, who, previous to the illumination, made it an indispensable duty to appear abroad decently dressed on a Sunday, would afterwards not only remain the whole day in their working dresses, to shew their contempt of the Christian Sabbath, but spend it at home in sottiness and stupidity. And yet Paine's Age of Reason, Godwin's Political Justice, &c, have remained upon their shelves, and in the full sight of their possessors during the whole time.[18]

The 'fatal deviations from order and decency' that characterize the domestic space of the radical lead, for Reid, to the 'muddy pools of vice', 'dreary skepticism' and 'self-murder'. The children of these 'enlightened husbands' 'stray into the fields, where they contract vicious habits', while the 'influence of a copious history of striking examples, and the sanctity of authority of ages is lost and evaded'.[19]

If the actual forms of literary and philosophical expression appropriated by radical culture are an intrusion into domestic space, they are also imagined, like Burke's Jacobins, as polluting. Gillray's 'New Morality', for instance, which served as the frontispiece for the first issue of *The Anti-Jacobin Review* in 1798, includes a 'Cornucopia of Ignorance' from which texts by prominent radicals like Wollstonecraft, Paine and Holcroft, as Claudia Johnson writes, 'spilled into an ignominious heap'.[20] The imagery has obvious scatological overtones – radical literary culture is also excremental. The masses of pamphlets and radical texts that litter the grotesque spaces of radical and revolutionary activity seem to proliferate uncontrollably in a manner reminiscent of the reign of Dullness and the apocalyptic and similarly excremental world of Grub Street in Pope's *The Dunciad*. Such texts are a medium of metaphysical seduction – the conspiratorial work of 'literary caballers', 'intriguing philosophers', 'political theologians and theological politicians'

James Gillray, 'New Morality'

Isaac Cruikshank 'The Friends of the People'

(*RRF*, p. 93). In Isaac Cruikshank's 'The Friends of the People', for example, the masses of texts that surround Priestley and Paine are also accompanied by piles of weapons which promise to literalize titles like 'Revolutions', 'Plots' and 'Treason'. Reid's description of London Corresponding Society division meetings as sites of consumption registers the centrality of these textual artefacts no less than it does the effusive outpourings of radical speakers: 'Next to songs, in which the clergy were a standing subject of abuse; in conjunction with pipes and tobacco, the tables of the club-rooms were frequently strewn with penny, two-penny, and three-penny publications, as it were so many swivels against established opinion.'[21] In a similar vein the second 1794 *Report of the Committee of Secrecy* identifies the threatening nature of radical literary expression as lying in the fact that it formally mimics that heterogeneous nature of its constituency (the serialized, ragged crowd of consumers) both in its own heterogeneity and in the extent to which it utilizes popular modes of expression. According to the report the London Corresponding Society tried to disseminate ideas and convert the 'lower orders' into the 'instruments of the most dangerous and desperate designs' through means carefully selected to blend inconspicuously into the world of lower-class subliterary consumption and reception.

The measures employed for this purpose appear to have been deliberately prepared, and every contrivance used to mix them (in the shape most likely to captivate attention) with the ordinary occupations or amusements of those on whom they were intended to operate. Accordingly lectures have been delivered on political subjects, calculated from their very extravagance to catch the attention of the audience, and in the course of them every topic has been employed that could inflame their minds, alienate them from the laws and constitution of their country, and habituate them to principles of sedition and rebellion. The most violent publications of the same effect have been secretly, but generally, circulated in hand bills, both in the metropolis and in the remote parts of the country. Every point that could excite discontent, according to the pursuits, interests, or prejudices of different classes has been successfully dwelt on, and always in such a manner as to connect it with the leading design. The attempt to accomplish this has appeared in the shape even of hand bills and songs; seditious toasts; and a stupid selection of tunes which have been most in use in France since the revolution, have been applied to the same purpose, of endeavouring to render deliberate incitements to every species of treason similar to the mind of the people.[22]

In the report transgression ferments in a certain kind of reading community and in textual objects otherwise hidden from view, but which, in the report itself, are examined, itemized and minutely dissected in what amounts to a display of official ocular mastery. The authority of such disciplinary discourses resides in their elaborate performance of disclosure – in their ability to infiltrate, uncover and visualize transgression.

The report, like anti-Jacobin discourse more generally, presents its own scopic authority as a compensation for the cognitive failure of its readers, to whom the transgressions of Jacobinism are otherwise not readily obvious. The reader is thus also positioned as a spectator integrated into a certain moral economy, invested in the maintenance of social order and reinforced in the certitude of this affiliation by the spectacularized excesses of transgression. As Peter Stallybrass has written, 'the "nameless thing" is transformed into the endlessly reproducible spectacle of the grotesque, the exotic, and the low'. This spectacularization of heterogeneity and of topographical difference also 'establishes the homogenizing gaze of the bourgeois subject'.[23] But it would be wrong to assume that the subject of this gaze is just synonymous with a proscriptive disciplinary intent oriented to the policing of Jacobin dissemination. As I've already suggested, Burke himself realized that his own representations of transgression, in their variously carnivalesque and grotesque extremes, could also solicit the possibility of a spectacular pleasure in excess of their disciplinary intent. In his *Letter to a Member of the National Assembly* Burke writes:

> the retrograde order of society has something flattering to the dispositions of mankind. The life of adventurers, gamesters, gipsies, beggars and robbers, is not unpleasant. It requires restraint to keep man from falling into that habit. The shifting tides of fear and hope, the flight and pursuit, the peril and escape, the alternate famine and feast, of the savage and the thief, after a time, render all course of slow, steady, progressive, unvaried occupation, and the prospect only of a limited mediocrity at the end of long labour, to the last degree tame, languid and insipid.
>
> (*W&S*, vol. 8, p. 301)

The pleasure content of Burke's own writing, and that of his imitators like Moore and Elliot, embodied in the violence of the Parisian mob or in the depravity of a Paine or a Rousseau, alludes to and substitutes for the *frisson* of the 'retrograde order' of revolution. Burke's representations of revolutionary transgression, to the extent that they exceed their strictly proscriptive function and permit a certain kind of voyeurism, also incorporate into their own structure the possibility of pleasurable culture-consumption, the pleasure of simulated proximity to forbidden and dangerously transgressive desire. Foucault's early work perhaps best captures the curious pleasures concealed in the folds of disciplinary discourses, pleasures he will later theorize as mandated by these very discourses. If a paranoid bourgeois imagination strove to contain the dangers of transgression, 'these same dangers, at the same time, fascinated men's imaginations and their desires. Morality dreams of exorcising them, but there is something in man which makes him dream of experiencing them, or at least approaching them and releasing their hallucinations'.[24] This pleasure is what, ultimately, counts as the repressed of anti-Jacobin discourse. The attempt to police desire also solicits desire, visualizes it and, in the form of text, caters to its satisfaction.

MASS CULTURE AND THE GOTHIC COMMODITY

After the 'two acts' of 1795 had made radical association a treasonable offence, the kind of community examined in the 1794 report became a legal impossibility. By 1801 the former populist leader John Thelwall had returned to writing Gothic-sentimental poetry. His volume *Poems, Chiefly Written in Retirement* included the long dramatic poem 'The Fairy of the Lake', an explicitly Gothic text at least partly designed to exploit the popularity of Gothic literary forms. In his 1803 review of this volume Francis Jeffrey articulated the logic of the connection between Jacobinism and the forms of print-culture epitomized by Gothic textual production. Commenting on Thelwall's prefatory memoir Jeffrey writes:

In every page of this extraordinary Memoir we discover traces of that impatience of honest industry, that presumptuous vanity, and precarious principle, that have thrown so many adventurers upon the world, and drawn so many females from their plain work and embroidery, to delight the public by their beauty in the streets, and their novels in the circulatory library.[25]

'The analogy between Thelwall and a street-walking, novel-writing woman', Michael Scrivener comments, 'suggests that both are guilty of disturbing a natural order in which women perform menial tasks and men from the "middling class" stay behind the shop counter; also, Jeffrey draws implicit contrast between a legitimate literary culture unconcerned with buying and selling and a presumptuous democratic culture marked entirely by the most immoral kind of economic exchange, prostitution.'[26] Jeffrey's reference to literary females who flaunt themselves on the street and their novels in the circulatory library is also an attack on the economics of Gothic literary production typified by the massive output of the Minerva Press, many of whose writers were women.[27] Indeed, in the 1790s and beyond, Gothic literary production was for many critics synonymous with literary prostitution: sensationalism, consumerism, plagiarized story lines and the degradation of the text as both commodity and spectacle signified a transgression against propriety and against authorized literary culture. As André Parreaux and E. J. Clery have pointed out, periodical criticism of the Gothic fad frequently published satirical novel-writing 'recipes' intent on exposing the monotonous, mechanically manufactured and potentially massified nature of Gothic plots.[28]

> *Take* – An old castle, half of it ruinous.
> A long gallery, with a great many doors, some secret ones.
> Three murdered bodies, quite fresh.
> As many skeletons, in chests and presses.
> An old woman hanging by the neck; with her throat cut.
> Assassins and desperadoes, '*quant. suff.*'
> Noise, whispers, and groans, threescore at least.
> Mix them together, in the form of three volumes, to be taken
>   at any of the watering places before going to bed.[29]

The recipe, as an instance of what Clery calls the 'demonology of novel reading', also underlines the perception that Gothic literary production was a feminized genre integrated into a world of fashion, consumption and imitation: 'the addicted consumer becomes a cog in the fashion machine, internalizing the code only to spew it out again in a novel of her own'.[30]

It was another best-seller of the 1790s, however, that most insistently made the connection between Jacobin textual production and Gothic literature – the initially anonymous *The Pursuits of Literature*, in fact written by Thomas James Mathias and published accumulatively between 1794 and 1797. Mathias's satirical poem, in four dialogues with lengthy prefaces and footnotes, is a classic of anti-Jacobinism, and reads like a *Dunciad* for the 1790s. It is faithful to the imagery of Jacobinism as a hidden atavism lurking dangerously out of sight, and summons this concealment as the justification for its own assertion of scopic authority.

> Jacobinism in her natural, ferocious, and unsoftened features has for a season slunk away from the public loathing in Great Britain; but we may depend upon it, she yet 'lies couching head on ground, with catlike watch;' though in this country the monster has lost many of her offspring, whom true reason and sober philosophy have torn from her ... But surely the most powerful light should still continue to be thrown on their secret caverns and skulking places; for the sleeping and inactive will be her prey.[31]

For Mathias it was Burke who most effectively illuminated the dark space of Jacobinism – 'his lightening shone through their dark recesses'[32] – revealing the hell with which he was surrounded. Mathias is invested in performing the same kind of visualization, mimicking Burkean rhetoric in descriptions of revolutionary excess: the Frenchman's 'ruffian daggers' and 'orgies of blood and lust', 'the violence, the presumption, the audacity, the arrogance, the tyranny of man, drunk with self-idolatry'.[33] This excess is closely bound up with the world of literary dunces: Priestley 'writes on all things, but on nothing well', Paine cries 'Hold! that margin let me measure,/ and rate the separate value of each treasure', and Godwin is described as 'a mongrel, or an exotic' who knows nothing about writing 'and of Belles Lettres nearly as much as can be attained, or rather picked up, in a modern academy in some London Square, or at Islington'.[34]

The preface to the fourth and final dialogue of the poem is almost exclusively concerned with exposing the potential political dangers of literary consumption. 'Literature, well of ill conducted, is the great engine by which all civilized states must ultimately be supported or overthrown', runs Mathias's famous declaration of political stakes.[35] But in an age in which the spread of literacy enabled peasants to read Paine's *Rights of Man*, or 'our unsexed female writers' to 'instruct, or confuse, us and themselves in the labyrinth of politics, or turn us wild with Gallic frenzy', there is one text which Mathias wants to single out as exemplary of the 'arts of lewd and systematic seduction' – Matthew Lewis's *The Monk*.[36]

> That there are very good descriptions of castles and abbeys in this novel? So much the worse again, the novel is more alluring on that account. Is this a time to poison the waters of our land in their spring and foundations? Are we to add incitement to incitement, and corruption to corruption, till there neither is, nor can be, a return to virtuous action and regulated life?[37]

Mathias condemned *The Monk* because he believed that the depravity, cruelty and violence of the novel could actually seduce its readers into imitative dissipation and transgression. In doing so he confused the interpretive context that the novel implied with that of radical textual production, which had always oriented itself to the mobilization and organization of its readership. This confusion is itself interesting. In imagining Jacobin pamphleteers as agents of impending anarchy, atavism and philosophical savagery oriented to an idolatrous worship of man without regard for the conventions of social order, Mathias enacted the standard reactionary account of Jacobinism as dangerously transgressive. The unleashing of repressed energy and revolutionary violence demolishes prior socialization and facilitates the eruption of man as a natural being – a savage. By including *The Monk* in this critique, Mathias assumed that consuming representations of this violence was tantamount to participating in it. Popular reading practices and popular political violence were intimately related, if not synonymous.

The slippage between populist violence and the consumption of Gothic texts is aptly captured by Jane Austen in *Northanger Abbey*. When Catherine Morland remarks 'I have heard that something very shocking indeed, will soon come out of London', Eleanor Tilney imagines she is referring to a riot. The ever-rational Henry takes it upon himself to resolve the confusion:

> 'My dear Eleanor, the riot is only in your brain. The confusion there is scandalous. Miss Morland has been talking of nothing more dreadful than a new publication which is shortly to come out, in three duodecimo volumes, two hundred and seventy-six

pages each, with a frontispiece to the first of two tombstones and
a lantern – do you understand? – And you, Miss Morland – my
stupid sister has mistaken all your clearest expressions. You
talked of expected horrors in London – and instead of instantly
conceiving, as any rational creature would have done, that such
words could only relate to the circulating library, she immediately
pictured to herself a mob of three thousand assembling in
St. George's Fields; the Bank attacked, the Tower threatened, the
streets of London flowing with blood, a detachment of the 12th
Light dragoons, (the hopes of the nation), called up from
Northampton to quell the insurgents…'[38]

Henry's assumption that transgressive collective violence and
Gothic texts constitute two discrete object domains that only a fool
could confuse belies the extent to which the two are both
metonymically and causally connected in the discourse of Gothic
consumption: populist violence is a stock component of the Gothic
text, while certain reading practices are imagined as causally related
to populist violence. While Paulson notes that the irony of
Catherine's remarks is 'that the exaggeration of the sign falls short
of the grim reality',[39] we might also say, bearing in mind Mathias,
that the exaggeration indexes a new object of critique – neither
popular violence nor popular literature, but popular or mass culture
appealing to the desire of the consumer, as a blanket term envelop-
ing both.

The imbrication of popular, consumerist desire and the process
of reading Gothic texts is made evident in the verse 'Preface' to *The
Monk*. Here Lewis introduces his own novel as implicated in the
process of object-cathexis that defines the monadic subjectivity of
both consumer-capitalism and of libertinage. Addressing the novel
itself he writes:

> Methinks, Oh! vain, ill-judging book,
> I see thee cast a wishful look,
> Where reputations won and lost are
> In famous row call Paternoster.
> Incensed to find your precious olio,
> Buried in unexplored port-folio,
> You scorn the prudent lock and key,
> And pant well bound and gilt to see
> Your Volume in the window set

Of Stockdale, Hookham, or Debrett ...
    Assuming now a conjurer's office, I
Thus on your future fortune prophesy: –
Soon as your novelty is o'er,
And you are new and young no more,
In some dark dirty corner thrown,
Mouldy with damps, with cobwebs strown,
Your leaves shall be the Book-worm's prey;
Or sent to Chandler-Shop away,
And doomed to suffer public scandal,
Shall line the trunk, or wrap the candle!

(*Monk*, pp. 33–4)

While the novel, like an eager debutant, pants to leave the security of private space for the market to which it wishes to subject itself, the process of consumption in which it will be caught involves its seizure and subsequent disposal when, in the act of consumption, it becomes abject – 'book-worm's prey'. This is, needless to say, the logic of consumption as it is represented in the Gothic text itself. As recent scholarship on late-eighteenth-century Gothic literature has pointed out, a process of object-cathexis is at the centre of the Gothic text. The libertine, typically, pursues an object (a spectacular-ized or sentimentalized female) only to realize that possession does not fulfil desire. Desire always exceeds, is never satisfied by this or that object, and thus compels the endless, cyclical quest for a gratification that never comes. This is the dynamic that Eve Sedgwick elucidates in her discussion of the veil in Gothic litera-ture. If the veil promises a sexual plenitude beyond its surfaces, it also 'very often hides nothing, or death, or in particular some cheat that means absence and substitution'. Accordingly sexual impulses are figured as error – 'as the driving, transitory illusion that a specific object can adequately answer to desire'.[40] Peter Brooks dis-cusses this aspect of *The Monk* in conjunction with Sade's *Philosophy in the Bedroom*: desire in both 'follows a logic which discovers the inevitable destruction of everything it depends upon, its own inher-ent destructiveness and self-destructiveness'.[41] The process of object-cathexis, violation, consumption and eventual abjection, which in Lewis's novel will take place over the body of the senti-mental heroine, is, as Lewis's Preface indicates, the same as that which characterizes the act of reading. Reading is also an act of self-destructive, self-defeating desire, which the textual commodity registers in its futile attempt to outlive public interest and demand. The text must present itself as more than a consumable object – it must represent itself as a transcendence of its own materiality in order to hold out the illusory promise that it will avoid abjection. The commodity is always a disavowal of its own temporality, materiality and inevitable obsolescence in the marketplace.

As a commodity that represented the idea of transgression, of the repressed beyond the prosaic world of the everyday, *The Monk*'s most immediate struggle was with the market for literary texts – the other texts 'bound and gilt' and 'in the window set/ of Stockdale, Hookham, or Debrett'. If Lewis's work could not obtain 'the approbation of the critic', wrote the *Critical Review*, 'it has secured, what Mr. Lewis perhaps values more, the applause of the multitude'.[42] In the sixty odd years between the 1764 publication of Walpole's *Castle of Otranto* and Maturin's 1820 *Melmoth the Wanderer*, Frederick S. Frank estimates that approximately five thousand Gothic novels were published.[43] Many of these were chap book versions of established bestsellers, predictable imitations, theatrical adaptations or magazine serializations, motivated quite explicitly by the demands of the market.[44] If literary consumption was geared to the sensationalism and terror of the Gothic, it was incumbent upon new participants in the market to out-shock their competitors as a means of transcending the commodity form and the constraints of linguistic representation with the promise of an experience worth paying for, a reading experience that promised to be more than the mere material experience of the textual-object. This is in fact the paradox of the commodity – the object that appears to be a virtually magical transcendence of its object status and its actual use-value, such that it can represent, embody, be the desire of the consumer and in so doing assume an exchange-value that is no longer consonant with its material reality. This transcendence is what the Marquis de Sade hints at in his brief discussion of *The Monk* in 'Idée sur les Romans'. Commenting on the new novels of terror he writes that 'sorcery and phantasmagoria constitute almost their entire merit'. He is referring to their content, obviously, but also perhaps to the magical allure of the commodity form. At the end of the eighteenth century, Sade writes, after 'revolutionary shocks' had been felt across Europe, 'the novel became as difficult to create as it was monotonous to read'. The experience of history itself already contained, for those that had lived through the revolution, 'more misfortune in four or five years than the most famous novelist in literature could paint in a century'. A writer like Lewis then 'therefore found it necessary to call Hell to his aid in order to draw up a title to our interest and to find in the country of chimeras that which we are only too easily acquainted with when we scan the history of man alone in this age of steel'.[45] The magic of the commodity finds itself replicated in the literal magic that the writer must represent in order to even compete with the horror of history at the end of the century. Both imply the drive beyond material and historical experience that marks the pleasure of literature as well as its fetishistic character.

In this equation terror and the pleasure of consumption have a relationship of direct correlation. 'The horrible and the preternatural have usually seized on the popular taste', writes Coleridge in his review of *The Monk*. For Coleridge the popularity of the Gothic signifies a kind of enervation which is registered in the excessiveness of the Gothic text itself. 'Powerful stimulants', he writes, 'can never be required except by the torpor of an unawakened, or the languor of an exhausted appetite.'[46] Coleridge reads spectacles of excess as indicative of a lack of sensibility and of the degradation of mass culture, which puts its consumers into a kind of death-sleep of indolence and hedonism as part of the act of culture-consumption itself. In a footnote to *Biographia Literaria* this critique is extended to novel reading in general, which is portrayed as both a narcotic and a compensation for mental vacancy. Projecting images to the mind of the reader, the mechanics of novel reading are almost cinematic in their spectacularity, and indeed Coleridge's condemnation of them seems to anticipate new visual technologies that will realize the effects he describes on a genuinely mass level. The 'devotees of the circulating library', Coleridge writes, indulge in

a sort of beggerly day-dreaming during which the mind of the dreamer furnishes for itself nothing but laziness and a little mawkish sensibility; while the whole *material* and imagery of the doze is supplied *ab extra* by a sort of mental *camera obscura* manufactured at the printing office, which *pro tempore* fixes, reflects and transmits the moving phantasms of one man's delirium, so as to people the barrenness of an hundred other brains afflicted with the same trance or suspension of all common sense and all definite purpose.[47]

Wordsworth's 1802 'Preface' to *Lyrical Ballads* suggests how this critique of mass cultural forms could also draw upon the oppositions that organize Gothic-sentimental narrative. In the 1802 preface Wordsworth opposes a rural sensibility, evoked by 'plain' and 'emphatic' language, to those 'arbitrary and capricious habits of expression' that 'furnish food for fickle tastes, and fickle appetites'.[48] If the moral culture of sensibility is linked to the pathos of the rural idylls that *Lyrical Ballads* dwells upon, the erosion of this culture is embodied in the market for cultural commodities, in urban amusement typified by Gothic texts and theatrical productions:

> For a multitude of causes, unknown to former times, are now acting with combined force to blunt the discriminating powers of the mind, and unfitting it for all voluntary exertion to reduce it to a state of almost savage torpor. The most effective of these causes are the great national events which are daily taking place, and the encreasing accumulation of men in cities, where the uniformity of their occupations produces a craving for extraordinary incident, which the rapid communication of intelligence hourly gratifies. To this tendency of life and manners the literature and theatrical exhibitions of the country have conformed themselves. The invaluable works of our elder writers, I had almost said the works of Shakespeare and Milton, are driven into neglect by frantic novels, sickly and stupid German Tragedies, and deluges of idle and extravagant stories in verse.[49]

In this passage Wordsworth identifies the cyclical process of consumerist object-cathexis typified in the 'craving' for incident. As Jon Klancher writes, 'he describes the crude, almost behaviorist circle of a historically-conditioned need, a demand for "gratification," and a language that basely satisfies by creating ever greater need'.[50] In this passage, however, Wordsworth also summons a genealogy of authorized literary production. Shakespeare and Milton, the patriarchs of English literary culture, secure the possibility of a form of discursive praxis not contaminated by the market for cultural commodities – by the 'degrading thirst after outrageous stimulation'.[51] They have a talisman-like quality that Wordsworth will evoke in order to secure and protect his own poetic and moral authority from his often compromising proximity to mass cultural forms and the degraded world of economic and political populism: 'We must be free or die, who speak the tongue/ That Shakespeare spake; the faith and morals hold/which Milton held.'[52] This sense of poetic genealogy is linked to the filial communality that inhabits the rural idyll, and which is lost in the processes of alienation and monadic consumption that accompany urbanization. The oppositions implied by the 'Preface' (rural idyll/city, lyric poetry/'frantic novels', empathy/consumerism, authorized culture/mass culture) mark the conditions that accompany the rise of culture-consumption as a fall from a residual form of community, and accordingly register the poet's attempts to affirm the moral culture in which he sees himself as belonging. Nowhere is this dynamic more evident than in Book VII of *The Prelude*, in which the world of popular entertainment, culture-consumption and, potentially, popular violence is juxtaposed to the pathos of the world epitomized by the 'Maiden of Buttermere', whose sad story is already one that involves a narrative of libertine seduction and violation.[53] It is here that Wordsworth's Romanticism and Burke's *Reflections* come together very explicitly. Wordsworth echoes the phraseology of the *Reflections* in his account of Bartholomew Fair and, in the 1850 version of the poem, even included a tribute to Burke.

In his review of *The Monk*, however, Coleridge hopes, paradoxically, that the logic of consumption itself will undercut the popularity of the Gothic novel, that the laws of supply and demand will in fact demystify its appeal as a commodity: 'We trust, however, that satiety will banish what good sense should have prevented; and that, wearied with fiends, incomprehensible characters, with shrieks, murders, and subterraneous dungeons, the public will learn, by the multitude of the manufacturers, with how little expense of thought or imagination this species of composition is manufactured.'[54] But, interestingly, if Coleridge's critique of *The Monk* is initially introduced as a critique of mass-produced Gothic novels, he finishes by condemning the novel precisely for its ability, in its terror, to exceed the bounds of pleasure itself, such that the novel is reconstituted, beyond the banal terror of 'the multitude of the manufacturers', as the forbidden text of a desire that appears to transcend the materiality of literary circulation and consumption. The sufferings which Lewis describes, Coleridge writes,

> are so frightful and intolerable, that we break with abruptness from the delusion, and indignantly suspect the man of a species of brutality, who could find a pleasure in wantonly imagining them; and the abominations which he portrays with no hurrying pencil, are such as the observation of character by no means demanded, such as no observation of character can justify

because no good man would willingly suffer them to pass, however transiently, through his own mind.

The Monk, in this description, is an unreadable text for the normative subject of literary sensibility, existing beyond the boundary at which 'terror and sympathy are deserted by pleasure.'[55] Its unreadability, however, is what inscribes it with the allure of the commodity. In attempting to exile the novel beyond the boundary of public tolerance, Coleridge also constitutes it as the embodiment of repressed desire, literalized in the idea of the possession of a book that one cannot even read. Because the commodity is immersed in this spiral of receding desire, Coleridge's review in fact succeeds in evoking the magic, in both senses mentioned above, of Lewis's novel: its unreadability guarantees its readership.

SENTIMENTALITY AND THE LANGUAGE OF CONSUMPTION IN MATTHEW LEWIS'S *THE MONK*

As both Ronald Paulson and David Punter have noted of Lewis's novel, Ambrosio's libidinal excesses are connected to the violence of the Madrid mob.[56] Lewis presents the transgression of disciplinary constraints, sentimental propriety and moral responsibility as a release into the cyclical pleasures of consumerism that are latent not just in Ambrosio but, much more generally, in the multitude which inhabits public space. The novel opens and all but closes with a crowd scene. At its commencement the people of Madrid crowd into the Capuchin church ostensibly to hear Ambrosio preach. Their actual motivations, however, are varied in a way that is typical of what Klancher refers to as the 'anthologized crowd' characterized not by communal sympathy, but by serialized desire.[57] The opening page of the novel constitutes the crowd, 'collected by various causes', as a motley collection of interests and energies:

> The women came to show themselves, the men to see the women; some were attracted by curiosity to hear an orator so celebrated; some came, because they had no better means of employing their time till the play began; some, from being assured that it would be impossible to find places in the church; and one half of Madrid was brought thither by expecting to meet the other half.
>
> (*Monk*, p. 35)

The crowd is straightaway without any unified experiential content that could define it: it is a series of desires awaiting gratification. While these desires are not literally individualized in the passage just quoted, the figure of the anthologized crowd rhetorically performs individuation in the constitution of isolated interests. In Lewis's Madrid public space and the atomized crowd are coterminous such that the former is always marked by the latent violence of populist desire, whether in the Capuchin church, or in the streets outside where the gypsy woman tells Antonia's fortune. In the cataclysmic finale to the novel individualized desires erupt simultaneously in the destruction of St Clare and, in a 'moment of popular phrensy', the dismemberment and mutilation of the prioress. This outbreak of popular violence is also written as an act of collective consumption similar to that in which Lewis imagines the final obsolescence of his own text. The body of the prioress, once it satisfies the 'phrensy' of the people, is reduced to abjection: it becomes quite literally a non-object, the disgusting refuse of consumption.

> The rioters heeded nothing but the gratification of their barbarous vengeance. They refused to listen to her: they shewed her every sort of insult, loaded her with mud and filth, and called her the most opprobrious appellations. They tore her one from another, and each new tormentor was more savage than the former. They stifled with howls and execrations her shrill cries for mercy, and dragged her through the streets, spurning her, trampling her, and treating her with every species of cruelty which hate or vindictive fury could invent. At length a flint, aimed by some well-directing hand, struck her full upon the temple. She sank upon the ground bathed in blood, and in few minutes terminated her miserable existence. Yet though she no longer felt their insults, the rioters still exercised their impotent rage upon her lifeless body. They beat it, trod upon it, and ill-used it, till it became no more than a mass of flesh, unsightly, shapeless, and disgusting.
>
> (*Monk*, p. 344)

The fury and atavism of the mob find a constant parallel in that of Ambrosio, who has literally been seduced beyond the bounds monkish discipline. The language of mob fury, of 'phrensy', is also the language of individual transgression. If, as I have suggested, the crowd is also a potential public of consumers, it will not be surprising to find that Ambrosio's liberation is precisely a liberation into the hedonistic and monadic subjectivity of consumerism. Like the crowd, he seeks gratification with a violence that devours its object, violates it and ultimately reduces it to abjection. *The Monk* constantly enacts the cyclical, repetitive path of desire, the consumption and destruction of its object. It imagines liberation as the possession and consumption of women, such that the 'ill-use' to which the prioress is subjected by the crowd finds its correlative in Ambrosio's relationship to Rosario/Matilda and later Antonia. The flip side of the commodity as a mystical object is its obsolescence once its magic has been consumed: its reduction to base materiality, the destruction of its aura, its relegation as refuse, as variously corrupted and rotting matter, condemned to some 'dark dirty corner ... mouldy with damp, with cobwebs strown'.

Ambrosio's relationship to Rosario/Matilda plays out this relationship. The appeal of Rosario is initially a sentimental one which solicits sympathy in Ambrosio. In Ann Radcliffe's novels, which Lewis is in part parodying, as in Burkean political philosophy, the sentimentalized female is portrayed in a similar way. The compassion, sympathy and devotion she solicits seem contingent on a disavowal of her sexuality such that she apparently remains immune to objectification. She is, in other words, the emblem of communal sentiment antithetical to the logic of consumption. She embodies a moral culture and community both resistant to and threatened by the democratizing, relativizing forces of market capitalism. But in Lewis's novel the initial sympathy Ambrosio feels is contingent on the apparent absence of heterosexual desire: Rosario, though effeminate, at least appears to be male and the homosocial aspect of his/her relationship with Ambrosio seems to guarantee its platonic quality. *The Monk* is interested in revealing the repression inherent in these very conventions, in demonstrating that the moment of sentimental identification, with the Radcliffean heroine say, is also the activation of a psychology tending towards possession and sexual violation. The extent to which the sentimental heroine is outside of libidinal economies, and hence unavailable to them, guarantees the process of object-cathexis in which she becomes the object of libertinage. This evocation of consumerist desire at the moment of its apparent occlusion is the repressed content of the sentimental tableau. Once an object of desire has been constituted, initially on the basis of its unattainability or distance from its potential subject, who is always summoned as such, its aura endows it with an autonomy that beckons this subject into the liberty of unrestrained consumption. In this movement the assumption of sensibility, of a moral culture embodied in the reader's response to a certain image, is radically problematized. In *The Monk* spectacles that are expected to evoke sympathy, insofar as they reference the cult of sensibility and its representational conventions, solicit the libidinous interest of the metamorphosed Ambrosio. When Rosario in fact turns out to be a woman – Matilda – in love with Ambrosio and threatening to kill herself, the slippage of sensibility into sexuality is comically apparent. With the dagger poised a potentially sentimental, pathos-filled moment is converted into one of licentious rebirth, as the beautiful, suffering heroine becomes an object of pornographic phantasm.

> she lifted her arm, and made a motion as if to stab herself. The friar's eyes followed with dread the course of the dagger. She had torn open her habit, and her bosom was half exposed. The weapon's point rested upon her left breast: and, oh! that was such a breast! The moon-beams darting full upon it enabled the monk to observe its dazzling whiteness: his eye dwelt with insatiable avidity upon the beauteous orb: a sensation till then unknown filled his heart with a mixture of anxiety and delight; a raging fire shot through every limb; the blood boiled in his veins, and a thousand wild wishes bewildered his imagination.
>
> 'Hold!' he cried, in a hurried, faltering voice; 'I can resist no longer! Stay then, enchantress stay for my destruction!'
>
> (*Monk*, p. 87)

This passage, in which Ambrosio's desire – 'a thousand wild wishes' – already has affinities with the image of the mob makes explicit the repression inherent in the sentimental tableau constructed around the suffering heroine. The moonbeams, in sentimental discourse a sure sign of feminine modesty, light upon the breast such that the 'beauteous orb' itself becomes a source of light. Sentimental conventions very similar to those that Mary Wollstonecraft used to occlude female sexuality from the field of representation (as we'll see in the next chapter) actually solicit rather than pacify a violent male libido. Consider, by way of comparison, the simultaneous evocation and effacement of sexuality in the following, typically sentimental description of the dishevelled Adeline in Radcliffe's *The Romance of the Forest*:

Her features, which were delicately beautiful, had gained from
distress an expression of captivating sweetness: she had
             'An eye
       As when the blue sky trembles thro' a cloud
       Of purest white.'
A habit of grey camlet, with short slashed sleeves, shewed, but
did not adorn, her figure: it was thrown open at the bosom, upon
which part of her hair had fallen in disorder, while the light veil
hastily thrown on, had, in her confusion, been suffered to fall
back. Every moment of farther observation heightened the surprise of La Mott, and interested him more warmly in her favour.
Such elegance and apparent refinement, contrasted with the des-
olation of the house, and the savage manner of its inhabitants,
seemed to him like a romance of imagination, rather than an
occurrence of real life. He endeavoured to comfort her, and his
sense of compassion was too sincere to be misunderstood.[58]

In this passage, enacting but also disavowing the libidinal dynamic
in which the figure of the veil is implicated, La Mott revealingly
imagines that he is beholding not a real person, but an image. If the
image of the sentimental heroine is apparently resistant to commodity status, evoking compassion ('too sincere to be misunderstood') instead of desire in all but the morally reprobate, her
resistance is also thoroughly spectacularized: she is an overtly material (textual) entity constituted by and constituting the sentimental
narrative as itself a textual commodity. She is one tableau after
another, devised for a reader who derives both the pleasures of
sympathy and of consumption from the heroine's suffering. By dramatizing the intrusion of libertine desire into the sentimental scenario, converting it into a moment of pornography, Lewis's novel
also dramatizes the libidinal content of the conventional, Radcliffean
tableau. Ambrosio's response to Matilda is actually a demystification
of the reader's response to sentimental images which are always
more overdetermined than their explicit evocation of a culture of
sensibility (written in the above passage as compassion) suggests.
    Once Matilda is explicitly sexualized as a 'seducing object' and
the process of object-cathexis that typifies consumerism is acknowledged, she is also marked in Ambrosio's dreams by her unattainability for a monk still bound into the repressive disciplinary regime
of the monastery: 'lust-exciting visions floated before his eyes;
Matilda, in all the pomp of beauty, warm, tender and luxurious,

clasped him to her bosom, and lavished upon him the most ardent caresses. He returned them as eagerly; and already was on the point of satisfying his desires, when the faithless form disappeared, and left him to all the horrors of shame and disappointment' (*Monk*, p. 104). Once he possesses Matilda fully, however, she ceases to hold any attraction. Her 'wanton expression' and 'luxurious fire' become vulgar and tawdry in comparison to Antonia, who is simultaneously constructed as a new and unattainable object of desire. Comparing Antonia with Matilda, Ambrosio exclaims to himself:

> Oh! sweeter must one kiss be, snatched from the rosy lips of the first, than all the full and lustful favours bestowed so freely by the second. Matilda gluts me with enjoyment even to loathing, forces me to her arms, apes the harlot, and glories in her prostitution. Disgusting! Did she know the inexpressible charms of modesty, how irresistibly it enthrals the heart of man, how firmly it chains him to the throne of beauty, she never would have thrown it off. What would be too dear a price for this lovely girl's affections?
>
> (*Monk*, p. 243)

The realization that Matilda has become a harlot, a commodity, is what constitutes Ambrosio's loathing, while the fact that Antonia is imagined as a sentimental transcendence of the female as commodity accounts for her appeal. Nevertheless this appeal is still only intelligible in terms of commodification; Ambrosio thinks of it as represented by a price beyond his comprehension (or his ability to pay). Whereas he can tear down the picture of the Madonna (in fact a portrait of Matilda, to which he had once prayed, declaring 'The prostitute!', 'Antonia's empire' is one that is similarly constituted by the spectacular, through which Ambrosio once again encounters his object of desire in initially sentimental terms, and thus as phrased in an idiom that marks its distance and unattainability.

Ambrosio as consumer is also a spectator, riveted to the voyeurism in which sentimental identification slips into the rapaciousness of the libertine. When Matilda, still bound to serve her former lover, gives him the magic mirror in which he can behold Antonia in the privacy of her own apartment, the spectacular nature of the sentimental heroine becomes abundantly clear and, once again, the reader enters into a voyeuristic complicity with Ambrosio as the sentimental tableau becomes part of a pornographic scenario:

The scene was a small closet belonging to her apartment. She was undressing to bathe herself. The long tresses of her hair were already bound up. The amorous monk had full opportunity to observe her voluptuous contours and admirable symmetry of person. She threw off her last garment, and, advancing to the bath prepared for her, put her foot into the water. It struck cold, and she drew it back again. Though unconscious of being observed, an in-bred sense of modesty induced her to veil her charms; and she stood hesitating upon the brink, in the attitude of the Venus de Medicis. At this moment a tame linnet flew towards her, nestled its head between her breasts, and nibbled them in wanton play. The smiling Antonia strove to shake of the bird, and at length raised her hands to drive it from its delightful harbour. Ambrosio could bear no more. His desires were worked up to phrensy.

(*Monk*, pp. 268–9)

Antonia is already likened to an art-object here, the Venus de Medici, recalling the initial description of her veiled at the Capuchin church. Once again it is clear that Lewis wants to debunk the illusions of Radcliffean sentimentality, by emphasizing that the sentimental heroine is as much a part of a male fantasy as the explicitly sexualized images of Matilda. This might also be an attack on the oppositions of Burkean sentimentality, implying that Burke's famous image of Marie Antoinette at Versailles, 'glittering like the morning star' (*RRF*, p. 169), and of the mob attempting to ravish or murder her, are not strictly opposed; that the constitution of the object of desire and the mad pursuit of its consumption are causally connected moments. The violence of the crowd and the violence of the libertine, Lewis's novel suggests, are both structured as liberatory escapes into the enthralment of hedonism. Certainly the numerous attempted rape scenes, in which Ambrosio attempts and finally succeeds in violating Antonia, evoke Burke's bedchamber scene, suggesting that the sentimental identification Burke had intended to promote amongst his readers actually participates in the same economy of voyeurism and consumption that *The Monk* evokes for its readers.

And just as Lewis imagined his novel finally as 'book-worm's prey', Antonia is finally doomed to abjection once she is consumed. The crypt in which she is finally raped by Ambrosio is, in terms of the dynamics of consumption I've been describing, an appropriate location.

By the side of three putrid half-corrupted bodies lay the sleeping beauty. A lively red, the forerunner of returning animation, had already spread itself over her cheeks; and as wrapped in her shroud she reclined upon her funeral bier, she seemed to smile at the images of death around her. While he gazed upon their rotting bones and disgusting figures, who perhaps were once as sweet and lovely, Ambrosio thought upon Elvira, by him reduced to the same state. As the memory of that horrid act glanced upon his mind, it was clouded by gloomy horror; yet it served but to strengthen his resolution to destroy Antonia's honour.

(Monk, p. 363–4)

The rotting corpses and the reanimated Antonia are not presented here in opposition. The corpses in fact figure Antonia's fate as an object held within the libidinal field of libertine desire. Indeed the abject female in Gothic literature is a constant index of the obsolescence created by consumption. The desired, sentimental heroine and the discarded, redundant, rotting or morbid female are two aspects of the same dynamic. They relate to each other as the two faces of the commodity form. In a way Lewis's novel can be read as a demystification of the spectacularized female in its insistence that Antonia and Matilda are caught in and constitute the same economy of desire. It is the bleeding nun incident that perhaps best articulates this doubled image of femininity. Agnes de Medina, attempting to disguise herself as the ghost of the infamously debauched Beatrice de las Cisternas, is in fact momentarily superseded by the real ghost, who is then mistaken as Agnes, such that the sentimental heroine and the female spectre inhabit the same space like alternate afterimages. In constantly performing this doubling, which we find in a more complex and displaced form in Radcliffe's novels, the Gothic text enacts a curious, though often unconscious knowledge of its own status as a commodity. In this process the Gothic heroine herself emerges as a figure for commodified pleasure. In the form of discarded, decaying bodies, the text speaks strangely to the experience of literary consumption, as Lewis's Preface indicates. The terror, violence and 'libidinous minutia' (Coleridge's phrase) of *The Monk*, moreover, place the reader-consumer of the text in a position that is curiously analogous to Ambrosio's. Once Ambrosio is reborn as the subject of a rampant consumerism that relentlessly objectifies its female prey, so too is the reader reconstructed as that monstrously reprobate subject whom Coleridge imagined taking delight in reading and imagining the images Lewis presents, images in which violation and abjection embody both the shock and the enjoyment of reading. In this way the liberation/enslavement to objectified forms that Ambrosio experiences is mimicked by the reader, only we are riveted to the spectacle that Lewis has presented as a way of momentarily tending towards the space of the Coleridgean unthinkable. Lewis places a magic mirror in the hand of his reader equivalent to that which Matilda gives Ambrosio. As was the case in Coleridge's image of the camera obscura, a kind of visual technology indexes the extent to which the novel is implicated in a market for cultural goods, amusement and increasingly massified forms of entertainment. The reception and content of the novel thus curiously mimic each other, as the act of reading transgresses the bounds of socialization in a manner analogous to Ambrosio's transgression. Libertinage, in other words, has become an allegory for the act of reading. But in reading the transgressions of Ambrosio and the Madrid mob, the reader's apparent transgression is also bracketed by the process of reading itself. It never moves beyond the limits of a specific kind of space and activity. The constitution of consumerism as the repressed of disciplinary and proscriptive structures also simultaneously permits exactly what is outlawed – consumption. In this way the repression of desire also reconstitutes desire in terms that are self-circumscribing: 'The sensual and dark rebel in vain,/Slaves by their own compulsion', as Coleridge wrote in another context.[59]

If the language of Gothic textual production is the medium in which consumption is rendered palpable, consumption itself, we might say, reproduces a topography of containment. The connection between private reading practices and forms of incarceration, we'll see, is one that both Mary Wollstonecraft and Maria Edgeworth raise. In its own way the space of reading is as finite as the dungeons, convents and prisons with which Gothic texts are preoccupied. It produces 'desire', 'liberation' and 'freedom' in a way that consolidates the social and economic relations of consumer-capitalism. This is the sense in which reading emerges as a disciplinary practice at precisely the moment that texts, across a variety of apparently discrete discursive sites, constitute themselves as the containment and solicitation of a consumerist psychology variously understood as libertinage and populism. It is not just that a novel like *The Monk* and, less obviously, anti-Jacobin texts that recount revolutionary violence, represent transgressive desire. They do much more than this: they also offer themselves as objects of desire, and offer the process of their own consumption as the limit of desire. The pleasure of reading, and the constitution of literature as the domain of this pleasure, are thus locatable in a very specific political and economic matrix. They are historically synonymous with an overdetermined set of representational practices striving to understand and to contain the apparent anarchy of the market-place, of mass cultural forms and of political populism in the wake of the French Revolution. In the process they constituted a very material regime of power-knowledge-pleasure complicit with the consolidation of consumerism and commodity capitalism. What Foucault describes as the moment at the end of the eighteenth century, in which what 'we should rigorously define as literature came into existence', was also a moment in the consolidation of the forms of pleasure that still mark us as the subjects of capital.[60]

5
Domestic Revolutions: Mary Wollstonecraft and the Limits of Radical Sentimentality

At the end of the eighteenth century figures like Burke and Thelwall, at opposite ends of the political spectrum, could both use sentimental conventions to convey their social visions, testifying to the centrality of sentimentality in political discourse and debate. Thelwall's 1793 *The Peripatetic* is representative of this 'politico-sentimentality' in its radical form. Thelwall, as we have seen, depicts the processes of land enclosure, property monopoly and the ensuing displacement of rural populations leading to the creation of an urbanized proletariat, as assaults on an idyllic image of family life. The pathos of the transition from the rural idyll to urban decrepitude and enervation solicits a kind of sympathy that, Thelwall assumed, embodied an intuitive, but apparently communally normative sense of justice – a sympathetic responsiveness analogous to what Hume referred to as the 'intercourse of sentiments'. In Thelwall's deployment of sentimental conventions sympathy and a nascent political consciousness were synonymous. We recognize a similar version of politico-sentimentality in Wordsworth's 'Salisbury Plain' poems and in works like 'The Ruined Cottage'. Yet Thelwall, unlike his better known contemporaries, was also a political activist engaged in the formation of what could be described as a proletarian public sphere in excess of a middle-class cultural revolution. Thelwall imagined a series of interactive sites in which workers and artisans excluded from the parliamentary process could grasp their political disenfranchisement as the basis of a collective identity. The political culture built up around the London Corresponding Society and Thelwall's public lectures was oriented to the mobilization of a public of subjects hitherto marginalized from established forms of political expression.

The language of this mobilization was also, however, a language of discipline. Thelwall called for 'temperate reform', 'moderation and good order', rather than the violence and popular vengeance associated with the French Revolution and the subsequent Terror.[1] Integral to this discipline was the sympathy which Thelwall's speeches constantly tried to evoke in his auditors. Fostering rational political activity also meant fashioning sentimental subjects responsive to the image of the idyll, and thus cognizant of the social and economic processes threatening it. Political patriots, in other words, also had to be, if not actual family men, at least oriented to an image of family as the embodiment of moral and political norms.

Thelwall makes this connection explicit in the poetry he wrote while awaiting trial for treason, along with Thomas Hardy and other London Corresponding Society delegates, in 1794:

> There are, degenerate! – to the future blind –
> Who deem the Patriot fervour – the firm soul
> That spurns Oppression, and the base controul
> Of Tyranny, should be to him resign'd,
> To whose lone bosom for protection clings
> No tender Bride – to whose embraces springs
> No smiling infant, to awake the mind
> To social tenderness. – Ah, fond mistake![2]

The image of the ideal wife/mother is a persistent one in radical literary culture and is epitomized perhaps no more literally than in a eulogy for the wife of Thomas Hardy published and probably written by Robert Lee during the incarceration and trial of the LCS members. The epigram to the poem reads, 'died a martyr to the sufferings of her Husband'. Lee's account of Mrs Hardy's death is a work of both vulgar sentimentality and hagiography in which the commitment and constancy of a woman is both the bedrock of political life and the sign of its gravity for the male protagonist absent from the scene recounted – the domestic interior. Lee's eulogy represents legal incursions into the private space of LCS family men, culminating in the arrests and trials of 1794, as assaults on the now unprotected women who reside there in fatally empathetic union with their husbands.

> Behold the scene, the piercing scene appear!
> Imagination drops a pitying tear.

Bereft of thee, thy tender partner pines,
Thinks of thy state, and dangers new divines;
Till in her bosom bleak despair conceives,
Nor beam of hope the pungent pain relieves;
Tho' thy misfortune all her efforts claim,
The hand of nature bears upon her frame:
Feeble, and unassisted, hear her cry,
'For thee O husband! 'Tis for thee I die!'[3]

If this image is one of republican virtue, loyalty and sacrifice, it is also one of domestic isolation, neglect, despair and morbidity in which the bereft heroine pines away in the deadening seclusion of private space.

The possibility of political life for the male patriot seems to be contingent on this stifling existence, on the absence of women in public space. As Joan Landes has shown, Jacobin political culture depended on this exclusion.[4] It is not only, or even primarily that the family idyll guarantees some kind of public commitment to what are construed as natural, communal bonds of sympathy, but that males can conduct themselves rationally and heroically in public only if otherwise errant or potentially anarchic passions are bracketed in and relegated to the private, where they are externalized in the female body. Accordingly, the threat of public women was also the threat of a kind of sexual transgressiveness and libidinalized object-cathexis inevitably equated to some form of prostitution or courtly decadence. Indeed Thelwall's prison poetry figures tyranny, the antithesis of enlightened political life, in terms of the public's subservience to a feminized image of 'Luxury' that repeats well established tropes of feminized libertinage, deception and dissipation.

O hell-born Tyranny! how blest the land
Whose watchful Citizens with dauntless breast
Oppose thy *first* approach! With aspect bland
Thou wont, alas! too oft, to lull to rest
The sterner virtues that should guard the throne
Of Liberty. Deck'd with the gaudy zone
Of Pomp, and usher'd with lascivious arts
Of glossing Luxury, thy fraudful smile
Ensnares the dazzled senses, till our hearts
Sink, palsied, in degenerate lethargy.

Then bursts the swoln destruction forth: and while
Down the rough tide of Power Oppression drives
The shipwreck'd multitude, no hope survives,
But from the whelming storm of Anarchy.[5]

Elsewhere Thelwall imagines 'pamper'd Luxury' lying 'Stretched
on her gorgeous couch' quaffing the strains 'of soul-seducing
flattery, while the train/Of Misery heave unheard the pleading
sigh'.[6] There are traces of Rousseau here, whose 1762 *Émile*, as Cora
Kaplan points out, emphatically established the need to police the
dangers of the feminine, through such notions as female decorum,
as the condition of a political enlightenment.[7] *Émile*, Claudia
Johnson argues, is symptomatic of the republican political tradition
more generally, a tradition which 'excludes women from citizenship because they are always and inescapably saturated by their
sexuality, whereas men are capable of abstraction from their bodies,
and thus are fit to function in the public sphere'.[8] Certainly the radicalism of someone like Thelwall shared a good deal in common
with this tradition. In the 1790s radical sentimentality was often
based on a similar segregation of the private from the public, which
served as a way of quarantining the feminine and ensuring the
undisturbed continuation of the project of radical politics. The
female, at least at the level of representation, is the emblem of filial
communality, and the victim of the spatializing disciplinarity that
banishes her to domestic confinement in order to contain passions
that, in Thelwall's poetry, are equated with irrationality, seduction
and mystification. The female is thus both sentimentalized and sexualized. She solicits both sympathy, as the 'tender bride' who registers the weight of political injustice, and a desire which remains
submerged in the folds of sentimental representation. As Mary
Jacobus writes, 'She is the term by which patriarchy creates a
reserve of purity and silence in the materiality of its traffic with the
world and its noisy discourse.'[9] But she is also more than this: she is
the veiled object of a desire banished from the public sphere.

Wollstonecraft was not affiliated with the LCS in any way. She
belonged to a public of writers who pursued a radicalism committed
to a more exclusive bourgeois enfranchisement. Gary Kelly describes
Wollstonecraft, along with writers like Mary Hays and Helen Maria
Williams, as part of a professional middle-class engaged in a bourgeois cultural revolution directed against a court-dominated
society.[10] But just as the proto-socialist politics of someone like

Thelwall emerged with, but pushed beyond, the ideological limits of the bourgeois public, so too did Wollstonecraft's work ultimately exceed the gendered semiotic of the political culture in which she was herself deeply involved. Her writing during the 1790s displays the complexity of her relationship to a republican political tradition that was still, at least at the level of ideology, uneasy about 'public' women and prone to reproducing the gendered stereotypes of sentimental romance, despite the fact that certain select women, like Wollstonecraft herself, were central to it. A novel like Godwin's 1799 *St Leon*, anchored as it is around a fictionalized portrait of Wollstonecraft as a prototypical image of the angel in the house, demonstrates the need to contain the sort of feminism that Wollstonecraft, by the time of her death in 1797, had come to embody. *A Vindication of the Rights of Woman* epitomizes many of the problems involved in forging a feminist consciousness-raising practice in a culture that took heterosexual conjugality as one of its most centrally normative components. In constantly, and sometimes selfconsciously, encountering these limits, the *Vindication* verges on auto-critique; it approaches the realization that feminine experience is precisely the alienated experience of discursive entrapment, or enclosure. The 'tender bride' archetype necessitates the occlusion of sensuality and voluptuousness, pejorative terms for critics of courtly conduct, as the condition of responsible and enlightened family life. This manifests in, as Johnson puts it, 'a revulsion at degraded bodiliness' and a corresponding need for a modesty that conceals the body.[11] But as Eve Sedgwick's study of Gothic tropes suggests, the concealment of the body and, related to it, the figure of the veil which effaces sensuality, are also the conditions upon which a certain kind of objectification takes place as an anticipation of what is initially out of sight, occluded, contained. Representations of modesty, in other words, might also reproduce the very voluptuousness they sought to elide. The *Vindication* is well aware of this dynamic. Wollstonecraft confronts this problem in a series of reflexive, even ironic passages that attempt to occlude once and for all the sensuality of the body by veiling it with language itself, turning text and the experience of reading into the locus of escapist pleasure that seems to promise the possibility of gender relations beyond the limits of objectification and domestic enclosure. Only in this way can she conjure away the female body *and* represent the conjugal union of the radical idyll. The kind of textuality that the *Vindication* produces at these moments, however, also, produces enlightened conjugality as the effect of Romantic and sentimental conventions. An affirmative aesthetic experience, in other words, becomes the supplement necessary to resolve the impasse of the *Vindication*'s emancipatory project, yet also turns out to be centrally implicated in the neutralization of this project insofar as it leads to the containment of critical consciousness (oriented to the transcendence of gender-based objectification) in an imaginative space – the space of private reading, reverie and day-dreaming.

This approach to the *Vindication* departs from established feminist readings of Wollstonecraft in ways that deserve explication. Some recent work on the *Vindication* reads the text as an attempt to ventriloquize a masculinized discourse of political enlightenment. For Wollstonecraft to perform male rationality she needs to contain the dangers of the feminine in a way that repeats the repressiveness of, for example, Rousseau's *Émile*. 'By defending women against Rousseau's denial of their reason', writes Kaplan, 'Wollstonecraft unwittingly assents to his negative, eroticized sketch of their emotional lives.'[12] Mary Jacobus phrases this complicity in a way that suggests Wollstonecraft's submission to a phallocentric, symbolic order that marginalizes the 'feminine': 'this access to male dominated culture may equally be felt to bring with it alienation, repression, division – a silencing of the "feminine," a loss of women's inheritance'.[13] Both of these accounts indicate a pervasive tendency to read Wollstonecraft's *Vindication* as both claiming for women the privileges of masculinized rationality, and claiming for itself the status of rational, political discourse opposed to an apparently 'feminine' sentimentality. Accordingly, images of cross-dressing, mimicry and gender confusion seem appropriate ways of describing Wollstonecraft's politics. As Mary Poovey writes, Wollstonecraft, in her earlier *Vindication of the Rights of Men*, actually 'aspires to be a man, for she suspects that the shortest way to success and equality is to join the cultural myth-makers, to tide what seemed to her a fatal feminine flaw beneath the mask of male discourse'.[14] Anna Wilson similarly charts Wollstonecraft's problematic rehearsal of the masculinized modes of expression, deployed by Paine, as a simultaneous repression of a language of eloquence and sensibility identified as feminine.[15] While it is clear, however, that Wollstonecraft is invested in an image of rational femininity defined initially against images imbued with sentiment and sensibility, her idea of what counts as rational femininity in the *Vindication* also forces her to repeat these images. This is what is finally so confusing about the text. Despite its well documented attempt to repress the feminine, it remains, by its own account of flawed femininity, a persistently 'feminine' text, in its rehearsal of sentimental, proto-Romantic language very similar at times to the sentimental idiom for which she so roundly criticized Burke in *A Vindication of the Rights of Men*. If, as Wollstonecraft argues, sentimental textual production is the medium in which patriarchal myths of love are phrased, it is also the medium in which a dangerous sensuality implicated in this process is veiled and contained. Wollstonecraft's at times dense, autotelic language, which seems to embody the quasi-sensual pleasure of *reading* the absence of sensuality, is parodic in its excess. Indeed, the *Vindication*, I'll argue, registers an awareness of its own limitations, and of how these are ideologically conditioned, in the explicitness of its withdrawal into language as a way beyond the problem of the body. In doing so it enacts the centrality of affirmative culture to the gender relations of late-eighteenth-century patriarchy.

Wollstonecraft's resignation to the logic of affirmative culture, which is readable in her very self-conscious textual performance of and absorption in sentimental, melancholic posturings, indexes the absence of the praxis that her final novel, *The Wrongs of Women; or, Maria*, will attempt to imagine: a praxis in which the experience of ideology can be grasped as the basis of collective subject predication and communal solidarity. The inability to demystify the social relations defining women's lives from within the bounds of sentimentality, radical or reactionary, needs to be grasped as the objective fact of feminine experience. To do this requires a space outside of the polarized field bounded by feminized domesticity and masculinized publicity. The throne of power, Wollstonecraft writes in the *Vindication*, 'is built across a dark abyss, which no eye must explore, lest the baseless fabric totter under investigation' (*RW*, p. 270). This image of socially inscribed ignorance cannily anticipates the one that Marx will use to describe the workings of bourgeois ideology – 'the hidden abode of production' in which the exploitative processes of capital are carried on unexamined.[16] Wollstonecraft's image of the 'dark abyss' carries similar epistemic implications. It implies that knowledge of the conditions on which power is founded arises initially as a clarification and explication of the very conditions impeding this knowledge. Foregrounding affirmative textual production as its central interpretive topos, *The Wrongs of Woman* finally reveals that this knowledge is not reducible to an abstract process of inquiry that can take place irrespective of the discursive limits imposed by specific spheres of production, but requires a discursive infrastructure oriented to the interactive explication of the experience of closure itself: beyond the limits of radical sentimentality, beyond the limits of the hearth, a feminized public sphere.

DOMESTIC ENCLOSURE AND THE TEXT OF ESCAPISM

At the heart of *A Vindication of the Rights of Woman* is an image of communality that stands in direct opposition to a functionally integrated society of property, class and gender inequality. This functionally integrated society, which is similar to Burke's image of a harmonious political order in the *Reflections*, is permeated by various degrees of legal coercion and ideological conditioning that bind individual subjects into fixed and hierarchical positions in a manner conducive to the functional efficiency of both residual patriarchy and emergent capitalism. This takes place in violent disregard for what Wollstonecraft, in accordance with radical natural rights theory, suggests is an intrinsic humanity. The process of social integration reproduces this violence across the whole gamut of social practices (in education, etiquette and the law, for example) ratifying and legitimizing itself as the necessary condition for social harmony, and maintaining monadic self-interest (possessive individualism, freedom in the market) as the normative foundations of sociability. The standing army is an archetypal and microcosmic image of this problem in the *Vindication*, in that it establishes a hierarchical and authoritarian structure which is experienced not as an external imposition on the bodies in its control, soldiers and officers, but as the internal principle of subjectivity itself. The disorganization of critical facilities in this hierarchy, Wollstonecraft suggests, enables it to reproduce its authority as a more or less natural fact. Hence:

A standing army, for instance, is incompatible with freedom; because subordination and rigour are the very sinews of military discipline; and despotism is necessary to give vigour to enterprises that one will directs. A spirit inspired by romantic notions of honour, a kind of morality founded on the fashion of the age, can only be felt by a few officers, whilst the main body must be moved by command, like the waves of the sea; for the strong wind of authority pushes the crowd of subalterns forward, they scarcely know or care why, with headlong fury.

(*RW*, p. 97)

The imposition of a disciplinary structure, in which autonomous, critical consciousness is effaced, does not present itself as coercive because it simultaneously eradicates the conditions on which its violence would be readable. Wollstonecraft writes the absence of autonomous, non-integrated subjectivity as the condition and effect of military discipline. The naturalization of this effacement in the 'sinews of military discipline' is analogous to the manner in which the imperatives of private, domestic space construct women in a way that seamlessly integrates them into its spatial segregation:

in order to preserve their innocence, as ignorance is courteously termed, the truth is hidden from them, and they are made to assume an artificial character before their faculties have acquired any strength. Taught from their infancy that beauty is woman's sceptre, the mind shapes itself to the body, and roaming around its gilt cage, only seeks to adore its prison.

(*RW*, p. 132)

If the institutions of marriage and patriarchy position women as objects before the male libido, as the chattel of their husbands, the educational apparatus they are subjected to from an early age prepares them to experience this position not as a moment of alienation, but of fond recognition and self-confirmation. The fact of enclosure within a specific set of spatial and interactive possibilities is effaced by the construction of a subjectivity adequate to its confinement. A form of ideological interpellation, involving the production of a subject position synonymous with its social position and function, remains operative, but unreadable for the subject of ideology herself. While the manner in which Wollstonecraft frames the issue of false or conditioned consciousness holds out the possibility of grasping the fact of enclosure independently of its ideological mediation, the material conditions in which women live also seem to foreclose the possibility of demystifying their situation. For my purposes the most compelling sections of Wollstonecraft's text are its explications of how the discursive resources available to women compel them to repeat the logic of enclosure in forms of imagined escape or transcendence.[17] The site of domestic enclosure, it turns out, also necessitates a form of affirmative discursive practice. It is this mutually sustaining confluence of discursive and spatial enclosure that I want to trace in order to demonstrate how Wollstonecraft's text, to the extent to which it remains caught within the structures of affirmative culture, can also be read as parodying its own limitations.

If society has rendered women 'insignificant objects of desire' (*RW*, p. 83) Wollstonecraft's writing takes this idea of objectification very literally. As objects before a male gaze women are also subject to the apparently cyclical nature of consumerist object-cathexis in a manner that suggests some sort of collusion between a regressive and decadent court culture and the objectifying processes of a commercial society. Like all objects that promise gratification, women's ability to evoke desire is temporary. Their incorporation into the libidinalized dynamic of male consumption guarantees the destruction of that aura that informs their initial desirability. If they are objects, they are also consumable. The life of the female as object in the *Vindication* is analogous to the life of the commodity as Marx describes it in the *Grundrisse*: 'the commodity which has exchanged itself for another commodity through the medium of money steps outside circulation in order to be consumed, destroyed.'[18] In courtly society the female presents herself to a potential suitor, playing on her desirability, is possessed and consumed by him (whether in marriage or not) and then confronts her obsolescence as an object of desire once she is discarded into the dead space of domestic enclosure. The fate of woman as object becomes a continual and degrading struggle with her own redundancy, strangely literalized by Wollstonecraft in images of feminine dissipation and abjection. She is subject to all the vicissitudes of the object. With only her sheer materiality as the inevitably fleeting basis of her desirability she is 'made ridiculous and useless when the short-lived bloom of beauty is over' (*RW*, p. 83). Beyond a brief moment in which she embodies the desire of her suitor, 'the woman who has only been taught to please will soon find that her charms are oblique sunbeams, and that they cannot have much effect on her husband's heart when they are seen every day, when the summer is passed and gone' (*RW*, pp. 110–11), just as surely as passions 'sink into mere appetites, become a personal and momentary gratification when the object is gained, and the satisfied mind rests in enjoyment' (*RW*, p. 114). The experience of obsolescence that lurks throughout the

Vindication as the dark fate of the object – Wollstonecraft talks about 'superannuated coquettes' and women as ruins 'born only to procreate and rot' (*RW*, p. 157) – merely leads to an abject reinscription of object status, a continual renewal through the acquisition of fashion commodities and, corresponding to this, the deadness of the object itself, marked through the eradication of natural activity and vitality. Swift's image of the 'nymph' who takes apart her beauty and reveals it to be literally composed of objects, prosthetic body parts as well as fashion accessories, reflecting the status of the prostitute as a commodity, lingers close to the surface here.[19] 'Coquettish arts', designed to 'gratify the sensualist' (*RW*, p. 115) imply, for Wollstonecraft, a legalized form of prostitution once they are mediated through marriage: 'In a seraglio, I grant, that all these arts are necessary; the epicure must have his palate tickled, or he will sink into apathy' (*RW*, p. 113).

The subservience and lack of activity into which women are bound literally enervates their bodies and virtually reduces them to household fixtures as they are seamlessly incorporated into the domestic interior: 'men who, by their writings, have most earnestly laboured to domesticate women, have endeavoured, by arguments dictated by gross appetite, which satiety had rendered fastidious, to weaken their bodies and cramp their minds' (*RW*, p. 157). This process of enervation can translate into a literal physical wasting in, say, the image of the eponymous heroine's mother in Wollstonecraft's *Mary*, whose countenance 'even rouge could not enliven'. Caught in the 'sickly, die-away languor' of bodily dissipation 'her voice was but the shadow of a sound, and she had, to complete her delicacy, so relaxed her nerves, that she became a mere nothing': 'For years she divided her time between the sofa, and the card-table. She thought not of death, though on the borders of the grave.'[20] The process of obsolescence is written as both lingering, creeping sickness and chronic boredom. Wolf Lepenies has discussed the phenomena of boredom in terms of a sense of redundancy, class impotence and the impossibility of public, political activity, specifically experienced by the German bourgeoisie in the late-eighteenth and early nineteenth centuries. Boredom, Lepenies argues, is symptomatized by the compensatory flight into an imaginary realm of sentiment, *Weltschmerz* and melancholic sensibility: 'Weltschmerz, melancholy, and hypochondria resulted from the enforced hypertrophy of the realm of reflection, from imposed loss of the ability to exercise real power, and from the consequent pressure to justify one's situation.'[21] This response to boredom, which typifies the situation of the obsolete female in the *Vindication*, is also construed by Lepenies as a 'retreat into literature'. Reading becomes both the practice in which one can consume affective idyllic images, and also the physical activity through which one can produce oneself as melancholic in the guise of the reader. In the *Vindication* the boredom of domestic enclosure also necessitates the production of escapist texts that hold out the imaginative possibility of the plenitude so obviously lacking in the private interior. The private consumption of sentimental texts is a part of the ideologically inflected education that prepares women for the 'gilt cage', and it supplies the basis of a fantasy life once they are ensconced in it. This 'retreat into literature', into sentiment, aesthetic experience or the space of the imagination as it is available even in day-dreams, is exactly equivalent to what Herbert Marcuse refers to as affirmative culture. The domestic enclosure remains so impenetrable precisely because the discursive structures that sustain it – forms of fantasy and culture-consumption – also offer the possibility of an escape into imaginative space. The dissipated, morbid body of the couch-bound female suggests not only the effects of objectification, but an imaginative escape from physical enclosure and the body itself, which now seems oblivious to its actual, material degradation.

Wollstonecraft's critique of the ideal of romantic love and its function in the education of women is thus also a critique of the forms of textual production that sustain this ideal. The love idyll, which supplies the telos of sentimental fiction, effaces the qualities that Wollstonecraft believes are necessary in a marriage if it is not to rehearse the process of objectification. Romantic love, Wollstonecraft believes, is a momentary passion sustained by the artificial production of affections and appearances. Its logic is both performative and spectacular. Posited as an authentic telos, in sentimental fiction for example, it ratifies the patriarchal culture in which women wilfully produce themselves as love objects for a male gaze and marriage market. It is a deceptive fiction that actually induces women to behave as if it were real. 'The lively heated imagination … draws the picture of love, as it draws every other picture, with those glowing colours, which the daring hand will steal from the rainbow, that is directed by a mind, condemned in a world like this, to prove its noble origin by panting after unattainable perfection, ever pursuing what it acknowledges to be a fleeting dream' (*RW*, pp. 170–1):

An imagination of this vigorous cast can give existence to insubstantial forms, and stability to the shadowy reveries which the mind naturally falls into when realities are found vapid. It can then depict love with celestial charms, and dote on the grand ideal object – it can imagine a degree of mutual affection that shall refine the soul, and not expire when it has served as a 'scale to heavenly'; and, like devotion, make it absorb every meaner affection and desire. In each other's arms, as in a temple, with its summit lost in the clouds, the world is to be shut out, and every thought and wish that do not nurture pure affection and permanent virtue.

(*RW*, p. 171)

Wollstonecraft is referring to the sentimentality of Rousseau, but her comments could just as easily apply to someone like Ann Radcliffe, whose novels incessantly construct heterosexual love idylls as antithetical to the spectacular world of courtly conduct, culture-consumption and libertine desire. Love is the illusion that, in the form of the myth of the intimate sphere, compels the repetition of precisely those oppressive structures it thought it had left behind. It compels women to construct themselves as love-objects within the field of the male gaze by creating the semblance of having transcended vulgar materiality, fabricating the simplicity of appearance which 'adorns' Radcliffe's sentimentalized heroines. Yet once the initial aura of the object of romantic love has disappeared the idyll still persists as the telos of an imaginative life. Even having proven its fictitiousness in actual marriage, sentimentality still supplies an affirmative realm in which women, having 'fostered a romantic delicacy of feeling', 'waste their lives in imagining how happy they should have been with a husband who could love them with a fervid increasing affection every day, and all day' (*RW*, p. 117). If 'Novels, music, poetry, and gallantry' make women 'creatures of sensation', forming their character 'in the mould of Folly during the time they are acquiring accomplishments' (*RW*, p. 154), these same practices sustain them in marriage. As 'creatures of sensation' they are subject to the specious reasoning of sentimental writing that 'skillfully exhibits the objects of sense most voluptuously shadowed or gracefully veiled; and thus making us feel whilst dreaming that we reason, erroneous conclusions are left in the mind' (*RW*, p. 192). This realm of sentiment, which is also one of deception, amusement and culture-consumption, is the realm to which women, 'restrained from entering into more important concerns by political and civil oppression', are left to exercise their imaginations and intellects, such that 'sentiments become events, and reflection deepens what it should, and would have effaced, if the understanding had been allowed to take a wider range' (*RW*, p. 314).

Wollstonecraft's critique of sentimental notions of love focuses on the extent to which these seemingly enact a transcendence of the world of vulgar materiality, of objectification, and libidinalized male desire. Love, erroneously imagined as resistant to commodification, also involves an occlusion of the material, of the physical body, such that it can absorb 'every meaner affection and desire' and inaugurate a plenitude of 'pure affection' and 'permanent virtue' (*RW*, p. 171). This is, needless to say, the logic of sentimental representation, in which the idealized female as love object is either marked by a physical absence (Burke's Marie Antoinette seems to float ethereally just above the ground at Versailles), or by a figurative veiling that produces her as an object of sympathetic identification rather than desire (in *The Romance of the Forest* 'The languor of sorrow threw a melancholy grace upon her [Adeline's] features, that appealed immediately to the heart'[22]). Redeploying the figure of the veil, Wollstonecraft presents this occlusion of the sensual as the condition upon which it is reconstituted, as if libidinal desire is precisely aroused by the object which is somehow hidden from view. When objects are 'voluptuously shadowed or gracefully veiled' (*RW*, p. 192) the reader/spectator is both seduced by their (half) appearance and prevented from seeing them as they are. Veiling or effacing the physical, explicitly sensual body thus always participates in the solicitation of a voyeuristic economy of desire that is motivated in direct correlation to the performance of the degree to which the object is unavailable for cognition, the degree to which it is veiled. Accordingly, Matthew Lewis's *The Monk*, parodying Radcliffean conventions, presents Antonia's 'modesty' (her attempt to conceal her body, often literally behind a veil) as the basis of a desirability that guarantees the dangerous attentions of the libertine.

Yet while Wollstonecraft recognizes the complicity of sentimental conventions in the solicitation of patriarchal object-cathexis, her own representation of what enlightened domesticity might look like is based on exactly the same sort of veiling. The *Vindication* is obsessed with what Johnson calls 'gross corporeality' and represents the female body as an object requiring careful management and discipline.[23] In order to avoid the pitfalls of objectification, the female body must be rendered transparent or invisible such that a woman's intrinsic worth will be evident in its place: 'Women are always to seem to be this or that – yet virtue may apostrophize them, in the words of Hamlet – Seems! I know not seems! Have that within that passeth show' (*RW*, p. 202). In this formulation interiority in all its depth and richness must be produced as a surface, it must conceal the outer body which only 'seems', in order that it pass what is still only imaginable as a visual inspection – the test of sympathetic identification as the basis of legitimate communal and familial sentiments leading to enlightened, companionate marriage. As a mode of domestic amelioration this kind of sympathetic communality repeats exactly the kind of fantasy scenario that Wollstonecraft imagined under the rubric of love: the wish for an almost messianic transcendence of the physical world and material body in the constitution of a domestic idyll safely beyond the baneful influences of objectifying desire. Wollstonecraft imagines the family as a space of republican virtue, in which men and women come together of their own free wills, form a domestic community and responsibly fulfil the functions that (naturally) fall to their lot. Needless to say this model replicates the gendered writing of public and private space that marks the domain of radical activism, for example, as a male one, and the domain of domestic sacrifice (maternity and housekeeping, but also the mythologized role of the empathetic martyr) as feminized.[24] But what is extraordinary is that this replication of affirmative sentimentality is itself, Wollstonecraft acknowledges, a fiction that historical conditions, the sheer oppressiveness of material circumstances, compel her to think. If, as critics rightly claim, moments in the *Vindication* seem almost Burkean in their rhetorical intensity, our readiness to deconstruct an argument that lapses into the position it is critiqueing has to be tempered by the fact that Wollstonecraft is clearly aware of what she is doing. Commenting on the logic of her own ameliorative vision, she writes:

> I only re-created an imagination, fatigued by contemplating the vices and follies which all proceed from a feculent stream of wealth that has muddied the pure rills of natural affection, by supposing that society will some time or other be so constituted, that man must necessarily fulfil the duties of a citizen, or be despised, and that while he was employed in any of the

departments of civil life, his wife, also an active citizen, should be equally intent to manage her family, educate her children, and assist her neighbours.

(*RW*, p. 264)

If this vision wishes away objectified relations in order to usher in companionate marriage, Wollstonecraft is also confronted with the problem of having to evoke the aura of virtue, of modesty as the principle of marriage, and in so doing is aware that she must replicate precisely the kind of sentimentalized discourse she most wanted to avoid. Like the ennui-stricken subject of domestic enclosure she too is compelled to visualize a moment of enlightened domestic intercourse characterized by natural affection immune to objectifying scopic drives, commodification and the obsolescence and boredom that result from them.

In her chapter on modesty this paradox is clear. Her refusal of the object world results in the deployment of densely figurative, sentimentalized prose which ironically reinscribes material pleasure in the form of textual consumption. Modesty is itself evoked as a kind of muse whom Wollstonecraft wants to inform her own rhetoric until such textual phantasms are socially redundant. She thus projects a world beyond not only objectification, but beyond the textual mediums that imagine this world, and grasps this projection as a contingent one that ironically registers the extent to which the moment of plenitude (its ideal object or telos) is absent. The projection, in other words, is entirely contingent on sentimental discourse. It foregrounds its own textuality.

> Modesty! sacred offspring of sensibility and reason! – true delicacy of mind! – may I unblamed presume to investigate thy nature, and trace to its covert the mild charm, that mellowing each harsh feature of a character, renders what would otherwise only inspire cold admiration – lovely! Thou that smoothest the wrinkles of wisdom, and softenest the tone of the sublimest virtues till they all melt into humanity; thou that spreadest the etherial cloud that, surrounding love, heightens every beauty, it half shades, breathing those coy sweets that steal into the heart, and charm the senses – modulate for me the language of persuasive reason, till I rouse my sex from the flowery bed, on which they supinely sleep life away!
>
> (*RW*, p. 231)

In this passage Wollstonecraft realizes that the posturing of her own language suggests the extent to which what she considers a desirable state of critical consciousness is absent for her sex. The language of sentiment is summoned to function as the medium in which some sort of consciousness-raising might be initiated. The difficulty of moving beyond this idiom is marked in the fact that several pages later, shortly after a description of 'the shameless behavior of prostitutes, who infest the streets of this metropolis' (*RW*, pp. 232–3), the plenitude beyond the object world is imagined, by contrast, as a sort of co-mingling of souls that, on the one hand, effaces the object world and, on the other, reinvests it with the mysterious aura of 'true love'.

> She who can discern the dawn of immortality in the streaks that shoot athwart the misty night of ignorance, promising a clearer day, will respect, as a sacred temple, the body that enshrines such an immovable soul. True love likewise spreads this kind of mysterious sanctity round the beloved object, making the lover most modest when in her presence. So reserved is affection that, receiving or returning personal endearments, it wishes not only to shun the human eye as a kind of profanation, but to diffuse an encircling cloudy obscurity to shut out even the saucy sparkling sunbeams. Yet that affection does not deserve the epithet of chaste which does not receive a sublime gloom of tender melancholy, that allows the mind for a moment to stand still and enjoy the present satisfaction, when a consciousness of the Divine presence is felt – for this must ever be the food of joy.
>
> (*RW*, pp. 234–5)

In this passage love involves the cloaking of the body in 'mysterious sanctity' and 'cloudy obscurity', by which it is rendered immaterial. As Tom Furniss points out, Wollstonecraft's use of what she calls 'poetical fiction' at such moments in the text is very close to the images of sentiment and chivalry she sought to critique:

> Rather than exposing the naked truth of women's sexuality, Wollstonecraft's text retreats into a set of beautiful poetic fictions in a way which seems to repeat Burke's recourse to the pleasing illusions of life. Tales which should not be told are displaced by an all-too-familiar tale about women and modesty ... Thus Wollstonecraft unexpectedly cedes to Burke's and Rousseau's

view that women must be kept within the bounds of modesty's 'contracted horizon.' Her resolution to be employed about things rather than words breaks down when confronted with female sexuality and retreats into a language and a representation of women (a 'beautiful ... poetic fiction') which it sets out to refute.[25]

The *Vindication* does certainly turn on this dynamic of repetition, but in a sense I would argue that that is its whole point. Wollstonecraft is not naively falling into the trap of repeating Burkean conventions, she is dramatizing the extent to which a certain kind of language, typically Burkean as Furniss points out, marks the limit of feminist politics in the culture of radical senti- mentality. The language itself, in its materiality as text, becomes a compensatory object that alludes to the possibility of a reformation in gender relations, but which also reinscribes the limits of the exist- ing social order. If the body is conjured away, the materiality of lan- guage now stands in its place. This substitution is most evident when Wollstonecraft goes on to discuss her respect for relics as the signs of deceased friends. Here memory, as a kind of communion with the dead, is also a process of meditating on objects capable of evoking the world beyond them. The object is endowed with an aura, and 'of such stuff is human rapture made up': 'A shadowy phantom glides before us, obscuring every other object; yet when the soft cloud is grasped, the form melts into common air, leaving a solitary void, or sweet perfume, stolen from the violet, that memory long holds dear' (*RW*, p. 235). The aura is a purely rhetorical matter – one might say that it is quite literally language in its most emphat- ically figurative form. This elegiac idiom is crucial to the aesthetic experience of modernity. Wollstonecraft's idyllic reveries typically inscribe their own reliance on poetic language. In them rupture is always a repetition, and veiling the body a disclosure of language itself as an object of desire. If the female body is apparently gone, desire is reconstituted over the pleasure of the text as a sensual object. One form of sensuality is substituted for another. The density of sentimental, Romantic language is intelligible as an es- capist response to boredom and enclosure, a move towards the space of meaningful reading that high Romanticism will map. Wollstonecraft, it would seem, is finally acknowledging that the telos of sentimental education is only available at this imaginative level, that is as a repetition and consolidation of the limits of enclosure.[26]

The messianic, melancholic posturing of Wollstonecraft's language, the longing for a projected world of souls as the basis of
textual, imaginative and aesthetic pleasure, inscribes the absence of
a praxis capable of breaching domestic enclosure. Wollstonecraft's
melancholy registers this lack in the yearning for a world not only
beyond objectification, spectacularity and gender inequality, but
beyond the textual media and discursive sites that supplement
them. In her 1788 *Mary*, Wollstonecraft concludes the melancholic
plight of her protagonist with precisely this double wish: 'Her deli-
cate state of health did not promise long life. In moments of solitary
sadness, a gleam of joy would dart across her mind – She thought
she was hastening to that world *where there is neither marrying*, nor
giving in marriage.'[27] This idea recurs in the *Vindication*, but revealingly as the basis of a critique of enclosure:

> How women are to exist in a state where there is neither to be mar-
> rying nor giving in marriage, we are not told. For though moralists
> have agreed that the tenor of life seems to prove that *man* is pre-
> pared by various circumstances for a future state, they constantly
> concur in advising *woman* only to provide for the present.
> Gentleness, docility, and a spaniel-like affection are, on this
> ground, consistently recommended as the cardinal virtues of the
> sex; and, disregarding the arbitrary economy of nature, one writer
> has declared that it is masculine for a woman to be melancholy.
> She was created to be the toy of man, his rattle, and it must jingle
> in his ears whenever, dismissing reason, he chooses to be amused.
>
> (*RW*, p. 118)

By writing messianic transcendence as the antithesis of the object
world, literalized in the infantile images of the rattle and toy,
Wollstonecraft deploys a sentimental posture as the basis of a critical distance. The wish for the world beyond marrying and giving in
marriage thus also repeats the relegation of critical impulses to an
aesthetic, imaginative space synonymous with the practices of sentimental, Romantic reading, of which the *Vindication* is constantly
critical. The pleasure of critique is still the pleasure of the text, and
neither can breach the 'gilt cage' of domestic enclosure precisely
because they reduce critique to the discursive practices that sustain
a topography of segregation, boredom and imaginative transcendence. If the *Vindication* is finally aware of this impasse,
Wollstonecraft is as yet unable to offer an alternative to it.

TOWARDS A FEMINIST PUBLIC SPHERE

The *Vindication* demonstrates that thinking beyond the limits of sentimental discourse cannot occur as an abstract thought experiment. On the contrary, Wollstonecraft's critique of sentimental representational strategies compels her to repeat some of their assumptions. Whatever the irony of this repetition, she still rehearses the melancholic, Romantic gestures of aestheticized interiority mediated through textual consumption, and thus contains the possibility of breaching closure in the very practices of discursive production and reception that sustain the segregation of the domestic sphere and its gendered semiotic. In this repetition we can see that ideology critique cannot occur as an abstract practice of demystification independently of a specific spatial and discursive context. The disillusioned wife can intuit on the basis of her own experience that the love idyll is a fiction, but this knowledge does not help her to transcend the enclosure that compels her to imagine an idyllic realm of freedom and value. Culture-consumption, the escape into literature and interiority, are inseparable from the material organization of spaces and bodies, inseparable from determinate positions and discursive resources within the mode of production. As Slavoj Žižek argues so emphatically, ideology is 'in the reality of doing', rather than a purely epistemic matter: the subjects of ideology 'know that, in their activity, they are following an illusion, but still, they are doing it'.[28] Domestic enclosure could not be breached by an act of mind alone. The breach requires a structural alteration in the types of spaces and discursive practices available to women.

In her final, unfinished novel, *The Wrongs of Woman*, Wollstonecraft foregrounds the contingency of the *Vindication*'s repetitions, but also attempts to imagine discursive possibilities beyond the impasse that constrained her earlier writing of social and domestic amelioration. According to Mary Poovey the fact that the novel was not completed indicates the central problem of the text: the incompatibility of Wollstonecraft's 'political insights' with sentimentality as the medium conveying them.

It is Wollstonecraft's recognition of this incompatibility and – equally to the point – her resistance to this recognition that account for both the hesitations of composition and the contradictions that mark the text. In this, her final work, Wollstonecraft identified one aspect of what she held to be the tyranny of eigh-

teenth-century bourgeois institutions, yet because her own values
– indeed, her own self-definition – were inextricably tied up with
these institutions, she was unable to pursue her revolutionary
insights to their logical conclusion.[29]

We have already seen, with regard to the *Vindication*, the plausibil-
ity of this reading. Yet we have also seen that Wollstonecraft's im-
murement in the culture of sentimentality is phrased with knowing
irony. Poovey nevertheless astutely reads the ideological character
of sentimentalism – its ability to pacify the 'imaginative longings of
powerless individuals' and to provide 'substitute gratifications'
without disturbing the spatial segregation of private and public
spheres. Yet she reads *The Wrongs of Woman* as still finally contained
by these limits, as ultimately complicit with enclosure: 'Maria's
celebration of the "humanizing affection" of the individual actually
constitutes Wollstonecraft's retreat from the insight to which she
was so close in *The Rights of Woman* [sic]: the recognition that the individual's – his or her position within class, gender, economics, and
history – really delimits freedom and virtually defines the "self".'[30]
In registering the contingency of sentimental textual production
and individualized interiority, their relationship to and complicity
with enclosure, Wollstonecraft's work seems somewhat more complicated than the simple repetition of monolithic superstructural
formations Poovey implies. *The Wrongs of Woman*, I want to suggest,
manages to go considerably further than Poovey allows in its
attempt to rupture discursive constraints. Wollstonecraft's last novel
attempts to rework heterosentimental structures in order to displace
them and ironically reveal their mystificatory character before a
new notion of community; a space and a discursive praxis oriented
to the interactive articulation of the experiential content of women's
lives in the over-determined patriarchy of the period. Claudia
Johnson has referred to this community as 'homosocial'.[31] As she
persuasively argues, the novel involves a rejection of the ideology
of heterosexual love that also involves a move away from 'the moral
and political normativity of the male body in conservative and
radical discourse'.[32] Laurie Langbauer's psychoanalytically inclined
reading makes a similar point, arguing that the novel effects a
subversion of the symbolic order, moving 'from what has come to
be called the Name of the Father to the Name of the Mother'.[33]
What I want to suggest is that this shift away from certain forms
of sentimental discourse can also be read as a working out of

communicative and interactive possibilities that promise to actualize feminist politics in discursive practices. The novel takes us beyond the bind of sentimental discourse by enacting, as the basis of its own formal organization, alternative forms of telling that emphatically demystify the ideology of heterosexual love and thus make alternative forms of community possible. If, as Gary Kelly argues, Wollstonecraft participated in a middle-class cultural revolution, in the *Wrongs of Woman* we see the extent to which her own politics exceeded its limits. At the very least we can say that the novel foregrounds forms of alienation specific to women, constituting a kind of consciousness-raising practice in which the forces impeding activist knowledge can be examined without allowing this critical impulse to be reworked and contained in the escapism of affirmative culture. The figures of socially mediated ignorance which point to the deep affinity of Marxist and feminist thought, Wollstonecraft's 'dark abyss' and Marx's 'hidden abode', thus also imply a standpoint from which this epistemic blockage, metaphorically written as a failure of scopic authority, can be overcome in the formation of relatively objective knowledge about the mode of production and one's position within it. The consolidation of the communal and communicative structures capable of achieving this are themselves what count as activism, as political activity that materially revolutionizes the content, limits and possibilities of the mode of production.

The *Wrongs of Woman* opens with its heroine, Maria, confined in a madhouse, prevented from leaving her cell and permitted only minimal intercourse with her keepers. Beyond the grated window of her cell she can behold both literal and metaphorical images of communal disorder – 'a huge pile of buildings, that, after having been suffered for half a century, to fall to decay, had undergone some clumsy repairs, merely to render it habitable' (*WW*, pp. 76–7), and her fellow lunatics parading about the asylum's garden, representing the 'most terrific of ruins – that of a human soul': 'What is the view of the fallen column, the mouldering arch, of the most exquisite workmanship, when compared with this living momento of the fragility, the instability, of reason, and the wild luxuriancy of noxious passions?' (*WW*, p. 83). Madness is figured by Wollstonecraft as a disease of the imagination, as a heightened sensitivity to the object world, such that the asylum's inmates are continually pathologized by their relationship to the materiality of their environment: 'so active was their imagination that every new object which accidentally struck their senses, awoke to phrenzy their restless passions' (*WW*, p. 84). Madness, in other words, compensates for the monotony of incarceration in much the same way as imagination sustained the enclosure of the obsolete wife. Madness, we might say, is written as the result, not the cause of incarceration; a result of the boredom, isolation and communal impoverishment of a disciplinary structure that, like the army or the domestic enclosure, fashions the subjectivity of its inmates in a seamless relationship to its spatial dimensions.

This impoverishment and its unmistakable Gothic-sentimental resonances, which we will soon discover are the outcome of Maria's marriage to the vile and deceptive libertine-husband Venables, metaphorically emblemize the plight of women more generally. Incarceration and the institutional effacement of the female as a rational being are suggestive of the situation of domesticated wives in the *Vindication* and, in the story of Maria, a direct result of it. When the novel, very early on, becomes one about reestablishing communality beyond the isolation of the cell, it begins to organize itself around two distinct possibilities: on the one hand, community as a reconstruction of the heterosexual love-idyll in the medium of sentimentality and, on the other, community as a response to and an examination of the actual experience of gender inequality as it is perpetuated by the confluence of sentimentality and patriarchal legal structures. While the former, embodied in Maria's relationship with Henry Darnford, a fellow prisoner, constitutes the story line that seems to guide and organize the narrative, and which the narrator most insistently foregrounds, the latter is implied in the actual formal organization of the text. Janet Todd refers to the two narrative structures I'm describing here as, on the one hand, 'circular and repetitive' and, on the other, 'linear and developmental'. 'The circular', Todd writes, 'binds her [Maria] to male relationships', while 'the linear tends towards freedom and maturity'.[34] Beyond the sentimentalized surface of the novel, in which Maria forms both a precarious and ironized romantic connection with Darnford, this is a novel in which women form, or attempt to form, sympathetic bonds by recounting their own experiences to each other, such that the act of retelling becomes the very condition of a counter-community that unsettles and finally promises to displace the sentimental repetition that Maria enacts. Moreover it reveals the very contingency of this repetition as one rooted in the alienation of enclosure (incarceration) that Maria, locked in her cell, initially experiences. The novel, as

Poovey suggests, does indeed embody the incompatibility of Wollstonecraft's political insights and sentimentality, though not as a helpless reflection of superstructural contradictions, but rather as a performative demystification of them, and as an attempt to conceptualize tangible social possibilities beyond a delimiting present.

The two forms of communality I have just mentioned occur simultaneously. Maria's nascent relationship with her guard Jemima is phrased initially as the possibility of human interaction and sympathy: 'It is so cheering to see a human face, even if little of the divinity of virtue beam in it, that Maria anxiously expected the return of the attendant, as a gleam of light to break the gloom of idleness' (*WW*, p. 79). As Jemima develops a cautious friendship with her prisoner, she also facilitates clandestine meetings between Maria and Darnford. These meetings arise in the first place because Jemima brings Maria books belonging to Darnford in order to relieve the former's extreme idleness and ennui. Maria reads Dryden's *Fables* and Milton's *Paradise Lost* and, in the handwritten notes in these texts, first encounters the traces of Darnford, which then begin to consume her and evoke fantasies of the idealized being who produced them.

> She read them over and over again; and fancy, treacherous fancy, began to sketch a character, congenial with her own, from these shadowy outlines. – 'Was he mad?' She perused the marginal notes, and they seemed the production of an animated, but not disturbed imagination. Confined to this speculation, every time she re-read them, some fresh refinement of sentiment, or acuteness of thought impressed her, which she was astonished at herself for not having before observed.
>
> (*WW*, p. 86)

Maria, conditioned by the claustral space of captivity, solitude and boredom, now reads her own desire inscribed in the margins and between the lines of the printed text and in so doing becomes a version of the sentimental reader criticized in the *Vindication*: boredom is causally linked to the escapism of culture-consumption. Ironically, remembering that Rousseau was a central target of critique in the *Vindication*, it is *La Nouvelle Héloïse* that she embraces in order to distract herself from the thought of Darnford. With Maria surrounded only by 'petrified figures', her fellow inmates, and feeling as if she had been 'buried alive', Wollstonecraft performs the impatience of her imagination in a literalization of the idea of imaginative flight: Maria 'flew to Rousseau, as her only refuge from the idea of him, who might prove a friend, could she but find a way to interest him in her fate' (*WW*, p. 89). Yet her own reading practices and her imaginings of the romantic love idyll she is about to replay become quickly confused as Saint Preux and Darnford, reading and reverie, become indistinguishable. This confusion is enacted in Wollstonecraft's own very confused syntax and deployment of male pronouns:

> still the personification of Saint Preux, or of an ideal lover far superior, was after this imperfect model, of which merely a glance had been caught, even to the minutia of the coat and the hat of the stranger. But if she lent St. Preux, or the demi-god of her fancy, his form, she richly repaid him by the donation of all St. Preux's sentiments and feelings, culled to gratify her own, to which he seemed to have an undoubted right, when she read on the margin of an impassioned letter, written in the well-known hand – 'Rousseau alone, the true Prometheus of sentiment, possessed the fire of genius necessary to portray the passion, the truth of which goes so directly to the heart.'
>
> (*WW*, pp. 89–90)

Literature and Maria's own textually mediated fantasies merge in an ironic repetition of exactly the kind of sentimental textuality that Wollstonecraft examined in the *Vindication*. But still, while texts and then notes are exchanged between Maria and Darnford, who establish their affection and reveal interiority by literalizing the mechanics of the sentimental epistolary novel, it is Maria's relationship with Jemima that is both central to (she is the go-between and fulfils this role with increasing willingness as her empathy with Maria grows) and submerged in the mystified folds of sentimentality in which Maria is caught.

When Jemima begins to facilitate actual meetings between Maria and Darnford, the eerily artificial and performative nature of the love idyll is continually foregrounded for the reader, despite the narrator's propensity to replay, in free indirect discourse, Maria's naive response to Darnford in an apparently uncritical manner. As Nicola Watson writes, discussing the novel's relationship to Rousseau, 'The lovers desire, as it were, by the book, according to its letter, which triangulates and falsifies Maria's relation to Darnford to the point where she cannot perceive the man himself at all, preferring to rehearse the self-destructive story of excessive sensibility in the over-inflated (and by now worryingly hackneyed) terms of *La Nouvelle Héloïse*.'[35] Darnford himself, when he tells his own story, turns out to be a seemingly reformed philanderer who has refashioned himself into an image of the republican patriot, though his telling of his past casts doubts over the integrity of this transformation, implying a monadic attachment to the pursuit of both property and pleasure that will continue to cast a shadow over his apparent affection for Maria (who, we will find out, is also the bearer of a large inheritance). The way in which Maria cathects Darnford as the principle of redemption also replays Wollstonecraft's own version of the ideal marriage of mutual modesty, but now as an ironic displacement that foregrounds incarceration and communal impoverishment as the determining context of such fantasies.

> Having had to struggle incessantly with the vices of mankind, Maria's imagination found repose in portraying the possible virtues the world might contain. Pygmalion formed an ivory maid, and longed for an informing soul. She, on the contrary, combined all the qualities of a hero's mind, and fate presented a statue in which she might enshrine them. ... A magic lamp now seemed to be suspended in Maria's prison, and fairy landscapes flitted round gloomy walls, late so blank. Rushing from the depth of despair, on the seraph wing of hope, she found herself happy. – She was beloved, and every emotion was rapturous.
>
> (*WW*, p. 99)

As in Romantic critiques of novel reading and Gothic literary production, an image of emerging visual technology – the magic lamp – is deployed as an index of the impoverishment of culture-consumption. And lest the reader miss the irony here, the narrator reminds us of the dark space beyond Maria's imagined picture of Darnford: 'could he, feeling her in every pulsation, could he ever change, could he be a villain?' (*WW*, p. 100).

This fantasy scenario of sentimental surfaces, however, can itself be the initial medium for the form of communality that will ultimately displace it. Here we begin to glimpse something of the complexity of this predicament, which Poovey's reading seems to overlook. The realm of the imagination that enables a simulacrum of communal plenitude to be played out on the wall of the cell – 'a tomb of living death' – also functions as the horizon against which the experience of persecution and victimization is evoked. The pathos of the love idyll juxtaposed to the poverty of the cell constitutes the kind of sentimental spectacle that, in Thelwall's *Peripatetic* for example, was supposed to evoke sympathetic identification. The ideal (and idealized) image of sentimental communality that Jemima, as a spectator, sees played out before her engenders this kind of response and enables her to broach the closure of the idyll and tell her own story, converting it into a different kind of interactive and discursive space. As Johnson suggests, the love idyll is no longer bound by the limits of heterosexual affection, it has become a more open kind of community.[36] But this expansion of narrative possibilities is nevertheless dependent on the sentimental tableau as an image of a kind of normativity that can in some way appeal to Jemima.

So much of heaven did they enjoy, that paradise bloomed around them; or they, by a powerful spell had been transported into Armida's garden. Love, the grand enchanter, 'lapt them into Elysium,' and every sense was harmonized to joy and social extacy. So animated, indeed, were their accents of tenderness, in discussing what, in other circumstances, would have been commonplace subjects, that Jemima felt, with surprise, a tear of pleasure trickle down her rugged cheeks. She wiped it away, half ashamed; and when Maria kindly enquired the cause, with all the eager solicitude of a happy being wishing to impart to all nature its overflowing felicity, Jemima owned that it was the first tear that social enjoyment had ever drawn form her. She seemed indeed to breathe more freely; the cloud of suspicion cleared away from her brow; she felt herself, for once in her life, treated like a fellow-creature.

(*WW*, p. 101)

Jemima's life history, however, which occupies the next chapter, is one of constant seduction, abuse, abandonment, prostitution and destitution until, worn down by the cruelty of the world, she finally succumbs to its logic, taking up the paid post she presently occupies, herself becoming incorporated into the very apparatus that now imprisons Maria. Jemima's story has a sobering effect on the heroine, forcing her to reconsider her own idyllic fantasies:

the story she had just heard made her thoughts take a wider range. The opening buds of hope closed, as if they had put forth too early, and the happiest day of her life was overcast by the most melancholy reflections. Thinking of Jemima's peculiar fate and her own, she was led to consider the oppressed state of women, and to lament that she had given birth to a daughter.

(*WW*, p. 120)

The novel, at this point, has led us from a sentimental idiom into a more realistic and confronting form of telling that seems to undermine the sentimentality necessary to evoke Jemima's history in the first place. Barely a page later Maria discovers, through the agency of Jemima, that her daughter is in fact dead. Plunged into despair Darnford's proclamations of affection now become strangely decentred. We are still in the midst of a predominantly sentimental narrative, and Maria is certainly consoled by Darnford's overtures, but just as his glibly analytical interjections into Jemima's story had appeared both superficial and superfluous in the face of brute experience, so too do his proclamations of love now seem somehow trivial and devalued to the reader.[37]

The next seven chapters are taken up with Maria's memoir, which was intended for and addressed to her daughter as a pedagogical text premised on her own experience of marital abuse. Importantly the memoir is available to the actual reader of the novel as read by Darnford. Here the displacement of the sentimental narrative is unmistakable, enacted in Darnford being actually written out of the novel, once he becomes the nevertheless sympathetic reader through which Maria's story takes centre stage. Not only is he effaced in this way, but the fact that the memoir is addressed to an apparently dead daughter as a maternal legacy marginalizes him as its implied addressee. The male of the sentimental love plot is usurped in this prioritizing of maternal communication. There is a sense both of impropriety and voyeurism in the idea of Darnford's eyes roving over Maria's narrative as part of the process by which their relationship will repeat the illusions and abuses of Maria's marriage to Venables. The trace of the dead child, occupying the same place as Darnford (as the memoir's addressee) enables the reader to grasp two distinct forms of interaction and communality forming in opposition over the same experiential content: on the one hand, the Darnford–Maria love idyll as a repetition and mystification of Maria's experience, in which Maria's suffering 'veils' her in a way that presents her as an object before the male gaze, and, on the other hand, the mother–daughter communiqué, as the basis of a community structured around the superfluity of men and the demystification of gender-specific experience, which is presented as a pedagogical resource rather than as the basis of sentimental affect. Maria's story recounts Venables's appropriation of her as a sexual object and as the embodiment of her uncle's fortune, which he now is attempting to legally assume by confining her in a madhouse and preventing her attempts to flee the prison of marriage. The story itself replays the opposition between the two forms of communality the novel as a whole is built around. Venables is continually objectifying his wife, and even attempts to sell her into prostitution, while constantly verbalizing, with Mandevillian verve, his grotesque version of monadic male property rights : 'all the world were governed by their own interests; those who pretended to be actuated by different motives, were only deeper knaves, or fools crazed by books' (*WW*, p. 167). In contrast, Maria's whole life has been a series of beneficent encounters with other women, either victims themselves or those willing to assist her in her flight from her husband who, much like Falkland in *Caleb Williams*, assumes a kind of panoptic omniscience in the mind of the fugitive. In this narrative it is relationships between women that embody the only possibility of genuinely ameliorative potential, and this potential is generally evoked through the extent to which brutish masculinity destroys it in its furious and hedonistic drive to power and property. What patriarchy must foreclose most emphatically is the possibility of female association outside the limits of domestic enclosure.

By the time we know Maria's history Darnford, it is clear, has become a misrecognized repetition of Venables, though the two are revealingly at opposite ends of the contemporary political spectrum.[38] Darnford is a would-be republican, and Venables a defender of established forms of ownership and power. Indeed the overtly performative nature of Darnford's restrained response to the memoir actually replays the critical moment at which Maria is momentarily convinced that she loves Venables enough to marry him.

[Darnford's] eyes, glowing with a lambent flame, told her how much he wished to restore her to liberty and love; but he kissed her hand as if it had been that of a saint; and spoke of the loss of her child, as if it had been his own. – What could have been more flattering to Maria? – Every instance of self-denial was registered in her heart, and she loved him, for loving her too well to give way to the transports of passion.

(*WW*, p. 188)

When Venables, having feigned public indifference, silently and secretly donates a guinea to a distressed widow whose cause Maria has taken up, deliberately avoiding public recognition of the act, Maria believes she has fallen in love with him as her disappointment is suddenly transformed to transport: 'What a revolution took place, not only in my train of thoughts, but feelings! I trembled with emotion – now, indeed, I was in love. Such delicacy too, to enhance his benevolence! I felt in my pocket every five minutes, only to feel the guinea; and its magic touch invested my hero with more than moral beauty' (*WW*, p. 135). Unlike Darnford's response to the memoir, recounted by the third-person narrator who, again in free-indirect discourse, rehearses the naivety of Maria's spontaneous reaction, Maria's own first-person narrative is able to retrospectively demystify her response to Venables's performance of affection. What is a mystified series of responses and appearances in the third-person present of the novel is juxtaposed to Maria's more considered and ultimately objective embedded memoir, which thus becomes a portentous and ironic commentary on her unrecognized repetition of sentimental error. This juxtaposition foregrounds the two levels at which the novel takes place – mystified experience presented as a spontaneous response to the immediate context of enclosure, and critical reflection in the life stories that Jemima and Maria have both produced. It thus also suggests the necessity of a space in which experience can be reflected on and examined critically, if the mystified world of sentimental surfaces is to be grasped as ideologically implicated. This space is one of public discussion, story telling and interaction, in which spontaneous or intuitive responses to circumstances can be rearticulated in relationship to previous experiences that cast them in a very different light.

The kind of space I think the novel tries to imagine is similar to that constituted by consciousness-raising groups in which emotional responses to specific situations are re-examined in order to, as Satya Mohanty writes, 'provide evidence of the extent to which even our deepest personal experiences are socially constructed, mediated by visions and values that are "political" in nature, that refer outward to the world beyond the individual'.[39] Consciousness-raising work is not understood by Mohanty as the discovery of an essentializing identity, but as a process in which the subject attains an understanding of the ways in which existing social and political relations generate emotional responses that have the potential to furnish relatively objective knowledge about their conditions of possibility. The crucial point here is that, given the right kind of mediating process, relatively inarticulate emotional responses to specific instances of injustice can be rearticulated as the basis of a politically useful and generalizable critique of power relations. Wollstonecraft's novel, in its attempt to demystify the pleasure of sentimentality, manifest in what Daniel O'Quinn calls the moment of 'trembling' (Maria's 'tremulous private body' in the face of Venables's and then Darnford's performance of love[40]), attempts both to reveal the socially mediated nature of emotional responses and to represent the practices that would make this kind of cognition possible.

The novel is unfinished and the published version of it culminates only in a series of notes, headings and fragments, edited by Godwin, that tell us, lest we were in any doubt, that Darnford betrays Maria once they are both free. Out of these fragments we get perhaps the most emphatic evidence of Wollstonecraft's attempt to move beyond the limitations of affirmative culture. In a series of notes we learn that the novel was supposed to end with the suicide of its heroine, though a final fragment, apparently projected as the last half a dozen or so paragraphs, reveals a very different conclusion. Maria indeed attempts suicide, swallowing laudanum, in an effort to leave the impoverishment of the present: 'nothing remained but an eager longing to forget herself – to fly from the anguish she endured to escape from thought – from this hell of disappointment' (*WW*, p. 202). But on the brink of a death that steals upon her like slumber Jemima enters before her, like a vision, carrying her child, at which point Maria regurgitates the narcotic and recovers her senses. Jemima has apparently managed to plumb the depths of deception to which Maria's avaricious male relatives have gone in order to conceal her child from her. Tutoring the child on the journey back to Maria, Jemima has taught her to recognize Maria and say the word 'mamma' upon encountering her for the first time. 'The conflict is over!' Maria exclaims finally, 'I will live for my child!' (*WW*, p. 203). This denouement is premised on the realization of the mutual bonds between Maria, Jemima and the child, which have been forming despite the compulsive sentimentality of the Maria–Darnford plot, and embodies a moment of communal harmony in which the errors of this plot cannot be repeated precisely because there now is no male figure included in what appears to be a family unit – a community with the common experience of abuse and alienation as its basis. What, in the 1788 *Mary*, was an abandoned narrative possibility, the possibility of a relationship between Mary and Ann as a solution to the contradictions of the sentimental plot,[41] is here realized not as a principle of closure but as an open-ended series of possibilities that portends the dissolution of domesticity as it had hitherto been imagined, and its reconstruction as a counterhegemonic interactive space. What the *Vindication* was compelled to imagine as the site of republican domesticity, maternity and affirmative culture-consumption has become a feminized public sphere that, in its ability to demystify the alienating structures of a patriarchal society, also appears to undermine the ideological foundations of the bourgeois revolution of which it was a part.

FICTIONALIZING WOLLSTONECRAFT: GODWIN'S *ST LEON*

We get a very clear indication of the ways in which Wollstonecraft's feminism exceeded bourgeois norms by looking at Godwin's response to some of the critical positions that inform *The Wrongs of Woman*. Daniel O'Quinn's discussion of Godwin's editorial interventions into the unfinished text carefully and persuasively demonstrates how these interventions were more than merely 'epithetic', as Tilottama Rajan suggests. O'Quinn shows how Godwin's commitment to narrative coherence and closure manifests in attempts to explain the inconclusive nature of the text and to tie up what might appear to be inconsistencies – attempts which 'tend to minimize the character's [Maria's] delusive projections, and give them the status of narrative events'.[42] For example, in trying to account for the uncertainty around the question of whether or not Darnford and Maria have met prior to their incarceration (a question left unresolved by the novel itself), Godwin also seems to rule out the possibility that Wollstonecraft was using the irreality generated by subjunctive tenses to foreground the imaginative dimension of Maria's investment in Darnford. O'Quinn's reading is ingenious, but still speculative. In Godwin's *St Leon*, however, we get a very explicit indication of the extent to which Wollstonecraft's critique of the imbrication of reading and domestic enclosure at the very least unsettled Godwin's increasing investment in the sanctity of bourgeois conjugality and privacy. David Simpson has noted the extent to which Wollstonecraft's gender politics sat uneasily with Godwin. In his *Memoirs* of Mary Wollstonecraft, Simpson writes, Godwin 'complained of her "rather masculine" sentiments and her "rigid, and somewhat Amazonian temper" at the same time as he dismissed her as a "female Werter"'.[43] In *St Leon*, published in 1799, two years after Wollstonecraft had died shortly after giving birth to their daughter Mary, Godwin attempted to recreate an idyllic conjugal scenario anchored around the figure of Marguerite de Damville, whom he modelled on Wollstonecraft and her ideas.[44]

Even more so than *Caleb Williams*, *St Leon* is a novel about the impossibility of rationality, reform, beneficence and enlightenment in public. The public cultures of the court, of feudal militarism, of the inquisition, of religious reformation and ultimately of market capitalism are all shown, at various points in the novel, to generate deeply irrational forms of collective consciousness and action. Throughout the novel the eponymous hero is constantly and compulsively drawn into public and seduced by his desire for public adoration. Entering public space, however, always occurs at the expense of the intimacy and honesty that binds his family together. St Leon, in other words, must betray the private sphere, his wife Marguerite and their children, to participate in public life: he must choose monadic isolation to the community of the family. All of this is made very clear when, after a period of uninterrupted familial tranquillity, the domestic idyll is disturbed by the arrival of an old man, an Archimago-type figure, who offers St Leon the philosopher's stone and the elixir of life, on the condition that he vow never to share the knowledge with his family (or anyone else). The acquisition of these secrets, apparently giving St Leon the ability to realize his grandiose public aspirations, also marks him as an alchemist, an illuminati, a projector and a conspirator, forcing him to withdraw himself from the domestic idyll in order to establish a predictably gendered public/private dichotomy:

The merchant does not call his wife into consultation upon his ventures; the statesman does not unfold to her his policy and his projects; the warrior does not take her advice upon the plan of the campaign; the poet does not concert with her his flights and episodes. To other men the domestic scene is the relaxation of their cares; when they enter it they dismiss the business of the day, and call another cause. I only have concentrated in it the whole of my existence. By this means I have extinguished in myself the true energy of the human character. A man can never be respectable in the eyes of the world or in his own, except so far as he stand by himself and is truly independent.[45]

The point of the novel, of course, is to demonstrate the error of this version of possessive individualism, and to maintain that true happiness and contentment lie in the sympathy and community fostered within the private sphere. St Leon's refusal to acknowledge this for most of the novel brings on the destruction of his family and the death of his wife. His drive towards the public sphere is written as pathological and addictive and in this respect the novel can be read as yet another allegorization of how the urge towards monadic gratification destroys the filial. This move away from public culture (which seems to include the court, market economics and political radicalism) announces Godwin's move towards a high Romanticism more typical of Wordsworth and Coleridge than of his own work throughout the preceding decade. Gary Kelly describes this as a 'new sensibility' that, he points out, is also very explicitly a recantation of an earlier critique of private life set out in *Political Justice*.[46] In the 'Preface' to the novel Godwin makes this very clear:

Some readers of my graver productions will perhaps, in perusing these little volumes, accuse me of inconsistency; the affections and the charities of private life being every where in this publication the topic of the warmest eulogium, while in the Enquiry Concerning Political Justice they seemed to be treated with no great degree of indulgence and favour. In answer to this objection, all I think it necessary to say on the present occasion is, that, for more than four years, I have been anxious for opportunity and leisure to modify some of the earlier chapters of that work in conformity to the sentiments inculcated in this.[47]

For the purposes of my discussion of Wollstonecraft, what is interesting here is the manner in which this revision also seems to fixate on and rewrite moments in Wollstonecraft's work, such that they are made to affirm the gendered semiotic that, it seems clear, Wollstonecraft fought so hard to destabilize. This is most evident when St Leon and Marguerite, as Maria and Darnford had done, read as a way of consolidating mutual understanding and intimacy.

We were both of us well acquainted with the most eminent poets and fine writers of modern times. But when we came to read them together, they presented themselves in a point of view in which they had never been seen by us before. It is, perhaps, more important that poetry, and everything that excites the imagination or appeals to the heart, should be read in solitude, than in society. But the true way to understand our author in these cases, is to employ each of these modes in succession. The terrible, the majestic, the voluptuous and the melting, are all of them, in a considerable degree, affairs of sympathy; and we never judge of them so infallibly, or with so much satisfaction, as when, in the presence of each other, the emotion is kindled in either bosom at the same instant, the eye-beams, pregnant with sentiment and meaning, involuntarily meet and mingle: the voice of the reader becomes modulated by the ideas of the author, and that of the hearer, by an accidental interjection of momentary comment or applause, confesses its accord.[48]

Together Marguerite and St Leon read Dante, Petrarch, the Troubadours and, revealingly, the letters of Eloisa and Abelard, the model for Rousseau's *La Nouvelle Héloïse*. But whereas Wollstonecraft had presented the space of meaningful reading as one that was ultimately intelligible as a limit to political awareness, Godwin seems to obfuscate the insights of *The Wrongs of Woman* with his unproblematic faith in the private as a solution to the dangers of public irrationality. His version of conjugal reading ratifies the private in terms of the kind of exchanges that, in Wollstonecraft's novel, were revealed to be continuous with the disorganization of feminist consciousness. In this way the radicality of Wollstonecraft's work – a radicality that consisted in pushing beyond the limits of affirmative culture and the myths of intimacy and love it fostered – is nullified and the horizon of rational communal activity again becomes tied to a mythology of privacy, intimacy and consumption that ultimately writes the nuclear family as a form natural society pitted against the corruption of the public.

In Godwin's fictionalization of Wollstonecraft, rational femininity consists in dutifully fulfilling the functions of mother and wife, and most importantly in saving (or attempting to save) man from his own irrational drives in the public sphere. The novel tirelessly plays out this thematic: Marguerite de Damville is the embodiment of both a moral and a domestic economy that is defined against the dangers of the court, the city and the market. We can see the same typically Romantic gestures of retreat and renunciation played out in Thelwall's temporary withdrawal from political life at the end of the decade. For both Godwin and Thelwall the renunciation of the political for the private also required a strategic rewriting of the gender politics of the preceding decade. Moments like those glimpsed in *The Wrongs of Woman*, at which a nascent feminism threatens to destabilize the dichotomization of private and public space and the forms of discursive practice that normalize this dichotomization, have to be either ignored, misunderstood or rewritten so that, once again, private life becomes the limit of feminist activity. At the end of the 1790s I think we can see very clearly the process in which political impulses that threaten to exceed the limits of a bourgeois cultural revolution are recoded in terms of an aesthetic that we recognize as Romantic. This imbrication of the conjugal and the literary speaks to a sense of a missed opportunity. In terms of the critique of affirmative culture, which I have argued is central to the development of Wollstonecraft's work, Godwin's sublimation of the political into an aestheticized privacy can only be read as regressive.

6

Conjugal Love and the Enlightenment Subject: the Colonial Context of Non-identity in Maria Edgeworth's *Belinda*

The publishing history of Maria Edgeworth's second novel, *Belinda*, registers the anxieties of a society intensely involved in debates over the abolition of slavery and the proper management of British colonies in the West Indies. By the time the novel went into its third edition in 1810, the depiction of interracial marriage in the previous two editions (1801 and 1802) had been all but erased, principally at the suggestion of Edgeworth's father.[1] In these earlier editions of the novel Juba, the African servant of a Jamaican plantation owner, marries an English farmer's daughter and settles with her as a tenant on an English estate. The 1810 text removed the trauma of miscegenation for a reactionary audience not by omitting the Juba character completely, but by replacing him in this conjugal scenario with the ubiquitously named James Jackson. As Suvendrini Perera points out, this alteration appeased the most recalcitrant anti-abolitionist fears about racial mixing and the integrity of British women in a metropolis overrun by freed slaves.[2] The revisions do not efface Edgeworth's own abolitionist sympathies, which are evident elsewhere in the novel, but they do affect the politics of the text in ways that might at first seem unexpected. In *Belinda* Juba does not just participate in a narrative of developing egalitarian sentiment, he also demonstrates that a former slave, mired in the fetishism of Afro-Caribbean culture, can be transformed into a subject capable of displaying the rationality and autonomy that apparently typify an enlightened culture. In a novel of domestic enlightenment, in which characters move inexorably towards the

181

ideal of conjugal love and harmonious private space, Juba's marriage implicitly establishes the universality of these ideals and their
ability to mediate a community of equals comfortably beyond the
effects of prejudice, power and exploitation. Domestic enlightenment, in other words, takes on a genuinely world historical
significance largely through the presence of Juba as an index of its
ability to assimilate racial difference.

The text's gesture towards a racially integrated society, however,
indicates more than just liberal, humanitarian sentiment. As abolitionist texts from the period indicate, attempts to reform the West
Indian slave economy were motivated as much by economics as by
political benevolence. At the end of the eighteenth century it was
increasingly apparent that slave-labour was not only inefficient, but
also prone to various forms of non-cooperation and insurgency.
Many abolitionists accordingly argued that the economic benefits of
colonial production could only be guaranteed by converting the
master–slave relationship, which now appeared as a feudal relic,
into a contractual relationship between employer and employee. In
short the racialized hierarchies of the slave system were to be sublimated into the apparently egalitarian culture of wage-labour. If this
sublimation assumed the normalcy and universality of the bourgeois individual, it was also premised on the marginalization of
communal and cultural identifications that seemed to refuse or con-
tradict this norm. At stake was not just an enlightened subject and
its abstract principles of rationality, but more importantly a mode of
production fundamentally dependent on the agency of free and
equal individuals negotiating their own emphatically private interests in the marketplace. In *Belinda*, I want to argue, the apparent
universality of bourgeois individualism is figured through the conventions of the domestic novel, in which marriage and harmonious
private life not only mandate certain behavioural norms, but
also predicate resistant and otherwise unassimilable traces of non-
identity that must be renounced as the condition of enlightenment.[3]

Conjugal love and the integrity of domestic, familial bonds are
represented in the novel as inseparable from the norms of rationality, privacy and interiority that characterize what I am calling here
the enlightenment subject – the 'freeman' of the marketplace no
less than the free will of philosophical modernity. Conjugal love
measures the ability of Edgeworth's characters to interact independently of irrational motivations, to display the freedom and
autonomy that suggest obedience to innate laws of desire unbe-

guiled by the appearances of the phenomenal world. In this respect
Edgeworth's novel is consistent with those eighteenth-century
conduct manuals and educational tracts which, as Nancy
Armstrong has argued, understood domesticity and in particular
the 'domestic woman' as the counterpoints to the errors of an aristocratic culture oriented to a world of fashionable appearances.[4]
Indeed Edgeworth wrote a number of pedagogical texts, *Practical
Education* written in collaboration with her father being perhaps the
best known, designed to consolidate a subject uncompromised by
the decadence of fashionable society – a subject that, precisely
insofar as it was considered 'natural', could become, as Armstrong
suggests, a 'dominant social reality'.[5] Yet non-identity in *Belinda* is
more overdetermined than this repudiation of aristocratic culture
suggests. In opposition to the rational freedom of conjugal love and
the domestic woman, the novel's characters are constantly assailed
by fetishistic fashion and ritual objects that embody the non-
modern insofar as they encourage forms of social life based on the
suspension of rational individual choice. While the novel directly
implicates Afro-Carribean fetishism (obeah) in this notion of the
non-modern, its figuration of non-identity as primarily fetishistic
also correlates this with forms of political and sexual difference that
appear both latent in and residual in regard to the culture of developing capitalism. The process by which rationality overcomes these
various forms of fetishism is also the process in which subjects shed
their illusions and emerge simply as they would be were they in
Rousseau's state of nature, at which time they are suited to obey
their own proclivities in the formation of uncoerced conjugal
relations.

The novel ultimately invites us to read conjugality and fetishism
as the poles around which enlightenment culture organizes the
assimilation of difference, of potentially resistant forms of social life,
into the economy of capitalist exchange, in which individuals are
understood as possessive, private entities rooted in a secure and
humanizing domestic sphere. It essentially recodes the racialized
dichotomies of slavery around a new set of oppositional terms that,
as we will see, are far from the political innocence that Juba's
marriage might suggest. In establishing an opposition between
conjugality and fetishism the text epitomizes a kind of late-
eighteenth- and early-nineteenth-century writing that we might call
enlightenment pastiche, in that it incorporates other contemporary
texts and motifs, and subordinates them to a coherent and seamless

narrative which can then function as an allegorization of enlightenment. This quality constitutes a large part of the text's seductiveness, but it also points us to the more explicitly political and economic issues obliquely notated in its discursive appropriations. *Belinda* is a fascinating text partly because it rephrases the political debates of the 1790s in a way that makes an explicit connection between political radicalism in Britain and anti-colonial insurgency outside it: both are represented as forms of irrationality at odds with a genuinely enlightened culture based on the private sphere. In this respect it is possible to argue that the novel, while clearly committed to a bourgeois cultural revolution, is also extremely aware of the political forces that, insofar as they destabilize bourgeois norms, need to be contained or marginalized. In *Belinda* the triumph of conjugality also figures the disorganization of forms of political activity in excess of the interests of an emerging bourgeoisie.

The following chapter, in pursuing the novel's intertextuality, tries to bring the relationship between domestic enlightenment, colonialism and emerging capitalism into sharper focus. If the novel establishes non-identity as a refusal of conjugality, this already intertextual writing of non-identity will also need to be contextualized in terms of late-eighteenth-century representations of resistance and insurgency in colonial Jamaica, since these crucially inform Edgeworth's vision of the transition from fetishism to conjugality, and relatedly from slave-labour to wage-labour. But while the novel does seem to me to symptomatize the ideology of early capitalism in its increasingly global form, its intertextuality also prompts an examination of the ways in which valorized images of conjugality suggest their affinity with affirmative cultural production. The novel, in other words, is not simply a seamless rehearsal of bourgeois norms: its own formal organization invites us to examine the ways in which bourgeois culture seeks to integrate political and social difference into the forms of privacy, monadic subjectivity and possessive individuality that I have discussed in the previous chapters.

THE FAMILY AND ITS OTHER

In *Belinda* the marriage plot is also one in which misconceptions affecting the behaviour and modifying the apparently natural inclinations of the principal characters are gradually eliminated. The novel's eponymous heroine, needless to say, reveals this dynamic in its most typical form. When she makes her debut in London society, under the tutelage of Lady Delacour, she is immediately confronted with the error under which she is dismissed by her potential suitor, Clarence Hervey. As the niece of the matchmaking Mrs Stanhope she is read by the public in which she circulates as an object to be hawked on the marriage market – literally a commodity. '"Belinda Portman, and her accomplishments, I'll swear, were as well advertised, as Packwoods razor strops,"' she overhears at a masquerade (*Belinda*, p. 25). A little later Hervey himself repeats this sentiment: '"Belinda Portman's a composition of art and affectation"' (*Belinda*, p. 26). The main story line of the novel is that in which Belinda and Clarence assert their own true natures independently of the other economies of value to which they are subjected, in order finally to be able to interact without the mediation of misleading social conventions or expectations. In order to interact freely and rationally both must exit the camera obscura of a public sphere in which women are treated as objects mediating and motivating the transference of status and wealth. The dignity of the subject apparently withstands and transcends its mediated public appearance, and its intrinsic humanity must be defined in rigorous opposition to this. Simply as themselves are Belinda and Clarence equipped to realize conjugal love as an extension of what is most fundamental to them, allowing them, by the end of the novel, to conform to the model of familial harmony supplied throughout by the Percivals. This dynamic is repeated numerous times in the novel: in Lady and Lord Delacour's reconciliation, in Juba and Lucy's marriage, and in Virginia St Pierre's rediscovery of Captain Sunderland. In each case the drive towards conjugality involves the realization and exercise of a freedom apparently thwarted by social convention, and the assertion of an authenticity erased by the contingencies of public interaction, fashionable society and the prejudices inherent in both.

Representations of the family as the index of a nature unadulterated by convention or habit are, as we have seen, a commonplace of eighteenth-century aesthetic and political philosophy. Edmund Burke's 1756 vision of a natural society based on heteronormative sentiment, *A Vindication of Natural Society*, expresses this very clearly. In *Belinda* Anne Percival expresses the connection between conjugality and the ability of potential spouses to reveal their 'real' or 'natural' characters to each other independently of the deceptions of fashionable society, indicating the extent to which Burkean notions of natural society were assimilated into codes of conduct.

> In the slight and frivolous intercourse, which fashionable belles usually have with those fashionable beaux who call themselves their lovers, it is surprising that they can discover any thing of each other's real character. Indeed they seldom do; and this probably is the cause why there are so many unsuitable and unhappy marriages. A woman who has an opportunity of seeing her lover in private society, in domestic life, has infinite advantages; for if she has any sense, and he has any sincerity, the real character of both may be developed.
>
> (*Belinda*, p. 240)

In this passage the possibility of authentic subjectivity, of revealing one's 'real' character, is entirely contingent on one's distance from the deceptive world of public appearances. Yet Anne Percival's stress on the authenticity of character revealed in 'private society', like Burke's vision of natural society, is also a function of a specific view of public life as necessarily performative – a matter of taking up roles and putting on masks. Her disparaging description of 'belles' and 'beaux' figures the whole gamut of socially mediated distinctions which seem to signify a negated reserve of unmediated humanity: master/servant, colonizer/colonized, African/European, etc. In private lovers come together simply as human beings, as 'ends' in themselves rather than as functions of the economic or instrumental imperatives that force them to play out specific roles in which the baneful effects of power, exploitation and inequality are realized. The view that private life allows one to realize the bedrock of one's own humanity is sustained, it seems, in direct relationship to the degree to which the public sphere is conceptualized as the burdensome imposition of essentially false value systems. It is thus that the masquerade party becomes a microcosmic representation of public life for eighteenth-century writers interested in establishing the certainty of a self existing somewhere beyond these deceptions.

Throughout *Belinda* this version of the natural subject is also juxtaposed to forms of life which represent a deviation from nature precisely because they refuse or transgress the notions of propriety and responsibility embodied in the family. Revealingly these are connected to a substratum of difference intelligible as both fetishistic and atavistic: as savage not in the sense of Rousseau's primitivism, but in the sense of a more threatening and belligerent kind of non-identity. Under the corrupting influence of the cross-dressing Harriet Freke (whose very name suggests her heterodoxy) Lady Delacour's abnegation of maternal responsibility and, with the exception of a neglected daughter, her telling inability to sustain children beyond early infancy, is enacted in the literal corruption of her natural, maternal body. As a result of a duelling accident her breast has apparently become cancerous, not only leaving her unable to function as a wife and mother, but establishing a spectral identification with the figure of the Amazon, which recurs through the novel, and throughout late-eighteenth-century culture more generally, as the embodiment of a kind of feminine *jouissance* dangerously in excess of conjugal norms. The Amazon hypostatizes this excess in the mutilation of the maternal body, viscerally materializing the violation of an abstract notion of nature. Despite the novel's critique of Rousseau's views on female education, embodied in Clarence Hervey's seclusion of Virginia and his dream of fashioning the perfect wife, it is evident that Edgeworth nevertheless imagines rational femininity in terms of the maternal responsibilities that Lady Delacour initially renounces. As Elizabeth Kowaleski-Wallace writes, 'the novel insists on the inevitable appeal, indeed, the very "naturalness," of a particular domestic arrangement in which supreme satisfaction is to be garnered from the intimate relationship of a biological mother to her children'.[6]

Freke, on the other hand, enacts her refusal of stable gender roles in her propensity to dress and act as a man, and in her unmistakable homosocial inclinations. In a debate with Percival she declares herself a 'champion for the Rights of Women' in a conspicuous allusion to Wollstonecraft's *A Vindication of the Rights of Woman*.[7] Yet while Freke's declaration suggests abolitionist sentiments – '"I hate slavery!"' – it is also associated with a refusal of sociability and the anarchy of Jacobinism, the French Revolution and the subsequent Terror – '"Vive la liberté!"' (*Belinda*, p. 229). '"Should we find things much improved by tearing away what has been called the decent drapery of life?"' Percival reproaches her: '"Drapery, if you ask me my opinion," cried Mrs. Freke, "drapery, whether wet or dry, is the most confoundedly indecent thing in the world"' (*Belinda*, p. 230). The reference to Edmund Burke is unmistakable, and revealing when pursued. In his *Reflections on the Revolution in France* drapery, itself a kind of satorial deception, refers to the necessary conventions of sociability which are also, paradoxically, the natural affections of heteronormative privacy, highlighting the undecidability of nature and convention in Burke's political philosophy, and indeed in Edgeworth's novel. Describing the moral culture of the revolution, Burke writes:

> All the pleasing illusions, which made power gentle, and obedience liberal, which harmonized the different shades of life, and which, by a bland assimilation, incorporated into politics the sentiments which beautify and soften private society, are to be dissolved by this new conquering empire of light and reason. All the decent drapery of life is to be rudely torn off. All the super-added ideas, furnished from the wardrobe of a moral imagination, which the heart owns, and the understanding ratifies, as necessary to cover the defects of our naked shivering nature, and to raise it to dignity in our own estimation, are to be exploded as a ridiculous, absurd, and antiquated fashion.
>
> (*RRF*, p. 171)

The nature apparently revealed in this process of stripping is also an anti-nature. It is not compatible with the moral imagination, the heart does not own it, and it suggests the production of the reason that in Burke's anti-Jacobin writings is a euphemism for artificiality and specious political sophistry. Burke points not to a resplendent natural body, but to an atavistic regression, a state of moral abjection that elsewhere in the *Reflections* he will cast in quite specific anthropological terms. Describing the procession that led Louis XVI to Paris, he writes, it was 'a spectacle more resembling a procession of American savages, entering into Onondaga, after some of their murders called victories, and leading into hovels hung round with scalps, their captives, overpowered with the scoffs and buffets of women as ferocious as themselves, much more than it resembled the triumphal pomp of a civilized martial nation' (*RRF*, p. 159).

The naked body suggested in Freke's hatred of drapery is similarly savage, and indeed the metaphorics of Freke's exchange with Percival, and of the larger debates regarding sexual and political radicalism to which they refer, point to the problem inherent in the representation of the subject of uncoerced conjugality. The opposition between natural affections in private and the corrupted performativity of public life is rendered incoherent by the threatening image of a savagery that is an atavistic regression, a refusal of moral codes, but which is also the result of social and philosophical decadence, of culture in excess of moral decency. The impulse, shared by Burke and Edgeworth, to represent political dissidence (whether Wollstonecraftian or Jacobin) in terms of atavism, thus threatens to disrupt the production of meaning in their own texts, plunging the dichotomization of nature and convention into doubt. Just as the savage is both atavistic and contaminated by an excess of convention (whether it be fashion or philosophical speculation), so too is the natural, conjugal self – the domestic woman – the result of a disciplined adherence to regulative behavioural norms. This problem is underscored by a text like *Practical Education*, in which the production of the self emerges as an entirely social process. It is thus that a novel like *Belinda* must effectively neutralize the excess of a character like Freke in order to secure its coherence against the uncertainties inherent in its own representational strategies. Freke is not only a counterpoint to images of healthy conjugality, she is also an externalization and localization of the undecidability inherent in the nature/culture opposition on which the novel is largely based.

By asserting the connection between what G. J. Barker-Benfield describes as Lady Delacour's 'diseased-breast-cum Amazonianism',[8] Freke's masculinity and the dire Burkean vision of patricidal libertarian politics which eschews filial loyalties and moral sentiment, Edgeworth produces a writing of non-identity defined primarily by its antithetical relationship to a stable and sequestered domestic sphere also understood as a metaphor for the polity in general. The image of the militant female, the Amazon, is, of course, more overdetermined than this. As Laura Brown has argued, the figures of the Amazon and the masculine, cross-dressing female had currency throughout the eighteenth century, implying a simultaneously gendered and racialized version of difference, but also embodying the violence of the first phase of British imperial consolidation. In Brown's discussion Defoe's *Roxana* presents this confluence most typically. The Amazon trope is deployed, through the character of Roxana herself, to represent the violence of mercantile accumulation and of public economic agency as a murderous recoil upon filial bonds and the integrity of the family unit: 'As an Amazon, Roxana figures violence, and violence materializes at the end of the novel in the cold-blooded murder of her daughter by Amy, Roxana's surrogate and a successful "Woman of Business" in her own right.'[9] It is revealing then that Freke's version of the

'Rights of Woman' echoes Roxana's own manifesto of liberated femininity as a rejection of the 'Laws of Marriage' and an endorsement of a hybridized gender identity: '"I would be a *Man-Woman*,"' Roxana proclaims,[10] which is precisely how Freke is stigmatized throughout *Belinda* – Juba refers to her as a 'man-woman' and the label seems to stick (Belinda, p. 219). By the end of the eighteenth century the cross-dressed Amazon had become a culturally central image of non-identity. After the French Revolution and Burke's momentous production of Jacobinism as an abnegation of filial affections, the family, conjugality, and the integrity of the private become figures of national identity and integrity in the face of the Napoleonic threat. By having Freke ventriloquize Wollstonecraft's second *Vindication*, which was also read as an implicit defence of Jacobin politics, Edgeworth conspicuously positions her own text in proximity to the Burkean alliance of national duty and filial ties, while echoing the more confrontational polemics of anti-Jacobin texts like Richard Polwhele's 1798 doggerel *The Unsex'd Females* which, as Claudia Johnson argues, 'links women's political heterodoxy to sexual aberrance'.[11]

But if this substratum of non-identity seems to be hypostatized in Lady Delacour, whose own private space is a grotesque projection of her abject, non-maternal body, non-identity also remains oddly apocryphal throughout the novel. Freke's Jacobin manifesto doesn't fool anyone. Indeed before the ever-rational Belinda her diatribe is an insubstantial rehearsal of clichés that seem to have no meaningful substantive referent, confirming the earlier analogy between the popular oracle 'Mrs W–', the modern dealer in art magic' who foresees a 'lawless lover' for Lady Delacour, and Wollstonecraftian libertarianism in excess of the norms of conjugal responsibility Edgeworth defended.[12] And just as Wollstonecraftian feminism is portrayed as insubstantial populism and superstitious magic, performed with all the trappings of 'German *horrifications*' (*Belinda*, p. 47), it is, relatedly, unclear whether Freke's sexual heterodoxy is intrinsic or a performative series of signifiers – male clothing, whips etc., all of which have a fetishistic quality to them – with, again, no stable referent. In fact this seems to be Edgeworth's point. The unnaturalness of Freke is her performativity, the undecidability that erases the possibility of unmediated subjectivity with a series of public gestures that enact the irrelevance of the whole idea of intrinsic value. In contrast rationality is bestowed throughout the text only as objects, gestures and signs are properly decoded in terms of their real significance, reestablished in terms of some absolute transparency in which they are made synonymous with a referent. This interpretive process penetrates the magic of appearances, the fetishistic nature of public signifiers, with a rational display of causal relations. Insofar as it dispels error, this process also releases intrinsic subjectivity from the fetters of false consciousness. Lady Delacour, for example, only needs to discover modern medical science through Dr X and renounce the arcane practices of quack medicine, to cure her ailment, recover her 'natural' body and her corresponding capacity for functional conjugality.

It is precisely by representing non-identity as the insubstantial rehearsal of signs and gestures that the novel can contain the rhetorical disruptions that its representation of Freke creates, and thus guarantee its own coherence. Indeed in this respect Freke can be read as figuring, synecdochically, the crisis of signification intrinsic to the novel and readable in the undecidability of its own writing of the nature/culture opposition. By localizing this crisis in her the novel strives to contain its own non-identity with the certainties of its moral and social worldview. The collusion of the atavistic and the decadent in Freke is thus understood explicitly as a matter of signification, as a dubiety in the way signs retain meaning. It is thus that non-identity in the novel is also presented as a kind of fetishism, the state of being irrationally enthralled by objects and appearances that retain no intrinsic value except in the beguiled and infantilized consciousness of the fetishist. In *Belinda* the critique of fashion that sees the performativity and triviality of public appearances as a threat to domestic stability is also, and perhaps more importantly in a novel preoccupied with the West Indian sugar plantations, a critique of fetishism that directly implicates forms of political expression specific to Afro-Caribbean communities. The novel can make its egalitarian gesture in the bracketing of race precisely because the substratum of non-identity locatable in Freke is rewritten not as intrinsic alterity, but as the play of surface appearances and the false consciousness resulting from it. Hence Juba, by renouncing the fetishism of his own culture, can also return to the bedrock of universal subjectivity and take his place in the conjugal idyll.[13]

Again it is Freke who is associated with the irrationality of appearances in the narrative of Juba's enlightenment, this time not as a man-woman, but as the equally militant obeah-woman. When Juba inexplicably falls into a state of melancholic taciturnity that he interprets as life threatening, the cause of his trouble turns out to be his belief that he has been pursued to England by the powers of obeah, an Ashanti-based belief system prevalent in the slave and free Afro-Caribbean, or Maroon communities of the West Indies, and thought to motivate acts of anti-colonial violence, from banditry to open rebellion:

> with a sort of reluctant horrour, he told that the figure of an old woman, all in flames, had appeared to him in his bedchamber at Harrowgate every night, and that he was sure she was one of the obeah-women of his own country, who had pursued him to Europe to revenge his having once, when he was a child, trampled upon an egg shell that contained some of her poisons.
>
> (*Belinda*, p. 221)

It is left to Belinda to disabuse Juba of his superstitious affiliations to the non-modern, with a demonstration of the means by which Freke had maliciously fabricated the appearance of obeah magic by drawing a phosphorescent head. This process of decoding will be repeated when Lady Delacour is haunted by a vision she believes is the ghost of Colonel Lawless, but which once again turns out to be one of Freke's 'frolics' (*Belinda*, p. 311). The rational demonstration of Juba's error recalls Rousseau's demonstration of the scientific principles informing the conjurer's magic in the fairground passage of *Émile*, one of many instances in which the young Émile is led to discern the real causal mechanisms informing the beguiling and explicitly fetishistic appearances of the phenomenal world.[14] Edgeworth's novel links the resolution of conjugal story lines to a similar practice of explication. In this process non-identity is reduced to the status of error. It retains no intrinsic quality of its own, which is why its sublimation is not only possible, but virtually inevitable.

OBEAH AND THE AFRO-CARIBBEAN CONTEXT

The presence of obeah in the novel refers to a large body of documentary material written in and about Jamaica itself, revealing the political context in which Edgeworth's writing of identity and non-identity must be read.[15] In *Belinda* the everyday experience of metropolitan affluence is thoroughly implicated in colonial production.

The domestic interiors of the novel are full of commodities, like Mariott's macaw for instance, imported from the colonies, while Clarence Hervey's viability as a public wit is largely dependent on his acquisition of the knowledge culled from the process of imperial consolidation: 'from Irwin to sir William Jones, from Spain to India, he passed with admirable celerity, and seized all that could adorn his course from Indian antiquities or Asiatic researches' (*Belinda*, p. 113). The appearance of obeah as a further importation, and a sign of militant non-identity and anti-colonial insurgency, suggests the urgency of sublimating colonial subjects into the apparently egalitarian and rational culture of capitalist production. It also highlights the inefficiency of the residual model of centralized authority (something like the great chain of being) acted out by Lady Delacour and Hervey as a piece of Elizabethan pageantry. After defeating a Spanish traveller in a game of chess (the British conquered Jamaica from the Spanish, we should remember), Hervey assumes the character of Sir Walter Raleigh while Lady Delacour appears dressed as Queen Elizabeth to receive his tribute (*Belinda*, p. 114). The rehearsal of a fetishistic mode of political authority based on the magical appearance of the monarch obliquely points to the realities of colonial government that, for a late eighteenth-century British public, were represented in the image of obeah. By the end of the eighteenth century the prevalence of apparently obeah-inspired slave rebellions in the West Indian plantations demanded of colonial administrators and planters alike an entirely different modality of political control oriented to the assimilation of slave-labour into a binding social contract, thereby reducing the risks of insurgency and other forms of economic non-cooperation. How rational was it, after all, for a British population in the West Indies to expect the loyalty of a slave population solely on the basis of its assertion of arbitrary authority? As critics of the plantocracy constantly pointed out, colonial power in the West Indies was self-defeating precisely because the master–slave relation established a situation in which, as James Ramsay writes, 'to the degree of his capacity of coercion, every man becomes his own legislator, and erects his interest, or his caprice, into a law for regulating his conduct to his neighbour'.[16] The idea that 'power constitutes right', in other words, authorized insurrection as much as it did slavery. Indeed abolitionist texts in the period were frequently informed by an awareness not just of the brutality of slavery, but by the idea that slavery was simply not effective as a mode of management, precisely because it could not expect the loyalty of its labour force. Accordingly, British opposition to slavery is characterized by the convenient co-dependence of humanitarian sentiment and political economy: free-labour is not only more efficient than slave-labour, but the relations of production in which free-labour introjects the laws of property and the idea of contractual obligation guarantee the stability of the production process itself. In this respect the sublimation of slavery into wage-labour actually consolidates productivity, ensures the security of colonial property and political relations, and expands the global market for domestic produce.[17] The abolitionist characterization of the plantocracy epitomized this duplicitous critique: it pointed out the emphatically pre-modern, feudal structure of control in the colonies, evoking images of the dark ages and of so-called Asiatic despotism that suggested economic inefficiency as much as they did brutality. Obeah signifies a legitimation crisis for colonial society. It raises the issues of effective management and counterinsurgency as inseparable, and demands not so much the modernization of the slaves, but the modernization of the relations of production in which they exist.

Edgeworth's novel footnotes Bryan Edwards's widely read *History of the West Indies* as her source on obeah. In Edwards's text, as in numerous other accounts of militant Maroon societies, slave revolts and popular banditry in colonial Jamaica, obeah represents the recalcitrant core of cultural difference motivating acts of violent insurgency against the plantocracy.[18] It implies by extension the failure of colonialism to forge a mode of hegemony able to contain the political desire of a subjugated population, and the inherent dangers of a racial apartheid unable to effectively assimilate slaves into a regime of time-work discipline. Though obeah had a constant presence in accounts of Maroon insurgency in Jamaica, it was not really until the 1760 slave uprising known as 'Tacky's revolt' that it became the object of colonial counterinsurgency in a concerted way. Edward Long, one of Edwards's principal sources, devotes some attention to the relationship between obeah and insurrection, describing the confluence of conspiratorial enclaves and fetishism as follows:

> When assembled for the purposes of conspiracy, the obeiah-man, after various ceremonies, draws a little blood from everyone present; this is mixed in a bowl with gunpowder and grave dirt; the fetishe or oath is administered, by which they solemnly pledge themselves to inviolable secrecy, fidelity to their chiefs,

and to wage perpetual war against their enemies ... If defeated in their first endeavours, they still retain the solicitude of fulfilling all that they have sworn; dissembling their malice under a seeming submissive carriage, and all the exterior signs of innocence and cheerfulness, until the convenient time arrives, when they think it practicable to retrieve their former miscarriage.[19]

In this passage obeah not only enacts a kind of filial bond that seems intractable to Long, but also accounts for the always concealed resentment of the apparently submissive slave. What Homi Bhabha would call a kind of colonial mimicry, or 'sly civility', is ultimately referable to the injunctions of obeah.[20]

As both Edwards and Long indicate, obeah was perceived as a central motivating factor in the 1760 revolt, and indeed the colonial authorities went to some lengths to dispel its influence on the insurgents in the course of reasserting control of the island:

in the year 1760, when a very formidable insurrection of the Koromantyn or Gold Coast Negroes broke out in the parish of St. Mary, and spread through almost every other district of the island, an old Koromantyn Negro, the chief instigator and oracle of the insurgents in that parish, who had administered the fetish or solemn oath to the conspirators, and furnished them with a magical preparation which was to render them invulnerable, was fortunately apprehended, convicted, and hung up with all his feathers and trumperies about him; and his execution struck the insurgents with a general panick, from which they never afterwards recovered.[21]

The execution of the obeah practitioner is the political reality behind the demystification of obeah enacted by Belinda as part of Juba's enlightenment. It was intended to prove decisively the impotence of the fetish and thus to undermine the insurgents' cohesiveness and commitment. Obeah trials and executions were not isolated events in the wake of 1760, and a bill passed that year in fact names obeah as a crime punishable by death or transportation.[22] Yet attempts to dispel the power of obeah were not limited to these displays of judicial mastery obliterating the power of the fetish in the symbolic reassertion of colonial legitimacy and authority. As Edwards relates, other strategies included the display of European science as a power superior to that of the obeah practitioner: 'Upon other *Obeah-men*, who were apprehended at that time, various experiments were made with electrical machines and magic lanterns, but with very little effect, except on one, who, after receiving some very severe shocks, acknowledged that "his master's *Obi* exceeded his own."'[23] This is a bizarre and revealing passage. The power of European science is itself impotent until it is converted into a medium of violence. The enlightenment enacts itself as a parody in the colonies, forced to resort to the tawdry display of its 'magic' in a manner similar to Rousseau's fairground conjurer, forced to hypostatize its own metaphorics in the staged, technologistic production of en-lightenment and, failing both of these, finally forced to realize its superiority by extorting submission to the fetish of progress. The explication of scientific causality that marks Edgeworth's novel and Rousseau's *Émile* is repeated but also undermined insofar as scientific causality is itself reduced to the cult of technology and the technology of torture.

In Edwards's account of the Jamaican Maroon societies obeah is closely connected with the other dominant sign of non-identity in the West Indian colonies – the absence of strong conjugal bonds. Along with an immersion in obeah fetishism, Edwards relates the violence to which women were apparently subjected in Maroon communities and, beyond this, the brutality informing every aspect of their family life. Maroon wives, suffering under the neglect of polygamy, are treated 'as so many beasts of burden', while their children are subjected to what Edwards describes as a kind of patriarchy gone mad:

> This spirit of brutality, which the Maroons always displayed towards their wives, extended in some degree to their children. The parental authority was at all times most harshly exerted; but more especially towards the females. I have been assured that it was not an uncommon circumstance for a father, in a fit of rage or drunkenness, to seize his own infant, which had offended him by crying, and dash it against a rock, with a degree of violence which often proved fatal.[24]

This absence of filial affection masks the moral depravity and non-identity of the Maroon, and Edwards's retelling of it participates in the form of imperial subject-predication which typified Burke's impeachment speech: colonial history is written in Spivak's sentence 'White men are saving brown women from brown men.'[25] The absence of safe, sequestered private spaces in Maroon communities is literally enacted in what Edwards describes as the sanctioned violation of private, filial relations and private bodies – the violent reduction of the private to the public, embodied in fathers forcing their daughters into prostitution, forcing them to become 'public' women:

> Nothing can more strikingly demonstrate the forlorn and abject condition of the young women among the Maroons, than the circumstance which every gentleman, who has visited them on festive occasions, or for the gratification of curiosity, knows to be true; the offering their own daughters, by the first men among them, to their visitors; and bringing poor girls forward, with or without their consent, for the purpose of prostitution.[26]

It is worth pointing out the extreme ambiguity of the colonial subject (the gentlemen) referred to in this passage. While Edwards registers his moral outrage as a form of colonial paternalism analogous to the mode of predication Spivak describes, we can also read a colonial sex industry lurking in the idea of the curious gentlemen visitor. What is repressed in Edwards's valorization of family space and his criticism of Maroon communities is precisely the transgressive desire of the colonial subject itself. The writing of non-identity, the confluence of filial depravity and obeah as inherently premodern, can only be sustained through this repression, which ensures the production of the European subject as a morally endowed agent of benevolent paternalism.

Edgeworth's 1802 story 'The Grateful Negro', set in the colonial context constantly alluded to by *Belinda*, brings the connections between obeah, conjugality and insurgency into more coherent and articulate ideological proximity. Like the other stories in *Popular Tales*, 'The Grateful Negro' is a tale of propitious economic management as much as it is one of paternalism. The story begins by introducing two plantation owners – Jefferies, who 'considered the negroes as an inferior species, incapable of gratitude, disposed to treachery, and to be roused from their natural indolence by force',[27] and Edwards, a benevolent reformer who opposes slavery and advocates in its place the gradual conversion of the slave system into one of contractual wage-labour, carried out by freemen: '"If we hired negroes for labourers, instead of purchasing them for slaves, do you think they would not work as well as they do now? Does any negro, under the fear of the overseer, work harder than a Birmingham journeyman, or a Newcastle collier, who toil for themselves and their families?"'[28] Accordingly, Edwards encourages the private cultivation of land by his slaves and places considerable emphasis on the related cultivation of the virtues of private life outside of the production processes essential to the everyday workings of the plantation. The role of conjugality in all of this is foregrounded when Edwards buys two slaves from Jefferies, Caesar and Clara, in order that they can marry and be spared the vicissitudes of the market in which their violent separation impends. The gratitude Caesar feels towards his new master is a direct extension of conjugal love, and now conflicts with his prior commitment to an insurgent conspiracy, the object of which is to 'extirpate every white man, woman, and child, in the island'.[29] The success of the conspiracy now depends on the other insurgents compromising Caesar's loyalty to Edwards, and enforcing his involvement in a plan that is now apparently incompatible with the quasi-contractual arrangements of reciprocal benefit that reign on Edwards's plantation, and relatedly with the quasi-autonomy that his slaves experience in regard to residual communal and ritual ties. As one might expect, after having read *Belinda*, a fanatical obeah woman who, it turns out, is the chief instigator of this intended rebellion, is enlisted to extort Caesar's loyalty by threatening the integrity of the conjugal idyll he and Clara constitute. When Clara, as Juba had done, sinks into a melancholic lethargy, it is because she believes Caesar will die if he does not perform the obeah-woman's bidding.

Ultimately the fetishistic practices of obeah cannot erode the bond forged between Caesar and Edwards, a bond that is consolidated by the trust Edwards places in his slave when he gives Caesar a knife to prune a tamarind tree. This moment is one of highly symbolic exchange in which the transference of the knife is also the assertion of a cosmopolitan community in which the pathos of Edwards's apparently naive belief in the possibility of equality and intrinsic humanity solicits a typically sympathetic response from Caesar.

Caesar had no knife. 'Here is mine for you,' said Mr. Edwards. 'It is very sharp,' added he, smiling; 'but I am not one of those masters who are afraid to trust their negroes with sharp knives.'

These words were spoken with perfect simplicity: Mr. Edwards had no suspicion, at this time, of what was passing in the negro's mind. Caesar received the knife without uttering a syllable; but no sooner was Mr. Edwards out of sight than he knelt down, and, in a transport of gratitude, swore that, with this knife, he would stab himself to the heart sooner than betray his master![30]

Edwards's own apparently suicidal gesture, he almost dares Caesar to kill him, is also one of republican virtue in which the citizen would rather die than see his cherished ideal of civic reciprocity compromised. Caesar, in sympathy, similarly vows his commitment to this model of virtue, preferring death to betrayal, though it is revealing that the authority of the European character enables an unconscious performance of self-sacrificing virtue, while the African is obliged to a kind of performative excess – a point I will return to below. This exchange consolidates an affiliative bond that erodes recalcitrant cultural difference and transports Caesar into a realm that allows him to assume identity with the plantation owner. In a myth of civic origins colonizer and colonized come together simply as men, and the intrinsic humanity that informs the private space of conjugality shared by Caesar and Clara can be extended beyond these confines as, in principle, an identification with the intrinsic humanity of other contractual parties in public.[31] This equality is both the premise and the fiction of wage-labour as a form of contractual obligation. The moment at which Caesar alerts Edwards to the impending revolt, the moment at which he quite literally becomes a native informant, consigns both racial apartheid and its corollary, obeah fetishism as belligerent non-identity, to the prehistory of wage-labour, an economic agreement entered into freely by rational subjects, but which surreptitiously continues the violence and alienation of slavery in what Marx famously referred to as the 'hidden abode of production'.[32] In this process the place of work is itself an arcane realm that remains non-identical with bourgeois society's utopian self-image as a bastion of rights and liberties, as the 'very Eden of the innate rights of men'.[33]

CONJUGALITY AND AFFIRMATIVE CULTURE

The theatricality of Caesar's loyalty to Edwards in the passage just quoted, his 'transport of gratitude', is in stark contrast to Edwards himself, who is unaware that he is implicitly inviting Caesar to betray him. This difference marks the humiliating particularity of the African's admission into the enlightened fold, into a narrative of historical progress that effaces his cultural originality and consigns it, as Hegel infamously did, to the realm of 'Unhistorical, Undeveloped Spirit'.[34] In order that we are convinced of his loyalty to Edwards and his corresponding place in the scheme of universal emancipation, he must perform in histrionic gestures what the benevolent European can convey without disturbing his demeanour. In effectively offering his own heart to the knife he gives Caesar – a sharp one mind you – Edwards is already acting in accordance with a free and rational will, for which commitment to enlightenment notions of autonomy and equality is second nature. Caesar, on the other hand, in order to forestall the European anxiety that he is merely the mimic Edward Long describes, concealing murderous intent under a 'submissive carriage', must be allowed this private confession. The performance of civic virtue, this display from one's heart as it were, is thus also a performance of the non-identity irreducibly apparent in its erasure. Caesar's style of self-presentation calls attention to difference in order that it can be sublimated into the universality of sympathetic, unaffected humanity.

It is revealing then that, at the moment his integrity is in doubt, Clarence Hervey is called upon to perform his commitment to Belinda and dispel rumours that he has seduced Virginia St Pierre, by quoting from a volume of Thomas Day's sentimental abolitionist poetry. The passage Hervey reads 'with so much unaffected, unembarrassed energy' (*Belinda*, p. 351) that Lady Delacour for one seems convinced of his integrity, is not exactly of a piece with Caesar's effusions. Hervey is, after all, only reading – literally performing his sincerity by rehearsing a pre-existing model of sincere expression. The intertextual intricacy of this moment, though, does need some explication. Day's most famous poem, which Belinda and Vincent were reading moments before Hervey's entrance, is the popular abolitionist work 'The Dying Negro', written in the voice of a slave who has just stabbed himself rather than accept his bondage. '"For my part,"' Vincent remarks of the poem, '"I neither have, nor pretend to have, much critical taste; but I admire in this poem the manly, energetic spirit of virtue, which it breathes,"' while Hervey adds that '"this writer (Mr Day) was an instance, that genuine eloquence must spring from the heart"' (*Belinda*, p. 349). That the competing claims of Vincent and Hervey on Belinda, and their respective attempts to vindicate their intrinsic qualities, are played out in proximity to this poem (which clearly provides some of the material for the similarly titled 'The Grateful Negro') is revealing: the dying slave's performance of civic virtue is also a testament to his conjugal loyalty and, by extension, proof of universal norms of humanity that transcend race. Yet the sublimation of racial difference into an apparently universal intercourse of sentiments in Day's poem, which is fundamentally incorporated into Edgeworth's novel, also reveals the secretly social character of identity as such, that is the degree to which images of conjugal love are embedded in a field of social relations.

Day's poem, written in conjunction with John Bicknell and dedicated to Rousseau, is based on the apparently true story of a slave who had intended to marry a European servant with whom he worked in his master's house in England. To carry out his conjugal plans he absconded from his master's residence in order to be baptized. Upon the discovery of his absence, however, his unreasonable master ordered him transported to America. Rather than endure separation from his wife-to-be and the horrors of transportation, he stabs himself and, with his final utterances, narrates his expiring thoughts, which turn inevitably to his 'lov'd bride'. The premise of the poem is thus a kind of lack. The impossibility of realizing a conjugal idyll, of asserting universal humanity, and the corresponding remorse, figured as intense melancholy, of remaining trapped in the racialized hierarchies of colonial production, propel the narrator to suicide. Recalling his life as a slave, it is precisely in the dream state that fantasies of redemption and freedom assert themselves as the compensatory pleasure to which the slave flees, as if having humanity denied by the realities of slavery forces one to imagine the overcoming of this lack in a private fantasy. 'Slaves', the narrator says,

> ... like the dull unpitied brutes repair
> To stalls as wretched, and as coarse a fare;
> Thank heav'n, one day of misery was o'er,
> And sink to sleep, and wish to wake no more. –
> Sleep on! ye lost companions of my woes,
> For whom in death this tear of pity flows;
> Sleep, and enjoy the only boon of heav'n
> To you in common with your tyrants giv'n!
> O while soft slumber from their couches flies,
> Still may the balmy blessing steep your eyes;
> In swift oblivion lull awhile your woes,

And brightest visions gladden the repose!
　Let fancy, then, unconscious of the change,
　Thro' our own fields and native forest range;
　Waft ye to each once-haunted stream and grove,
　And visit ev'ry long-lost scene ye love!
　– I sleep no more – nor in the midnight shade
　Invoke ideal phantoms to my aid;
　Nor wake again abandon'd and forlorn,
　To find each dear delusion fled at morn;
　A slow consuming death let others wait,
　I snatch destruction from unwilling fate ...[35]

In this passage nocturnal fantasies of an African idyll are contingent on and rooted in the very practices of oppression in which the slave is caught. The nightly compensation, the minimal autonomy of privacy, rehearses a fantasy of escape which, precisely to the extent that the realities of slavery are suspended in this fantasy, sustains the slave economy. What makes the slave economy feasible, in other words, is that it does not seem to colonize every aspect of psychic life, but leaves a minimal space in which the slave can appease himself by retreating into his own humanity. Importantly the narrator likens this cycle of servitude and fantasy to a 'slow consuming death'. The 'highest visions' which 'gladden the repose' lull the slave into an oblivious sleep that enables him to forget the reality of his existence in an oppressive system. If this dream state indexes a kind of dissidence, a refusal of the degrading condition of slavery and the assertion of a purely human identity that the slave and master share, it also contains and pacifies this dissidence in the politically impotent realm of private fantasy. When the narrator declares 'I sleep no more' – a line that evokes *Macbeth*, but which will also resonate through the age of revolution as a decidedly ambiguous call to consciousness and agency – he also identifies the rejection of sleep, of a realm of imagined flight, to be the very essence of his revolt. He is done with the impotence of private fantasy. The narrator's own suicide, however, has also been a reaction to the reality of slavery, and the visions that now occupy him in death are thus predictably similar to the nocturnal fantasies he has just denigrated. They are visions of conjugality and nature in which men simply commune as men, unaffected and unhindered by instrumental directives. The slippage between a sleep that is part of the 'slow consuming death' of the slave system and a death that, like sleep, transports one beyond it, is unmistakable. Corresponding to this slippage, the ambiguous notion of 'transport' itself in abolitionist writing, signifying both an exalted spiritual state and passage to the plantations of the Americas, marks the contradictory character of images of liberated plenitude: if they point to the possibility of the private subject realizing its fullness outside of the production process, the very fact that this realization of completion and unity can only happen in private leaves the repressiveness of production untouched.

Another version of this dynamic is played out in the story of Virginia St Pierre, who is adopted by Clarence Hervey and nurtured by him in accordance with the thinking of Henri Bernardin de Saint-Pierre, whose *Paul and Virginia* documented a form of natural education taking place beyond the conventions and prejudices of a fallen world. Yet Hervey's pedagogical scheme, it is clear, is also an emphatic denial of Virginia's liberty and autonomy. Edgeworth deploys conventional Gothic images of incarceration and seclusion to describe Virginia's captivity and the misguided plan to educate her to be the perfect wife. Bored by her isolation, her literal entrapment inside a parodied version of enlightenment culture, and prone to reading Gothic-pathetic literature, her own freedom becomes inextricably bound up with romance conventions in which she imagines her salvation through the agency of a mysterious hero. Edgeworth is clearly attacking aspects of the pedagogical schemes inspired by Rousseau's theories of nature (schemes which Thomas Day also tried to implement) in order to criticize not only the denial of autonomy to women and the enforcement of their seclusion in private space, but the effacement of their actual natures: in renaming Rachel Hartley Virginia St Pierre, Hervey consolidates the fiction of enlightenment as a repression of her real identity. The negative impact of Hervey's scheme is compounded by Virginia's reading habits, that is her interest in Gothic and sentimental texts which encourage both ennui and an overactive fantasy life. In *Practical Education* the Edgeworths claimed that exposing children to this sort of writing 'lowers the tone of mind'.[36] As Heather Macfadyen argues, Virginia's reading habits represent the 'trope of female reading' which, like the performativity of fashionable reading initially embodied in Lady Delacour, and in opposition to Belinda's reading habits (which include Adam Smith and Anna Laetitia Barbauld), signifies a 'breach of domestic femininity'.[37] But the very idea of redemption that Virginia imagines, largely under the influence of the Gothic-pathetic texts she reads, is realized and thus vindicated in the actual appearance of her imagined savior in the form of Captain Sunderland. At this point Virginia too is integrated into the heteronormative romance plot that projects conjugality as a narrative telos, yet this narrative and the escapist fantasies nourished by the boredom of seclusion in private space now have a relationship of similitude, not opposition. Whereas Wollstonecraft's *The Wrongs of Woman* figures social amelioration as a necessary deconstruction of sentimental narrative conventions, *Belinda* seems to figure it as their realization. Insofar as Virginia's Gothic-romantic fantasies come true, as it were, they do so in a narrative of domestic enlightenment, enabling us to argue that Gothic romance and the domestic narrative are in fact derivations of each other. They are both narratives of wish-fulfilment that derive their appeal from the extent to which true love, sympathy and domestic stability are absent in the reality of lived experience. In this respect Virginia's reading habits and those of the actual reader of Edgeworth's novel are specularly related. As it did for Day's dying slave, conjugal love marks the resistance of fantasy to oppression, but it also negates and contains this resistance within the space of the imagination, daydreams, reverie and reading. Revealingly Captain Sunderland is verified as the chivalric hero by Virginia's father, who recalls the former's coincidental role in the pacification of a slave rebellion on his Jamaican plantation some years earlier. Conjugal proclivities and counterinsurgency in the colonies are not only compatible, but in fact prerequisites for each other, as the conjugal romance also insinuates the romance of effective government on the plantations as a similarly fictionalized narrative of heroism and civic virtue.

The fantasy of conjugality can be read as a kind of psychic defence mechanism protecting the subject from the trauma of alienation, from determinate production spheres in which something like innate desire seems to be denied. But in protecting the subject, in fortifying its private, psychic integrity, it also constitutes the subject as an autonomous entity, a possessive individual, equipped for life in the culture of emerging capitalism. The model of resistant private space that Day's poem projects in opposition to production in fact suggests the lived experiences of both bourgeois and proletarian populations already integrated into domestic capitalism and accordingly invested in forms of escapist fantasy, whether in private or through increasingly massified forms of entertainment in

public. In attributing this model to slave communities, Day anticipates the imminent sublimation of slavery into free labour, and
reads the slave as the subject of liberal humanism awaiting liberation. The paradox here is that Day's slave could only be liberated
into exactly the condition of slavery depicted in the poem, a condition characterized by the separation of labour from redemptive
private space and conjugal felicity. As Marx wrote, 'The bourgeois
viewpoint has never advanced beyond this antithesis between itself
and this romantic viewpoint, and therefore the latter will accompany it as legitimate antithesis up to its blessed end.'[38] In Herbert
Marcuse's theory of affirmative culture, literature, as we have seen,
is understood as central to this problem. Affirmative culture, as I
have used it throughout this study, signifies practices that negate
the reified relations that increasingly permeate and define metropolitan experience throughout the eighteenth century and beyond:
literature, art and idealist philosophy. They are affirmative because,
on the one hand, they affirm what cannot be articulated in relations
of production based on exchange value. On the other hand,
however, the extent to which they bracket this excess, recode it in
practices of culture-consumption, and confine it to the very forms of
individualism that legitimate the mode of production, effectively
affirms existing social and economic relations. The phrase
affirmative culture thus denotes a contradiction that must be articulated dialectically; bourgeois society posits a vision of universal
freedom and rationality that the realities of production cannot
realize except in forms of sequestered idealism. Affirmative culture
is thus a necessary structural component of the mode of production
precisely because of its negative value. It is through culture-
consumption, reading and reverie that the utopian impulses of
bourgeois society are gratified and pacified, realized privately
'without any transformation of the state of fact'.[39]

The dense intertextuality of *Belinda* tells not only of its engagement with an enlightenment discourse of cultural modernity, but
also of the central role of textuality and reading in the reception and
transmission of this discourse. Indeed there is barely a moment in the
novel at which the presence of enlightenment thought as text is not
felt, either in direct or more coded references. That its own multiple
writings of the conjugal plot are so mediated by prior textual objects
points to the contradiction of the enlightenment itself; its norms and
ideals, as Marcuse suggests of bourgeois culture, can only be tolerated at a distance from the actual processes of production with

which they are nevertheless complicit. That is to say, they can only be tolerated as text. In attempting to present the universality of these norms, in sublimating colonial production into capitalist production, Edgeworth's fictional project produces a version of difference (readable in fetishism and performativity) that survives the identitarian impulse to threaten the bourgeois production of conjugality, but that also suggests the inevitability of its eventual assimilation. Yet in obliquely referring to the imbrication of affirmative culture and conjugality in capitalism, the novel also points to the fundamental non-identity *within* bourgeois society: that is, bourgeois society posits an idyllic private realm which sustains the subject, but which is also incompatible with the dehumanizing forces that increasingly permeate the production process. The segregation of private and public spheres, on the one hand, and the positive unreality of utopian conjugal fantasies, on the other, ensure the precarious coexistence of enlightenment idealism and the empirical-historical realities of emerging capitalism. As the novel's highly performative closing tableau of conjugal felicity seems to indicate, the images of conjugality that legitimize Edgeworth's vision of enlightened universality are finally as unstable as the deceptions and magical fabrications that, throughout the text, suggest a distinctly pre-modern worldview. Yet these images are also inextricably integrated into the mode of production as a form of discursive practice that is crucial to the process of subject predication, to the imagining of redemptive privacy and authenticity despite the instrumental imperatives of public life. They cannot be simply conjured out of existence by an act of will or mental volition precisely because they are seamlessly incorporated into the infrastructural organization of society. If they are, in a sense, illusions, the illusion is itself material, as Wollstonecraft's work so emphatically demonstrates. That Edgeworth's espousal of enlightenment idealism is carried out in conjunction with the abolition movement compels us to interrogate it all the more thoroughly, lest we believe that, safely under the aegis of humanitarian progress, capitalism should be spared the intrusiveness of critical scrutiny at precisely the moment in its history when it begins to assimilate both colonial production and resistant cultures into its increasingly global fold.

Notes

INTRODUCTION: LITERATURE AND THE PUBLIC SPHERE IN THE 1790s

1. See James Chandler, 'Hallam, Tennyson, and the Poetry of Sensation: Aestheticist Allegories of a Counter-Public Sphere', *Studies in Romanticism*, vol. 33, no. 4 (Winter 1994) p. 527.
2. Special issues of *Studies in Romanticism*, vol. 33, no. 4 (Winter 1994) and *Prose Studies*, vol. 18, no. 3 (December 1995) on the public sphere, have recently foregrounded the importance of Habermas for literary studies.
3. See Raymond Williams, *Culture and Society 1780–1950* (Harmondsworth: Penguin, 1961) pp. 48–64.
4. Kevin Gilmartin, 'Popular Radicalism and the Public Sphere', *Studies in Romanticism* vol. 33, no. 4 (Winter 1994) pp. 550–1.
5. Terry Eagleton, *The Function of Criticism* (London: Verso, 1984) p. 36.
6. See, for example, Jon Klancher, *The Making of English Reading Audiences, 1790–1832* (Madison: University of Wisconsin Press, 1987), Iain McCalman, *Radical Underworld: Prophets, Revolutionaries and Pornographers in London, 1795–1814* (Cambridge: Cambridge University Press, 1988), and Günther Lottes, *Politische Aufklarung und plebejisches Publikum: Zur Theorie und Praxis des englischen Radikalismus im späten 18. Jahrhundert* (Munich: R. Oldenbourg Verlag, 1979).
7. Orrin Wang, 'Romancing the Counter-Public Sphere: a Response to *Romanticism and its Publics*', *Studies in Romanticism*, vol. 33, no. 4 (Winter 1994) pp. 579–80.
8. See Gary Kelly, *Revolutionary Feminism: the Mind and Career of Mary Wollstonecraft* (New York: St. Martin's Press, 1992), which is premised on the idea that radicalism in the 1790s was primarily representative of a middle-class cultural revolution.
9. John Brenkman, *Culture and Domination* (Ithaca, NY: Cornell University Press, 1987) pp. 63–4.
10. See William Wordsworth, *The Prelude: the Four Texts. 1798, 1799, 1805, 1850*, ed. Jonathan Wordsworth (Harmondsworth: Penguin, 1995) 1850 version, 12: 208–15 and Samuel Taylor Coleridge, *Poems*, ed. John Beer (London: Everyman, 1993) p. 353.
11. See Nick Roe's discussion of Wordsworth's relationship to Godwinian thought in *Wordsworth and Coleridge: the Radical Years* (Oxford: Clarendon Press, 1988) pp. 192–8.
12. Helen Maria Williams, *Julia*, 2 vols (London: 1790; reprinted by Garland Publishing, New York, 1974) vol. 1, p. 14.
13. Ibid., vol. 1, p. 19.
14. Wordsworth, 'Preface' to *Lyrical Ballads*, in *Poems*, vol. 1, ed. John O. Hayden (Harmondsworth: Penguin, 1990) p. 881.

15.   Herbert Marcuse, *Negations: Essays in Critical Theory*, trans. Jeremy J. Shapiro (Boston: Beacon Press 1968) p. 95.
16.   Ibid., p. 114.
17.   See also Peter Bürger's *Theory of the Avant-Garde* trans. Michael Shaw (Minneapolis: University of Minnesota Press, 1984), which develops Marcuse's essay into a more comprehensive account of artistic 'autonomy' as an ideological category.
18.   See John Brewer, 'Commercialization and Politics', in *The Birth of a Consumer Society: the Commercialization of Eighteenth-Century England*, eds Neil McKendric et al. (Bloomington: Indiana University Press, 1982) pp. 197–262.
19.   Ibid., p. 217.
20.   Terry Eagleton's *The Rape of Clarissa* develops some of Habermas's comments on Richardson, arguing that Richardson should be seen as an 'organic intellectual' at the forefront of England's bourgeois cultural revolution. This leads Eagleton to suggest that Richardson's novels are not 'literature' in any simple sense, but indicative of a more heterogeneous, hybridized intersection of discursive strands. 'Richardson's novels are not only or even primarily literary texts: they entwine with commerce, religion, theatre, ethical debate, the visual arts, public entertainment. They are both cogs in a culture industry and sacred scripture to be reverently conned. In short, they are organizing forces of what, after German political theory, we may term the bourgeois "public sphere".' See *The Rape of Clarissa: Writing, Sexuality and Class Struggle in Samuel Richardson* (Minneapolis: University of Minnesota Press, 1982) p. 6.
21.   David Hume, *A Treatise of Human Nature*, ed. L. A. Selby-Bigge (Oxford: Clarendon Press, 1978) p. 603. See John Mullan, *Sentiment and Sociability: the Language of Feeling in the Eighteenth Century* (Oxford: Clarendon Press, 1988) and G. J. Barker-Benfield's *The Culture of Sensibility: Sex and Society in Eighteenth-Century Britain* (Chicago: University of Chicago Press, 1992) for general accounts of sensibility in the period.
22.   See Benedict Anderson, *Imagined Communities: Reflections on the Origins and Spread of Nationalism* (London: Verso, 1983), which discusses the relationship between the development of print culture and the formation of communities mediated by it. Kathleen Wilson's 'Citizenship, Empire, and Modernity in the English Provinces, c. 1720–1790', *Eighteenth-Century Studies*, vol. 29, no. 1 (1995) pp. 69–96, usefully relates Anderson's insights to eighteenth-century Britain.
23.   Klancher, p. 24.
24.   James Anderson, 'On the Advantages of Periodical Performances', *The Bee* vol. 1 (1740–1), p. 14, quoted in Klancher, p. 23.
25.   Max Horkheimer, 'Authority and the Family', *Critical Theory: Selected Essays* trans. Matthew J. O'Connell (New York: Continuum, 1972) p. 114.
26.   See Pheng Cheah, 'Violent Light: the Idea of Publicness in Modern Philosophy and in Global Neocolonialism', *Social Text* 43, vol. 13, no. 2 (1995), p. 169.

27. Claudia Johnson, *Equivocal Beings: Politics, Gender, and Sentimentality in the 1790s: Wollstonecraft, Radcliffe, Burney, Austen* (Chicago: University of Chicago Press, 1995) p. 3.

28. Slavoj Žižek, *The Metastases of Enjoyment: Six Essays on Women and Causality* (London: Verso, 1994) p. 55.

29. Michel Foucault, *Madness and Civilization: a History of Insanity in the Age of Reason*, trans: Richard Howard (New York: Vintage Books, 1988) p. 64. E. P. Thompson's *Whigs and Hunters: the Origin of the Black Act* (London: Penguin, 1990) and Peter Linebaugh's *The London Hanged: Crime and Civil Society in the Eighteenth Century* (Cambridge: Cambridge University Press, 1992) both show how the eighteenth century was the period in which legislative practices expanded definitions of criminality in line with the requirements of private property and developing capitalism.

30. Max Byrd, 'The Madhouse, the Whorehouse and the Convent', *Partisan Review*, XLIV, no. 2 (1977) p. 268.

31. See David Simpson's discussion of Blake and 'America', in *Romanticism, Nationalism, and the Revolt Against Theory* (Chicago: University of Chicago Press, 1993) pp. 159–64.

32. Foucault, *Madness and Civilization*, pp. 207–8.

33. Ibid., p. 210.

34. Foucault, *The Order of Things: An Archeology of the Human Sciences* unidentified translation (New York: Vintage Books, 1973) p. 300.

35. Simon During, *Foucault and Literature: Towards a Genealogy of Writing* (London: Routledge, 1992) p. 86.

36. Foucault, 'Language to Infinity', *Language, Counter-Memory, Practice*, ed. Donald F. Bouchard (Ithaca, NY: Cornell University Press, 1977) pp. 60–1.

37. The recent collection of essays entitled *Habermas and the Public Sphere*, ed. Craig Calhoun (Cambridge, Mass: MIT Press, 1992) contains a representative cross-section of theoretical and historiographical responses to *The Structural Transformation*.

38. The 'totality of the context of mystification' is similar to Pierre Bourdieu's notion of 'habitus' as a horizon of experience and action which is not so much ideologically mediated as it is, simply, ideology as the totality of interpellating effects deployed by a given mode of production. Habitus demarcates a 'socially constituted system of cognitive and motivating structures, and the socially structured situations in which agents' interests are defined, and with them the objective functions and subjective motivations of their practices.' See Pierre Bourdieu, *Outline of a Theory of Practice* trans. Richard Nice (Cambridge: Cambridge University Press, 1977) p. 76.

39. Karl Marx, *Early Writings*, ed. Quintin Hoare (Harmondsworth: Penguin, 1975) p. 230.

40. Hannah Arendt, *The Human Condition* (Chicago: University of Chicago Press, 1958) p. 46.

41. Chandler, 'Hallam, Tennyson, and the Poetry of Sensation', p. 535.

42. See Paula R. Backscheider, *Spectacular Politics: Theatrical Power and Mass Culture in Early Modern England* (Baltimore, Md: John Hopkins University Press, 1993) p. 231.
43. Klancher, p. 99.
44. Louis Althusser, *For Marx* trans. Ben Brewster (London: New Left Books, 1977) p. 151.

CHAPTER 1 EDMUND BURKE'S IMMORTAL LAW: READING THE IMPEACHMENT OF WARREN HASTINGS, 1788

1. Thomas Paine, *Rights of Man* (1791; Harmondsworth: Penguin Books, 1985) pp. 49–50.
2. Linda Zerilli, *Signifying Woman: Culture and Chaos in Rousseau, Burke and Mill* (Ithaca, NY and London: Cornell University Press, 1994) p. 61.
3. Mary Wollstonecraft, *A Vindication of the Rights of Men* in *The Works of Mary Wollstonecraft*, vol. 5, eds Janet Todd and Marilyn Butler (London: William Pickering 1989) p. 8.
4. Tom Furniss, *Edmund Burke's Aesthetic Ideology: Language, Gender, and Political Economy in Revolution* (Cambridge: Cambridge University Press, 1993) pp. 1–13.
5. See Burke's 'Articles of Impeachment' (14, 21, 28 May 1787), *W&S*, vol. 6, pp. 125–258.
6. On the sentimental character of Burke's representation of India see Frans De Bruyn, 'Edmund Burke's Gothic Romance: the Portrayal of Warren Hastings in Burke's Writings and Speeches on India', *Criticism: a Quarterly for Literature and the Arts*, vol. 29, no. 4 (Fall 1987) pp. 415–38.
7. Burke, *A Vindication of Natural Society* (London, 1757), in *Pre-Revolutionary Writings*, ed. Ian Harris (Cambridge: Cambridge University Press, 1993) p. 14.
8. Claudia Johnson, *Equivocal Beings Politics, Gender and Sentimentality in the 1790s: Wollstonecraft, Radcliffe, Burney, Austen* (Chicago: University of Chicago Press, 1995), p. 3.
9. Sara Suleri, *The Rhetoric of English India* (Chicago: University of Chicago Press, 1992) p. 51.
10. Ibid., p. 52
11. Eagleton, *Heathcliff and the Great Hunger: Studies in Irish Culture* (London: Verso, 1995) pp. 42–6.
12. Paine, p. 118.
13. Michael Warner, 'The Mass Public and the Mass Subject', *The Phantom Public Sphere*, ed. Bruce Robbins (Minneapolis: University of Minnesota Press, 1993) p. 239.
14. Burke, *Vindication*, p. 14.
15. See, for example, Joan B. Landes, *Women and the Public Sphere in the Age of the French Revolution* (Ithaca, NY: Cornell University Press, 1988).
16. Anne McClintock, *Imperial Leather: Race, Gender and Sexuality in the Colonial Context* (London: Routledge, 1985) p. 44.

17. Frans De Bruyn, 'Edmund Burke's Gothic Romance', pp. 424–5.
18. Burke to Philip Francis (c. 3 January 1788), *The Correspondence of Edmund Burke*, ed. H. Furber (Cambridge: Cambridge University Press, 1669) vol. 5, p. 372.
19. The details Burke relates were based on John Patterson's report on the 1783 rebellion in Rangpur. See *W&S*, vol. 6, p. 413, n. 1.
20. Burke used this phrase in his 'Speech on Nabob of Arcot's Debts' (28 February 1785), *W&S*, vol. 5, p. 521.
21. Gayatri Chakravorty Spivak, 'Can the Subaltern Speak?', *Marxism and the Interpretation of Culture*, eds Cary Nelson and Lawrence Grossberg (Chicago: Illinois University Press, 1988) p. 296.
22. Burke, *A Philosophical Enquiry Into the Origin of our Ideas of the Sublime and the Beautiful* (1756; Oxford: Oxford University Press) p. 79.
23. Ibid., p. 42.
24. Tom Furniss's discussion of the undecidability that informs the category of the sublime in the *Reflections* provides a helpful way of thinking about this duality. Furniss notes that 'the sublime is a mode by which bourgeois society defines itself through the exclusion of the "barbarous" past. Yet the sublime can also be read as the return of that which polite commerce represses within itself and which structures its own ethos.' See Furniss, *Aesthetic Ideology*, p. 147. The undecidable structure of sublimity that Furniss discusses here is analogous to the undecidable nature of pleasure evoked by the speech.
25. Slavoj Žižek, *The Metastases of Enjoyment: Six Essays on Women and Causality* (London: Verso, 1994) p. 75.
26. Ibid., p. 75.
27. Major [John] Scott, *A Third Letter from Major Scott to Mr Fox on the Story of Deby Sing* (London, 1789) p. 8.
28. [Ralph Broome], *The Letters of Simpkin the Second, Poetic Recorder of all the Proceedings Upon the Trial of Warren Hastings in Westminster Hall* (London, 1789) pp. 12–13.
29. Žižek, *The Metastases of Enjoyment*, p. 55.
30. Frans De Bruyn, *The Literary Genres of Edmund Burke: the Political Uses of Literary Form* (Oxford: Clarendon Press, 1996) p. 14.
31. See, for example, Furniss, *Aesthetic Ideology*, pp. 138–63, De Bruyn, *The Literary Genres of Edmund Burke*, pp. 163–208 and Zerilli, *Signifying Women*, pp. 60–94 – three exemplary and sophisticated readings of the *Reflections*.

CHAPTER 2 WILLIAM GODWIN AND THE PATHOLOGICAL PUBLIC SPHERE: THEORIZING COMMUNICATIVE ACTION IN THE 1790s

1. See E. P. Thompson's *The Making of the English Working Class* (New York: Random House, 1964), pp. 17–185, and Albert Goodwin's *The Friends of Liberty: the English Democratic Movement in the Age of the*

French Revolution (Cambridge: Harvard University Press, 1979) for detailed accounts of the political climate of the 1790s.

2. Kristen Leaver, 'Pursuing Conversations: *Caleb Williams* and the Romantic Construction of the Reader', *Studies in Romanticism*, vol. 33 (Winter 1994) p. 592. My argument in the following chapter takes up many of the issues already discussed by Leaver. Whereas Leaver, however, argues that Godwin ultimately retreats into a 'vision of literature as a private, inner world', I want to suggest that his work, by examining the always-already mediated nature of this retreat, can be read back another way as explication of the impediments to structurally differentiated forms of political life.

3. John Reeve's Association for Preserving Liberty and Property Against Republicans and Levellers, for example.

4. Godwin's critique of Thelwall and the LCS is made explicit in his *Considerations on Lord Grenville's and Mr. Pitt's Bills* (see discussion below). See Don Locke, *A Fantasy of Reason: The Life and Thought of William Godwin* (London: Routledge & Kegan Paul, 1980) pp. 100–104, for a discussion of Godwin's turbulent relationship with Thelwall. Critical literature on Godwin naturally enough situates the tensions I'm discussing here in the broader context of political radicalism in the 1790s, though often failing to grasp that what is at stake in Godwin's relationship to radical activism is not a doctrinaire political difference. As Locke points out, Godwin and radical activists like Thelwall basically shared the same political beliefs. See Locke, p. 65. Godwin questioned not the doctrines, but the forms of interactive discursive praxis he saw embodied in corresponding societies, popular political meetings and radical journalism. Garrett A. Sullivan's essay '"A Story to be Hastily Gobbled Up": *Caleb Williams* and Print Culture', *Studies in Romanticism*, vol. 32, no. 3 (Fall 1993) pp. 323–37, makes this very point, focusing on the forms of discursive production embodied in radical culture, and Godwin's anxiety regarding these. Sullivan argues that Godwin's rejection of Jacobin print-culture and public oration was the result of an elitism that pitted established forms of public interaction, embodied by Addison and Steele's writing and located in the coffee house, against forms of interaction linked to, on the one hand, the mass circulation of textual commodities, and, on the other, to polyphonous forms of public discourse embodied in popular journals.

5. It is worth pointing out that such explicit critiques of Thelwall and the LCS may have also been strategic attempts by Godwin to exempt himself from official censure while still being critical of the government.

6. Godwin, *Considerations on Lord Grenville's and Mr. Pitt's Bills, Concerning Treasonable and Seditious Practices and Unlawful Assemblies* (London, 1795) p. 19.

7. Ibid., p. 20.

8. See, for example, 'The Rise, Progress and Effects of Jacobinism', in *The Anti-Jacobin Review and Magazine*, which argued that the efficacy and popularity of Paine's *Rights of Man* resided in its solicitation of 'vulgar

and undistinguishing minds', and its appeals to the vanity of labouring classes which were thus flattered into political affiliations with the prospect of their own empowerment. See *The Anti-Jacobin Review and Magazine, or, Monthly Political and Literary Censor*, 3 vol. (London, 1798–99) vol. 3, pp. 95–6. See also T. J. Mathias's *The Pursuits of Literature* (London, 1797), which similarly links Jacobin political philosophy to print-capitalism.

9. Godwin, *Considerations*, p. 75.
10. Ibid., pp. 81–2.
11. See Thelwall's *The Peripatetic*, which was subtitled *Sketches of the Heart, of Nature and Society; in a Series of Politico-Sentimental Journals* (London, 1793).
12. Claudia L. Johnson, *Equivocal Beings: Politics, Gender and Sentimentality in the 1790s: Wollstonecraft, Radcliffe, Burney, Austen* (Chicago: University of Chicago Press, 1995) pp. 1–14.
13. Eric Rothstein gives a detailed account of the allusions to Richardson in Godwin's novel. See Rothstein, *Systems of Order and Inquiry in Later Eighteenth-Century Fiction* (Berkeley: University California Press, 1975) pp. 211–12. For an elaboration on Falkland as a representation of Burke, see James T. Boulton, *The Language of Politics in the Age of Wilkes and Burke* (London: Routledge & Kegan Paul, 1963) pp. 226–32.
14. We see this reversal, archetypally, in the image of the captive that Yorick conjures in Sterne's *A Sentimental Journey* (Harmondsworth: Penguin Books, 1986) pp. 97–8. For examples of radical textual production that sentimentalize the scene of incarceration, see John Thelwall's *Poems Written in Close Confinement in the Tower and Newgate, Under a Charge of High Treason* (London, 1795) and Charles Piggott's preface to his *A Political Dictionary* (London, 1795).
15. See James Thompson, 'Surveillance in William Godwin's *Caleb Williams*', in *Gothic Fictions: Prohibition/Transgression*, ed. Kenneth Graham (New York: AMS, 1989) pp. 173–98.
16. Foucault, *Discipline and Punish: the Birth of the Prison* trans. Alan Sheridan (Harmondsworth: Penguin Books, 1985), p. 213.
17. John Fielding, 'Circular of October 19, 1772', reprinted in Leon Radzinowicz, *A History of English Criminal Law and its Administration from 1750*, vol. 3 (New York: Macmillan, 1957) p. 482.
18. The same opposition between private space, presided over by a maternal figure, and hostile public structures will organize Godwin's next novel, *St Leon*, in which the pathologies of the public sphere will be in part identified with the accumulation of capital, represented allegorically in the philosopher's stone.
19. See John Bender, *Imagining the Penitentiary: Fiction and the Architecture of Mind in Eighteenth-Century England* (Chicago: University of Chicago Press, 1987), chapters 1, 2 and 6 especially.
20. Gary Handwerk, 'Of Caleb's Guilt and Godwin's Truth: Ideology and Ethics in *Caleb Williams*', *ELH*, vol. 60, no. 4 (Winter 1993) pp. 949–50.
21. Godwin, *The Enquirer: Reflections on Education, Manners, and Literature* (London, 1797) p. 136. The significance of this essay and the terms it sets out have been discussed initially by David McCracken in

214 *Notes*

'Godwin's Literary Theory: the Alliance Between Fiction and Political Philosophy', *Philological Quarterly*, vol. 49, no. 1 (1970) pp. 113–33, and more recently as the basis of Tilottama Rajan's metafictional reading of Godwin's work. Rajan describes the moral as 'the authoritarian intention' of a work, while the tendency is 'an intersubjective and historically developing significance, generated by the productive interaction of intention and its representation and subsequently of the text and its reading'. See 'Wollstonecraft and Godwin: Reading the Secrets of the Political Novel', *Studies in Romanticism*, vol. 27, no. 2 (Summer 1988) p. 224.

CHAPTER 3   POLITICO-SENTIMENTALITY: JOHN THELWALL, LITERARY PRODUCTION AND THE CRITIQUE OF CAPITAL IN THE 1790s

1. E. P. Thompson, *The Making of the English Working Class* (New York: Random House, 1964), p. 160.
2. Karl Marx, *Capital*, vol. 1, trans. Ben Fowkes (Harmondsworth: Penguin, 1976) p. 875.
3. Marcuse, *Negations: Essays in Critical Theory*, trans. Jeremy J. Shapiro (Boston: Beacon Press, 1968) p. 95.
4. Quoted in David Erdman, *Blake: Prophet Against Empire* (New York: Dover, 1977) p. 219.
5. Parodic uses of recognizably Burkean rhetoric were a mainstay of radical texts directed towards artisans and workers in the period. Eaton's *Politics for the People* used images of swine and hogs in its addresses to a readership of 'brother grunters' while radical pamphlets frequently assumed the speaking positions of their opponents as a way of parodying reactionary discourse. *The Pernicious Effects of the Art of Printing Upon Society, Exposed* (London, 179?), for example, warns of the dangers involved in a popular and free press, repeating reactionary discourse as ridiculous in its feudal intolerance.
6. For detailed discussions of Thelwall's political philosophy, see Günther Lottes, *Politische Aufklärung und plebejisches Publikum: zur Theorie und Praxis des englischen Radikalismus im späten 18. Jahrhandert* (Munich: R. Oldenburg Verlag, 1979), pp. 267–99, 327–34, Claeys's introduction to *The Politics of English Jacobinism: the Writings of John Thelwall* (University Park: Pennsylvania State University Press, 1995) pp. xxxv–lvi, and Iain Hampsher-Monk, 'John Thelwall and the Eighteenth-Century Radical Response to Political Economy', *The Historical Journal*, 34 (1991) pp. 1–20.
7. Marx, *Capital*, pp. 873–904.
8. See Stephen Addington, *An Inquiry into the Reasons For and Against Inclosing Open-Fields* (Coventry, 1772).
9. Marx, *Capital*, p. 280
10. Quoted in Thompson, *The Making of the English Working Class*, p. 144.

11. See Thompson 'Hunting the Jacobin Fox', *Past and Present*, no. 142 (February 1994) p. 100.

12. For details of this visit see Nicholas Roe, 'Coleridge and Thelwall: the Road to Nether Stowey', in *The Coleridge Connection*, eds Richard Gravil and Molly Lefebure (London: Macmillan, 1990) pp. 60–80.

13. We can compare this loss of faith in the possibilities of public life with contemporaneous moments in high Romanticism: with Wordsworth's phobic picture of London in Book VII of *The Prelude*, or with Coleridge's 'Dejection: an Ode', which juxtaposes imagination to the 'loveless ever-anxious crowd'.

14. Thelwall, *The Tribune*, 3 vols (London, 1795–6) vol. I, p. 277.

15. Marx, *The Eighteenth Brumaire of Louis Bonaparte*, trans. Ben Fowkes in *Surveys From Exile: Political Writings. Volume 2*, ed. David Fernbach (Harmondsworth: Penguin, 1992) p. 148.

CHAPTER 4 GOTHIC CONSUMPTION: POPULISM, CONSUMERISM AND THE DISCIPLINE OF READING

1. Peter Brooks, 'Virtue and Terror: *The Monk*', *ELH*, vol. 40, no. 2 (Summer 1973) p. 259.

2. David Punter, '1789: the Sex of Revolution', *Criticism: a Quarterly for Literature and the Arts*, vol. 24 (Summer 1982) p. 206.

3. See Paulson, *Representations of Revolution (1789–1820)* (New Haven, Conn.: Yale University Press, 1983) pp. 219–23.

4. E. J. Clery, *The Rise of Supernatural Fiction, 1762–1800* (Cambridge: Cambridge University Press, 1995) pp. 134–5.

5. See Michel Foucault, *The History of Sexuality, Volume 1: An Introduction*, trans. Robert Hurley (Harmondsworth: Penguin Books, 1978) pp. 1–49, where Foucault articulates these ideas with regard to the discursive production of sex in the nineteenth century.

6. 'The Rise, Progress and Effects of Jacobinism', *The Anti-Jacobin Review and Magazine, or, Monthly Political and Literary Censor*, 3 vols (1798–99; London, 1799) vol. 1, pp. 712–14.

7. Ibid., *The Anti-Jacobin*, vol. 3, pp. 95–6.

8. 'An Essay on the Use of Polysyllables – Addressed to the Authors, Speakers, and Readers of the Corresponding Society', *The Anti-Jacobin*, vol. 2, p. 221.

9. Jon Klancher, *The Making of English Reading Audiences, 1790–1832* (Madison: University of Wisconsin Press, 1987) p. 35. See also Arthur Young, *Travels in France in the Years 1787, 1788, and 1789*, ed. Jeffrey Kaplaw (Garden City, NY: Doubleday, 1969) p. 465, which is paraphrased in Klancher's discussion.

10. 'The Literary Fund', *The Anti-Jacobin*, vol. 3, p. 100.

11. Arthur Young, *The Example of France a Warning to Britain* (Dublin, 1793) reprinted in *Political Writings of the 1790s*, 8 vols, ed. Gregory Claeys (London: William Pickering, 1995) vol. 8, p. 122.

12. William Atkinson, *A Concise Sketch of the Intended Revolution in England* (London, 1794) reprinted in *Political Writings of the 1790s*, vol. 8, p. 189

13. See Ronald Paulson, p. 65, and Isaac Kramnick, *The Rage of Edmund Burke* (New York: Basic Books, 1977) pp. 183–5.

14. Christopher Reid, 'Burke's Tragic Muse: Sarah Siddons and the "Feminization" of the *Reflections*', in *Burke and the French Revolution: Bicentennial Essays*, ed. Steven Blackmore (Athens: the University of Georgia Press, 1992) p. 2.

15. Thomas Moore, *Address to the Inhabitants of Great Britain on the Dangerous and Destructive Tendency of the French System of Liberty and Equality* (York, 1793), in *Political Writings of the 1790s*, vol. 8, p. 35.

16. Charles Harrington Elliot, *The Republican Refuted; in a Series of Biographical, Critical and Political Strictures on Thomas Paine's Rights of Man* (London, 1791), in *Political Writings of the 1790s*, vol. 5, p. 314.

17. Paulson, pp. 62–4.

18. William Hamilton Reid, *The Rise and Dissolution of the Infidel Societies in this Metropolis* (London, 1800) p. 32.

19. Ibid., p. 32.

20. Johnson, *Jane Austen: Women, Politics and the Novel* (Chicago: University of Chicago Press, 1988) p. xiv.

21. Reid, *The Rise and Dissolution of the Infidel Societies*, p. 8.

22. *Second Report from the Committee of Secrecy of the House of Commons* (London, 1794) p. 26.

23. Peter Stallybrass, 'Marx and Heterogeneity: Thinking the Lumpenproletariat', *Representations*, vol. 31 (Summer 1990) p. 79.

24. Michel Foucault, *Madness and Civilization: a History of Insanity in the Age of Reason*, trans. Richard Howard (New York: Vintage Books, 1988), pp. 207–8.

25. *Edinburgh Review*, no. 2 (April 1803) p. 200. Quoted in Scrivener, 'The Rhetorical Context of John Thelwall's *Memoir*', in *Spirits of Fire: English Romantic Writers and Contemporary Historical Methods*, eds G. A. Rosso and Daniel P. Watkins (London: Associated University Presses, 1990) p. 125.

26. Scrivener, 'The Rhetorical Context of John Thelwall's *Memoir*', p. 125.

27. On the Minerva Press see Clery, pp. 135–40.

28. André Parreaux, *The Publication of The Monk* (Paris: Libraire Marcel Didier, 1960) p. 34 and Clery, p. 147.

29. 'Terrorist Novel Writing', in *Spirit of Public Journals for 1797*, vol. 1 (London, 1789) pp. 223–5. Quoted in Clery, p. 147

30. Clery, p. 147.

31. T. J. Mathias, *The Pursuits of Literature* (London, 1805) p. xix.

32. Ibid., p. 279.

33. Ibid., pp. 4, 18.

34. Ibid., pp. 48, 76, 395.

35. Ibid., p. 244.

36. Ibid., pp. 244–5.

37. Ibid., pp. 248–9.

38. Jane Austen, *Northanger Abbey* (Harmondsworth: Penguin Books, 1985) pp. 126–7.

39. Paulson, p. 217
40. Eve Kosofsky Sedgwick, *The Coherence of Gothic Conventions* (New York: Methuen, 1890) pp. 146, 145.
41. Brooks, p. 260.
42. *Critical Review*, vol. 22 (1798) p. 476.
43. Frederick S. Frank, *The First Gothics: a Critical Guide to the Gothic Novel* (New York: Garland, 1987) p. ix.
44. See Robert D. Mayo, *The English Novel in the Magazines, 1740–1815* (Evanston, Ill.: Northwestern University Press, 1963).
45. Marquis de Sade, *Selected Writings* (London: Peter Owen, 1964) p. 287.
46. [Samuel Taylor Coleridge], *Critical Review*, vol. 19 (1797) p. 194.
47. Coleridge, *Biographia Literaria* (London: Everyman's Library, 1991) p. 28.
48. William Wordsworth, 'Preface' to *Lyrical Ballads and Other Poems*, in *The Poems Volume 1*, ed. John O. Hayden (Harmondsworth: Penguin, 1990) p. 870.
49. Ibid., pp. 872–3.
50. Klancher, p. 137.
51. Wordsworth, *Poems*, p. 873.
52. Wordsworth, 'It is not to be thought of that the Flood', ibid., p. 561
53. As Donald Reiman points out, the historical 'Maiden of Buttermere' (Mary Robinson) was seduced and abandoned by the bigamist John Hatfield. See 'The Beauty of Buttermere as Fact and Romantic Symbol', *Criticism: a Quarterly for Literature and the Arts*, vol. 26, no. 2 (Spring 1984) pp. 139–70, for an invaluable discussion of the textual sources informing Wordsworth's use of the story.
54. [Coleridge], *Critical Review*, vol. 19 (1797) p. 194.
55. Ibid., p. 195.
56. Ronald Paulson, pp. 219–25, and David Punter, pp. 206–7.
57. Klancher, p. 82.
58. Ann Radcliffe, *The Romance of the Forest* (1791; Oxford: Oxford University Press, 1991) pp. 6–7.
59. Coleridge, 'France: an Ode', *Poems* (London: Everyman Library, 1993) p. 283.
60. Michel Foucault, 'Language to Infinity', *Language, Counter-Memory, Practice: Selected Essays and Interviews by Michel Foucault*, ed. Donald F. Bouchard, trans. Donald F. Bouchard and Sherry Simon (Ithaca, NY: Cornell University Press, 1977), p. 66.

CHAPTER 5 DOMESTIC REVOLUTIONS: MARY WOLLSTONECRAFT AND THE LIMITS OF RADICAL SENTIMENTALITY

1. Thelwall, *Sober Reflections on the Seditious and Inflammatory Letter of the Right Hon. Edmund Burke to a Noble Lord* (London, 1796) p. 78.
2. Thelwall, 'The Universal Duty', *Poems Written in Close Confinement in the Tower and Newgate Under a Charge of High Treason* (London, 1795) p. 13.

3. [R. Lee], *On the Death of Mrs. Hardy, Wife of Mr. Thomas Hardy, of Piccadilly; Imprisoned in the Tower for High Treason* (London, 1794) p. 3.

4. See in particular Landes's discussion of Rousseau's fear of public women in *Women and the Public Sphere in the Age of the French Revolution* (Ithaca, NY: Cornell University Press, 1988) pp. 66–89.

5. Thelwall, 'To Tyranny', *Poems Written in Close Confinement*, p. 2.

6. 'To Simplicity of Manners', ibid., p. 4.

7. See Cora Kaplan, 'Pandora's Box: Subjectivity, Class and Sexuality in Socialist Feminist Criticism', *Making a Difference: Feminist Literary Criticism*, eds Gayle Greene and Coppelia Kahn (London: Methuen, 1985) p. 156.

8. Claudia Johnson, *Equivocal Beings: Politics, Gender, and Sentimentality in the 1790s: Wollstonecraft, Radcliffe, Burney, Austen* (Chicago: University of Chicago Press, 1995), p. 42.

9. Mary Jacobus, 'The Difference of View', *Reading Women: Essays in Feminist Criticism* (New York: Columbia University Press, 1986) p. 28.

10. See Gary Kelly, *Revolutionary Feminism: the Mind and Career of Mary Wollstonecraft* (New York: St. Martin's Press, 1992), and *Women, Writing and Revolution 1790–1827* (Oxford: Clarendon Press, 1993), both of which advance this thesis.

11. Johnson, *Equivocal Beings*, p. 41.

12. Kaplan, 'Pandora's Box', p. 158.

13. Jacobus, 'The Difference of View', p. 27.

14. Mary Poovey, *The Proper Lady and the Woman Writer: Ideology as Style in the Work of Mary Wollstonecraft, Mary Shelley and Jane Austen* (Chicago: University of Chicago Press, 1984) p. 57.

15. Anna Wilson, 'Mary Wollstonecraft and the Search for the Radical Woman', *Genders*, no. 6 (Fall, 1989) pp. 88–101.

16. Marx, *Capital*, vol. 1, trans. Ben Fowkes (Harmondsworth: Penguin, 1976) p. 279.

17. Daniel O'Quinn has recently discussed this aspect of the *Vindication* as part of a 'feminist meta-discourse on literature and reading', manifest in a 'resistence to novels'. The broader category of affirmative culture, as a way of designating the role of the aesthetic in the maintenance of gendered power relations, however, also lets us account for Wollstonecraft's own ironic complicity with the very forms of discourse she criticizes. See 'Trembling: Wollstonecraft, Godwin and the Resistance to Reading', *ELH*, vol. 64 (1997) pp. 761–88.

18. Karl Marx, *Grundrisse*, trans. Martin Nicolaus (Harmondsworth: Penguin, 1993) p. 254.

19. See Jonathan Swift, 'A Beautiful Young Nymph Going to Bed', *Complete Poems* (Penguin: Harmondsworth, 1983) p. 453. See also Laura Brown's discussion of the relationship between Swift, commodification and feminized abjection in her *Ends of Empire: Women and Ideology in Early Eighteenth-Century English Literature* (Ithaca, NY: Cornell University Press, 1993) pp. 170–200.

20. Wollstonecraft, *Mary* and *The Wrongs of Woman* (Oxford: Oxford University Press, 1980) pp. 1–2, 4.

21. Wolf Lepenies, *Melancholy and Society*, trans. Jeremy Gaines and Doris Jones (Cambridge, Mass: Harvard University Press, 1992) p. 61.
22. Ann Radcliffe, *The Romance of the Forest* (1791; Oxford: Oxford University Press, 1991) p. 9.
23. Johnson, *Equivocal Beings*, p. 41.
24. See, Landes, *Women and the Public Sphere*, pp. 129–38, for a discussion of what she calls the 'ideology of republican motherhood' in Wollstonecraft's work.
25. Tom Furniss, 'Nasty Tricks and Tropes: Sexuality and Language in Mary Wollstonecraft's *Rights of Woman*', *Studies in Romanticism*, vol. 32 (Summer 1993) p. 204
26. Daniel O'Quinn's discussion of the *Vindication* argues that history emerges as an alternative to sentimental literature for Wollstonecraft, but that, at least in Wollstonecraft's account of it, this also seems to turn on a repetition of novelistic conventions. See 'Trembling', pp. 765–6.
27. Wollstonecraft, *Mary*, p. 68.
28. Slavoj Žižek, *The Sublime Object of Ideology* (London: Verso, 1991) p. 33.
29. Poovey, *The Proper Lady*, p. 96.
30. Ibid., 109.
31. Johnson, *Equivocal Beings*, 69.
32. Ibid., p. 60.
33. Laurie Langbauer, *Women and Romance: the Consolations of Gender in the English Novel* (Ithaca, NY: Cornell University Press, 1990) p. 95.
34. See Todd, *Women's Friendship in Literature* (New York: Columbia University Press, 1980) pp. 211–12.
35. Nicola Watson, *Revolution and the Form of the British Novel 1790–1815: Intercepted Letters, Interrupted Seductions* (Oxford: Clarendon Press, 1994) p. 52.
36. Johnson, *Equivocal Beings*, p. 67.
37. Johnson, appropriating Eve Sedgwick's model of triangulated desire for a lesbian poetics, describes this tension as one in which the 'heterosexual dyad represses female rather than male homosociality'. See ibid., 66.
38. Daniel O'Quinn writes that Maria's 'embedded narrative acts as an archeological critique of the surrounding narrative events in the asylum'. See 'Trembling', p. 769. O'Quinn's detailed discussion of Maria's embedded narrative develops a nuanced reading of Wollstonecraft's relationship to sentimentality that centres on the delusional nature of what he calls the tremulous bodily affect that indexes the mistake of imagining oneself into the sentimental narrative – as Maria does with both Venables and Darnford.
39. Satya Mohanty, *Literary Theory and the Claims of History: Postmodernism, Objectivity, Multicultural Politics* (Ithaca, NY: Cornell University Press, 1997) p. 207. Mohanty's discussion of consciousness-raising work draws on Naomi Schemen's, 'Anger and the Politics of Naming', in *Woman and Language in Literature and Society*, eds Sally McConnell-Ginet, Ruth Borker and Nelly Furman (New York: Praeger, 1980) pp. 174–87.

40. O'Quinn writes, 'The moment of trembling is important because it occurs at the moment when a woman's phantasmatic projection is successfully fitted to man's seduction strategy'. See 'Trembling', p. 772.

41. Claudia Johnson describes *Mary* as a 'weirdly elliptical protolesbian narrative'. See *Equivocal Beings*, p. 16.

42. 'Trembling', p. 778.

43. Simpson, *Romanticism, Nationalism and the Revolt Against Theory* (Chicago: University of Chicago Press, 1993) p. 106.

44. Pamela Clemit's introduction to the novel quotes a letter from Thomas Holcroft to Godwin indicating that Wollstonecraft was the model for Marguerite. See *St Leon* (Oxford: Oxford University Press, 1994) p. xvi.

45. *St Leon*, p. 138

46. See Gary Kelly, *The English Jacobin Novel 1780–1805* (Oxford: Clarendon Press, 1976) p. 227.

47. *St Leon*, pp. xxxiii–xxxiv.

48. Ibid., p. 40

CHAPTER 6   CONJUGAL LOVE AND THE ENLIGHTENMENT SUBJECT: THE COLONIAL CONTEXT OF NON-IDENTITY IN MARIA EDGEWORTH'S *BELINDA*

1. See Marilyn Butler, *Maria Edgeworth: a Literary Biography* (Oxford: Clarendon Press, 1972) pp. 494–5 and Suvindrini Perera, *Reaches of Empire: the English Novel from Edgeworth to Dickens* (New York: Columbia University Press, 1991) pp. 29–30. See Kathryn Kirkpatrick, '"Gentlemen Have Horrors Upon This Subject": West Indian Suitors in Maria Edgeworth's *Belinda*', *Eighteenth-Century Fiction*, vol. 5, no. 4 (1993) pp. 331–48 for a more detailed discussion of the changes made in the 1810 text.

2. See Perera, pp. 29–30.

3. My notion of non-identity is derived from Theodor Adorno's *Negative Dialectics*, which turns on an elucidation of the relationship between philosophical modernity and the drive towards identity. See *Negative Dialectics*, trans. E. B. Ashton (New York: Continuum, 1995).

4. See Nancy Armstrong, *Desire and Domestic Fiction: a Political History of the Novel* (Oxford: Oxford University Press, 1987) pp. 59–95

5. Ibid., p. 21.

6. Elizabeth Kowaleski-Wallace, *Their Fathers' Daughters: Hannah More, Maria Edgeworth, and Patriarchal Complicity* (New York: Oxford University Press, 1991) pp. 10–11.

7. G. J. Barker-Benfield discusses *Belinda* in the context of Edgeworth's response to Wollstonecraft. See Barker-Benfield, *The Culture of Sensibility: Sex and Society in Eighteenth-Century Britain* (Chicago: University of Chicago Press, 1992) pp. 386–95.

8. Ibid., p. 387

9. Laura Brown, *Ends of Empire: Women and Ideology in Early Eighteenth-Century Literature* (Ithaca, NY: Cornell University Press, 1993) p. 154.
10. Daniel Defoe, *Roxana* (1724; Oxford: Oxford University Press, 1981) p. 171.
11. Claudia Johnson, *Equivocal Beings: Politics, Gender, and Sentimentality in the 1790s: Wollstonecraft, Radcliffe, Burney, Austen* (Chicago: University of Chicago Press), p. 8. See also Susan Greenfield's '"Abroad and at Home": Sexual Ambiguity, Miscegenation, and Colonial Boundaries in Edgeworth's *Belinda*', *PMLA*, vol. 112, no. 3 (March, 1987) pp. 214–228, which offers a parallel reading of sexual ambiguity and the image of the Amazon in the novel.
12. Baker-Benfield, p. 388.
13. Gary Kelly's discussion of Elizabeth Hamilton's 1796 *Letters to Hindu Raja* and her 1800 *Memoirs of Modern Philosophers* highlights the association between irrational idolatry, Quixotism and political radicalism in anti-Jacobin fictions. The figure of the Quixote in anti-Jacobin novels, I'd argue, is closely allied to the irrationality of the fetish in Edgeworth's text. See Kelly, *Women, Writing and Revolution, 1790–1827* (Oxford: Clarendon Press, 1993), pp. 140–6 especially.
14. Jean-Jacques Rousseau, *Émile* (London: Everyman's Library, 1974) pp. 135–9.
15. See Alan Richardson's 'Romantic Voodoo: Obeah and British Culture 1797–1807', *Studies in Romanticism*, vol. 32 (Spring 1993) pp. 2–28, for a detailed survey of obeah in British sources and their relationship to British attitudes towards the West Indies.
16. James Ramsay, *An Essay on the Treatment and Conversion of African Slaves in the British Sugar Colonies* (London, 1784) p. 3.
17. These arguments are virtually ubiquitous in late-eighteenth-century abolitionist writing. See, for example, Ramsay, pp. 113–29 especially, but also Joseph Woods, *Thoughts on the Slavery of Negroes* (London, 1784) and John Gray, *An Essay on the Abolition, Not Only of African Slavery, but of Slavery in the British West Indies* (London, 1792).
18. See Bryan Edwards, *The History, Civil and Commercial, of the British Colonies in the West Indies*, 3 vols (London, 1794) vol. 2, pp. 90–101, and *An Introductory Account, Containing Observations on the Disposition, Character, Manners, and Habits of the Life of the Maroons*, published with *The Proceedings of the Governor and Assembly of Jamaica in Regard to Maroon Negroes* (London, 1796), Edward Long, *The History of Jamaica*, 3 vols (London: T. Lowndes, 1774) vol. 2, pp. 447–52, 473, and William Burdett, *The Life and Exploits of Three-Finger'd Jack, the Terror of Jamaica, with a Particular Account of the Obi* (Sommers Town: A Neil, 1801). See also Mavis C. Campbell, *The Maroons of Jamaica 1655–1796: a History of Resistance, Collaboration and Betrayal* (Granby, Mass.: Bergin & Garvey, 1988) pp. 176–8, for a discussion of the Maroon leader 'nanny', who also seems to have been an obeah practitioner.
19. Long, vol. 2, p. 473.
20. See Homi Bhabha, 'Of Mimicry and Men: the Ambivalence of Colonial Discourse', *October*, 28 (Spring 1984) pp. 125–133, and 'Sly Civility', *October*, 34 (Fall 1985) pp. 72–80.

21. Edwards, *History*, vol. 2, p. 96.
22. See ibid., vol. 2, pp. 96–101.
23. Ibid., vol. 2, p. 100.
24. Edwards, *An Introductory Account*, pp. xxx–xxxi
25. Gayatri Chakravorty Spivak, 'Can the Subaltern Speak?', in *Marxism and the Interpretation of Culture*, eds Cary Nelson and Lawrence Grossberg (Chicago: Illinois University Press, 1988), p. 296.
26. Edwards, *An Introductory Account*, p. xxxi
27. 'The Grateful Negro', in *Tales and Novels by Maria Edgeworth*, vol. 2 (London: George Routledge & Sons, 1893) p. 399.
28. Ibid., p. 403
29. Ibid., p. 405
30. Ibid., p. 412.
31. Moira Ferguson has discussed 'The Grateful Negro' in the context of abolitionist women's literature more generally, revealing the predominance of the tendency to valorize the transition from slavery to contractual obligation in explicitly sentimental terms. See Ferguson, *Subject to Others: British Women Writers and Colonial Slavery, 1670–1834* (New York: Routledge, 1992) pp. 231–4.
32. Karl Marx, *Capital*, vol. 1, trans. Ben Fowkes (Harmondsworth: Penguin, 1976), p. 279.
33. Ibid., p. 280.
34. G. W. F. Hegel, *The Philosophy of History*, trans. J. Sibree (New York: Prometheus Books, 1991) p. 99.
35. Thomas Day, *The Dying Negro: a Poem* (London, 1793) pp. 25–7.
36. Maria and Robert L. Edgeworth, *Practical Education*, 2 vols (London, 1801) vol. 2, p. 105.
37. Heather Macfadyen, 'Lady Delacour's Library: Maria Edgeworth's *Belinda* and Fashionable Reading', *Nineteenth-Century Literature*, vol. 48, no. 4 (March 1994) pp. 428.
38. Marx, *Grundrisse*, trans. Martin Nicolaus (Harmondsworth: Penguin Books, 1995) p. 162
39. Herbert Marcuse, *Negations: Essays in Critical Theory*, trans. Jeremy J. Shapiro (Boston: Beacon Press, 1968) p. 95.

Index